TWO MINUTE WARNING

How Concussions, Crime,
and Controversy Could Kill
the NFL (and What the
League Can Do to Survive)

Mike Freeman

TRIUMPH
BOOKS

The Library of Congress Cataloging-in-Publication Data
Freeman, Michael, 1966–
Two minute warning : how concussions, crime, and controversy could kill the NFL (and what the league can do to survive) /
Mike Freeman.
    pages cm
 ISBN 978-1-62937-083-5
 1. National Football League. 2. Football—Social aspects—United States. 3. Football—United States. I. Title.
 GV955.5.N35F75 2015
 796.330973—dc23

                                        2015012572

This book is available in quantity at special discounts for your group or organization. For further information, contact:
    Triumph Books LLC
    814 North Franklin Street
    Chicago, Illinois 60610
    (312) 337–0747
    www.triumphbooks.com

Printed in U.S.A.

ISBN: 978-1-62937-083-5

Design by Amy Carter

To Ella—

The greatest daughter of all

Why did football bring me so to life? I can't say precisely. Part of it was my feeling that football was an island of directness in a world of circumspection. In football a man was asked to do a difficult and brutal job, and he either did it or got out. There was nothing rhetorical or vague about it; I chose to believe that it was not unlike the jobs which all men, in some sunnier past, had been called upon to do. It smacked of something old, something traditional, something unclouded by legerdemain and subterfuge. It had that kind of power over me, drawing me back with the force of something known, scarcely remembered, elusive as integrity—perhaps it was no more than the force of a forgotten childhood. Whatever it was, I gave myself up to the Giants utterly. The recompense I gained was the feeling of being alive.

Frederick Exley, A Fan's Notes

"I came to the conclusion there was nothing else to do except end my miserable life."

—*Former New York Jets quarterback Ray Lucas,*
whose NFL career spawned 19 concussions
and a painkiller addiction

CONTENTS

INTRODUCTION

THIS BOOK IS ABOUT THE POWER OF A SPORTS LEAGUE—A LEAGUE
with such abilities and so wide a reach that a major television studio was frightened of it. The hack on Sony did more than provide Hollywood gossip to the media. It opened a window into
the NFL and that hammer it now wields—and how even some
of the most powerful entities in entertainment fear that power.

Sony is releasing a movie in 2015 called *Concussion*, about the
life of Bennet Omalu, the neurologist who discovered Chronic
Traumatic Encephalopathy (CTE) in the brain of Pro Football
Hall of Fame center Mike Webster. CTE is a frightening disease. These paragraphs, written by former NFL player George
Visger in January 2015 for *Esquire* magazine, are some of the
more succinct, yet powerful words on CTE. They show why
there is so much at stake for the NFL—and why Sony is doing
a movie on the subject.

> Studies have also shown that the younger you are
> when first concussed, the lower your threshold is for
> the next. And it doesn't take concussions to cause

brain damage. The brain is encased in a hard skull, with sharp bony ridges on the inside, and is surrounded by cerebral spinal fluid. Each of the thousands of sub-concussive hits an average high school player takes each season causes the brain to slosh around in the skull. Sometimes it hits the front of the skull and bounces back and hits the back of the skull. They call this a coup contrecoup injury, where the neurons get stretched. Neurons are partially composed of a stabilizing protein called tau protein and as the neurons get stretched repeatedly they get inflamed. The inflammation increases over time and over time the neurons begin to die. As they die, the sticky tau proteins disengage from the tubules and form amyloid plaques, which clump together and may block cell-to-cell signaling at synapses. This build up of amyloid plaques is a precursor to Chronic Traumatic Encephalopathy, or CTE.

One of the problems with head injuries in younger players is that your brain continues to develop into your twenties. Damage to a developing brain can worsen over the long term, leading to devastating effects in adulthood. Four years ago at age 52, doctors prescribed Lexapro to me for memory problems, in addition to the Lamictal, the anti-seizure medicine I'd been on for decades. Lexapro didn't seem to help, so they stacked Arricept and Namenda, both dementia medicines, on top of those two. Since my youth, I've lived with the repercussions of not taking football head injuries seriously. I was 22 when I had my first of what are now nine and counting football-caused emergency VP Shunt brain surgeries, and my football injuries have impacted not only my life, but have torn my family apart. In addition to football-caused gran-mal seizures, short-term memory problems have arisen from damage to my temporal lobes and anger management issues and poor judgment due to damage to my frontal lobe. My array of physical and psychological symptoms contributed to the loss of my environmental consulting business in 2011, my family's home in 2012, and my 20-year marriage to the mother of my three children in 2014.

As of September 2014, the Department of Veterans Affairs' brain repository in Bedford, Massachusetts, reported that 76 of the 79 brains of deceased NFL players showed CTE. Also, as of that 2014 date, researchers had examined the brains of 128 football players in total. The subjects had played football on either the professional, semi-professional, college, or high school level. Of those 128 players, 101 of them—or just under 80 percent—tested positive for CTE.

Dr. Ann McKee, the director of the brain bank, told PBS.org she believes the findings show a clear link between football and serious brain trauma. She added that "the higher the level you play football and the longer you play football, the higher your risk."

Publicized exposure for CTE would change everything in football, opening an arena of medical awareness the sport had never seen before. The Sony movie, with Will Smith as Omalu, is a dramatic adaption of that discovery and the subsequent fallout. It would do more than present an uncomfortable truth.

The disease represents the first challenge to the long-term future of the NFL.

Among the leaked information, as originally documented by BuzzFeed.com, was a memo sent to the Sony team working public relations for the movie from Allan Mayer, who heads a PR firm called 42West. Mayer wrote about his company's plans to counter what they expected—rightfully so—would be the NFL's attempt to discredit, even crush the movie.

Said Mayer in the leaked document: "*Concussion* is going to piss off the NFL. We should not try to pretend otherwise. Moreover, there is no concession we could make short of agreeing to cancel the project entirely that could possibly satisfy them. Our strategy should thus be based on the assumption that we are going to be facing a powerful adversary that may try to prevent the movie from being made—and, failing that, to ensure that as few people as possible see it or take it seriously."

BuzzFeed writer Lindsey Adler wrote: "Mayer warns of two tactics they fear the NFL will use to push back against *Concussion*. He first suggests the NFL will release information that they feel will devalue the validity of *Concussion*'s portrayal of their relationship with Dr. Omalu. Next, he warns the team at Sony that the NFL might try to use its influential partnerships [ESPN, Nike, 'a horde of celebrities'] to derail the marketing and promotion of *Concussion*.

"The second approach, which Mayer calls a 'pressure campaign' would not be far off from how the NFL managed to suppress the reach of a similar film: *League of Denial*, a 2013 documentary about Dr. Omalu, CTE, and the NFL. Last year, ESPN backed out of partnership on the documentary out of fear of damaging its relationship with the NFL. Unlike ESPN,

Sony does not rely heavily on access and partnerships with the NFL, but Mayer's memo supports the long held understanding that the NFL is an enemy that even the largest competitors don't want to 'piss off.'"

In other words, the NFL was able to intimidate one of its television partners, ESPN, into dropping a legitimate concussion expose because it might make the league look bad. Mayer's memo reveals that a huge movie studio feared the NFL would try to Swift boat them as well. In many ways, the memo—barely discussed in the football media (another sign of the NFL's power)—is one of the greatest indicators of pro football's current influence.

There was a time, not long ago, when a PR company would have never concerned itself with pushback from football. I don't mean the 1960s, or 1980s, or even the 1990s. Just a decade ago, a corporation would have patted the objecting NFL on the head and said, "Nice try, now go practice some punting." But now...now everything has changed. The sport is embedded in every aspect of American society. It dominates television, is among the most prevalent issues on social media, and is talked about from the White House to the outhouse. Nothing intimidates the NFL now. Probably not even the North Koreans.

This work is a look at that seemingly all-powerful NFL from many angles—different people, scenes, and situations—and a look at the NFL's future. A commissioner under fire. A race to make the game safer. The quarterback who could end up being the best we've ever seen. The football journalist who already is. The NFL's year from hell. The owner who fights for a racist nickname. The day the NFL righted a wrong some 25 years ago, and how it still impacts the game today. Violence on and off the field. The man who could help save the sport.

This is the examination of a year in the life of pro football, a sport that is wonderful and true, full of good people who do the right thing. But this is also a sport that has changed rapidly and not always for the better despite its stratospheric television ratings and glossier appeal. The NFL has always been a business, but that is true now more than ever. Worse, those business interests often are at odds with the simple mission of playing football and keeping its players from harm. What's become clear is that the NFL has, in recent years, compromised itself—compromised the safety of its players, in particular—to make more money.

The league's propensity to put profit above the human beings who play the game was even noticed by a former commissioner. In a *Rolling Stone* article published in 2015 it was Paul Tagliabue, Roger Goodell's predecessor, who did something I cannot remember any NFL commissioner ever doing before: criticized a fellow commissioner. Tagliabue spoke specifically about the at-times hypocritical stance Goodell—and by extension the league—has taken in disciplining players. He also mentioned how the NFL gives lip service to player safety but at the same time pushes to extend the regular season to 18 games. Speaking of the commissioner, Tagliabue's words might as well have been referring to the NFL as a whole: "If they see you making decisions only in economic terms, [players] start to understand that and question what you're all about. There's a huge intangible value in peace. There's a huge intangible value in allies."

Indeed, the NFL's future might not be as secure as many believe. There are even variations of that future (like alternate timelines in a *Star Trek* plot) in which children of the middle class or wealthy don't play football at all. Instead, they play safer sports, like basketball or baseball. Yet the poor will continue to play football because the sport will still be seen as a way out of poverty—despite the real danger of long-term brain damage.

Much of the reporting in this book is from the 2014–2015 season, which happened to be the most historic—on the field and off, good and bad—the league has ever seen. The majority of this book is original storytelling. I also use some stories, in full or in part, from my writing at Bleacher Report. Put simply, there hasn't been a more important year in the sport possibly since the 1970 merger. For the book alone, I conducted approximately 200 interviews.

Mostly, this is a new look at what seems impossible: a future in which the NFL is not the most popular sports league in the country. Such a future seems wholly improbable, but it's entirely realistic. This book explores how that could happen and how the NFL can prevent it.

I have no proof of an NFL bubble. If I had it, this would be an entirely different book. It would be an H.G. Wells novel, and I'm not equipped with a time machine. Hell, the NFL may say this book is indeed science fiction. Yet there are warning signs. One of the big problems stems from an old saying, the one about chickens coming home to roost. That applies to guys like Junior Seau. For decades, players like him suffered from the dizzying and horrible effects of head trauma. The NFL ignored those problems, or worse. Or the players and their union ignored them. Players even hid their symptoms from doctors to stay on the field (something that still happens today). Now, finally, those issues are coming to light.

In January 2015 Seau's family told *60 Minutes Sports* that Seau had been suffering greatly. "When he would come home from games, he would go straight to the room," his wife Gina said. "[He'd] lower the blinds, the blackout blinds, and just say, 'Quiet. My head is…is burning.'"

"I saw a man that right before my eyes [was] changing," his son Tyler Seau said. "He wasn't that happy-go-lucky guy anymore."

"It was hard," daughter Sydney said, "because we were all reaching for someone that wasn't exactly reaching back, even though we know—we knew—that he wanted to."

Seau committed suicide by shooting himself in the chest. I knew Seau well and interviewed him dozens of times. He was, outwardly, one of the nicest, most gregarious players I have ever been around in my 25 years of covering the sport. He once told me, early in his career: "Football saved my life. Not sure where I'd be without it." But I believe, at the end of his life, that he knew football was destroying him. I believe it is why he took his own life in the manner he did. Seau knew football had eroded his mind, and he wanted scientists to examine it upon his death. Stories like Seau's will only continue to emerge—and those stories are among the threats to football.

Off-field issues weren't the only ones last season. The January 4 playoff game between Detroit and Dallas had one of the more controversial plays in postseason history when game officials backtracked on a crucial pass interference penalty late in the game. The refs picked up that flag, and also did not call a penalty on Cowboys receiver Dez Bryant when he ran onto the field with his helmet off—a clear penalty itself. The botched calls basically handed the game to Dallas. Both acts were so egregious that even President Barack Obama felt compelled to comment on the play. He told the *Detroit News* that he couldn't "remember a circumstance in which a good call by one of the refs is argued about by an opposing player of the other team with his helmet off on the field, which in and of itself is supposed to be a penalty. The call is announced and then reversed without explanation. I haven't seen that before, so I will leave it up to the experts to make the judgment as to why that happened, but I can tell you if I was a Lions fan I'd be pretty aggravated."

The past year for the NFL was so remarkable, in mostly dire ways, that Obama and members of his administration actually commented on the NFL several times. In many ways, Obama's admonishment of the league felt unprecedented for a United States president.

Separately, all of the issues—domestic violence, accusations of child abuse, underinflated footballs, flawed leadership (in some cases), and botched calls in a big game—might not seem to be gigantic. Put together, they start to show the chinks in the league's armor. But how bad must it get before the NFL's ratings finally suffer from so many things going so wrong?

Will the NFL survive like certain corporations—the oil companies, cigarette makers, and banks who had public relations debacles and still prospered? The greed of bankers almost caused the world to collapse, yet banks are still powerful. Oil companies pollute oceans, and still they prosper. Cigarette makers sell poison and have some of the worst public relations of any business in human history, yet they are still rich. The NFL has made numerous public missteps, mistakes that would have sunk almost any other organization or sport, and it is still top dog. One difference between the sport and, say, an oil company causing the destruction of the Gulf of Mexico, is there are few mass alternatives to oil. Most economies don't run on solar power or dilithium crystals, so we need oil, and use it despite how repugnant the practices of oil companies may be. Football, contrarily, does have easily accessible competition.

The threats to football are more theoretical but still problematic, especially as science seems to increasingly link violence with players off the field. (Seau's entire personality changed, his decision-making was altered, and his temperament changed for the worse because of head trauma suffered while playing football.) Even potentially worse for football is an ongoing struggle with concussions. In a 2014 Wild Card game, Pittsburgh Steelers quarterback Ben Roethlisberger and tight end Heath Miller suffered from hard hits to the head late in the game. It was a game in which the Steelers were trailing. Roethlisberger's head smashed to the turf. Miller absorbed a helmet-to-helmet blow. Cameras would later show a close-up of Roethlisberger after the Steelers' medical staff had examined him. He clearly looked extremely dazed.

Did Roethlisberger have a concussion? It's unfair to play armchair medical doctor. He said after the game that he had "a little whiplash." We will never know. But here is what we do know, thanks to excellent reporting from the *Washington Post*: there was no way for the medical staff to know either, since their examination of Roethlisberger was too short to make an accurate determination. I personally watched the Steelers' medical team examine Roethlisberger, looking at his neck and head area. Roethlisberger was out for three plays and about four to five minutes of playing time. A doctor told the *Post* that a proper concussion examination can't be performed in that short a time. Roethlisberger was not serially monitored "over a period of time." He was out for three plays! A medical doctor for another NFL team agreed, telling me, "performing concussions tests in that little bit of time is impossible. It can't be done." He told me that a good concussion test takes approximately 20 minutes and many go longer.

The NFL's own concussion diagnostic tool reads in part: "Signs and symptoms of concussion may be delayed, and therefore it may be prudent to remove an athlete from play, not leave them alone, and serially monitor them over a period of time. WHEN IN DOUBT, TAKE A TIMEOUT."

The Steelers organization is one of the classiest—and best run—in all of professional sports. If they have a difficult time with diagnosing concussions, then every team does.

The concussion issues even extended to the Super Bowl. Patriots wide receiver Julian Edelman was smashed in the game by heavy-hitting safety Kam Chancellor with about 11 minutes remaining in the contest. Edelman stayed in the game for the rest of the series and then caught the winning touchdown pass. While an NFL source after the game said that medical officials checked Edelman for a concussion during the contest, Edelman was clearly not right. I was standing there when Edelman referred to Seattle as "St. Louis" in the postgame interview, and he was, in some moments, slurring his words slightly. When asked if he was still woozy, Edelman said he couldn't answer the question, citing the Patriots' in-house rule that players are not allowed to discuss injuries. (Months after the Super Bowl he gave the same answer when asked by the media again.)

We will see these injured and damaged players more and more, and more and more they will test our own boundaries, forcing us to constantly think about—and acknowledge—that the sport that so many of us love is doing real, long-term damage to human beings. If there ever comes a time when fans see the players as people and not commodities or gladiators or faceless entities on our fantasy rosters, everything could change. And the more information about their health becomes publicly available, the quicker that shift could come.

This story is just now beginning to hit the mainstream media. Fans still don't understand the connective thread between the violence of football and how it destroys the human mind. Once this connection is cemented, I contend, is when the popularity of football could suffer. And that change might happen rapidly.

Wrote Nathaniel Rich in the *New York Review of Books* in March 2015, "If some of the league's sins remain foggy to the average NFL fan, it may have something to do with the NFL's tenacious public relations policy. Goodell, the son of a New York senator, has sought the help of Republican pollster Frank Luntz to draft his public statements and advise league press strategy. This has resulted in Goodell's repeating the word 'integrity' incessantly during press conferences, and asserting that the rate of concussions has declined thanks to new safety protocols."

He added, "The question is not why the NFL can't be safer. It's why we—why Americans, since football is primarily a national obsession—crave its brand of violence. Do we watch simply for the visceral thrill, the same reason we might choose to buy a ticket for the upcoming film *Jurassic World* [a Super

Bowl sponsor]? Or is it an inoculation against real violence; that is, do we watch football in the same way that certain deviants watch extreme pornography to satisfy their perversions? Or perhaps we watch to avoid contemplating the greater [violence] occurring all around us—of foreign wars, civil rights abuses, environmental collapse...America is addicted to violence; America is addicted to football. We look up and find ourselves at a strange moment."

Even more importantly, some players are starting to—finally—understand the health risk football presents and speak out about it. Sean Morey, a longtime NFL player who in the spring of 2015 ran to become leader of the NFL Players Association, sent a letter to players outlining his platform. In the letter, Morey made several blunt—and I think brave—statements about the nature of the sport now. I can't remember a union head or person running to become one ever saying something remotely like it. One part of Morey's letter read:

> Owners continue to socialize their costs, privatize profits, and abuse their political influence to insulate themselves from uninsured liability, while diminishing the rights of our members. NFL Players must understand that we are a rapidly depreciating luxury good. We have decades of personal investment and a PhD in football, and yet we are considered migrant workers in a sharecropper system. Agents, Financial Advisors, Scouts, Coaches, and General Managers will all continue to generate revenue for the league as we are forced to retire and become a liability.

We are a rapidly depreciating luxury good...

I've always felt that the current crisis involving CTE was a by-product of both league and union inaction. In the documentary *The United States of Football*, Morey spoke about how he resigned from the union brain injury committee that he helped to cofound. "It became abundantly clear that I had been betrayed," he said. "Every player that ever played the game, every player that plays the game today, is being betrayed by their union. Because they're dismissing this issue [football causing serious brain trauma] because they don't want to incur additional liability, and they're trying to protect themselves."

McKee, who directs Boston University's CTE Center, was the first to discover a protein called tau, the telltale indicator of CTE. What McKee told the website BU Today is pertinent to the NFL's future. When asked about the implications of CTE on young athletes, McKee responded: "We need to understand the risks for young athletes and reevaluate whether or not young kids should even be playing this game. Their bodies are immature, their necks aren't very well developed, they're not very coordinated. Plus, they're literally walking bobbleheads with big heads, thin necks, and small bodies. Your brain is adult-size by age four, and it's relatively heavy for those little bodies. The only good thing is, they're low to the ground."

She added, "The thing that is shocking to me, and continues to be shocking, are the 25-year-olds who have died with this disease [CTE]. Not because of it—it's usually a suicide or an accidental death. I can't say that CTE caused their suicide. But for me, it's shocking to see neurodegenerative disease in a 25-year-old. It's horrible. And it's undeniable. We've seen it in enough twentysomethings now that you can't escape this. It's a shock to think, that guy looks so young, and he's dead. And he's dead with this."

The target on the NFL's rather ample backside has never been bigger, and social media exponentially widens it. A book written in the 1970s about the pills and violence doesn't have the same impact as claims today that can and do go viral. That is another factor potentially affecting the sport's future.

"Twenty five years ago, when I got into the NFL," owner Jerry Jones told the ESPN show *Mike & Mike* in January 2015, "it never occurred to me that we, in the NFL...that social issues...[would] be something that we could impact.... When I [first] got involved all I wanted to do was figure out how to pay for the Cowboys and figure out how to coach football "

The NFL has become so large that it is looked to as an example for how to do the right thing, and the NFL struggles mightily with this new leadership role. Interestingly, the NBA has not. The NBA has adapted more rapidly to the notion of players being social examples. Basketball players understand this point—NBA players are among the best behaved of all athletes. Today you do not see legions of basketball players getting into trouble like their counterparts in the NFL. (There are exceptions, of course.)

Mark Cuban, owner of the Dallas Mavericks, said something extraordinary on that same ESPN show. It went mostly unnoticed, but it was highly accurate. Decades ago, in the NBA, there were maybe three players who were brands, like Larry Bird or Magic Johnson. In the NFL, there were maybe two. "Now everybody in professional sports is a brand," he said. "And it's not just because that's their intent, but because of social media. You have your Twitter page, you're on Cyber Dust [a privacy app], you're on Facebook, you have Instagram, you have Tumblr, all these outlets. And not only do you have an outlet to present yourself and build your brand, but everyone else is watching you as well. And because everyone else is watching you, you change your behavior."

That is a point that almost every NBA player gets and a precious few NFL players do. NFL players have not changed their bad behavior, at least in large enough numbers, while NBA players have.

The same could be said for a number of NFL teams (not all but a lot) when it comes to management. Particularly when it comes to the draft, so many teams ignore players' off-the-field problems. "It's hard sometimes as an owner, general manager, coach, whatever it is," said Cuban, "when you know there's warts, not to just turn a blind eye. And I think that's what happened to the NFL."

The excellent site ProFootballTalk.com keeps an arrest tracker. It's exactly what it sounds like: it tracks arrests of every NFL player. In December 2014 it hit 40 days without an arrest for the first time since the tracker began in 2007. It was seen as a positive thing for the NFL (interesting in itself that there's almost a celebration when a player isn't arrested for 40 days). Of course, a short time later, the tracker was reset when several players were arrested.

Hall of Famer Lem Barney is one of the few current or former players to openly doubt the sport's long-term future. The *Los Angeles Times* reported that when speaking to a football academy in 2013, Barney, one of the best corners of all time, said professional football could disappear sooner than many think. "The game is becoming more deadly today," he told the newspaper. "I think it's the greatest game if you like gladiators.... I can see in the next 10 to maybe 20 years, society will [eliminate] football altogether."

If you want to know the challenge facing players, particularly when it comes to health issues, one example occurred when the NFLPA formed a committee to study the feasibility of lifetime medical care for all NFL players. The estimated cost: $2 billion. The cost was problematic enough, but no company would even insure them. The union instead went to a Health Reimbursement Account, an employer-funded system that uses tax advantages to fund health care costs. The fact that insurers wouldn't touch them is instructive.

In the winter of 2015 the head of the NFL union, DeMaurice Smith, faced five challengers vying for his job—including several, such as Morey, who were former players. That number of challengers to a sitting union head is believed to be the most ever. It's an indicator that despite the massive popularity of football, and the incredible amount of money it makes, there is an unsettling feeling among the player base and, indeed, across the sport.

There was a time when many of us believed football held the universe together. We played it at some level. We loved it the way we loved a person. For some of us, that love never stopped. But for others, our passion, our love for football, was drained by the controversies, the concussions, and the knowledge of what football has become. That revelation wasn't like learning how the meal was cooked; it was like finding out we were the meal. And that is football's greatest challenge: returning a fan who has weaponized cynicism back to that time when football meant everything.

1 THE WORST YEAR
IN NFL HISTORY

"Football is not for the well adjusted."

—The late George Young,
former New York Giants general manager

IS THIS HOW AN EMPIRE FALLS? DOES IT BEGIN WITH CRACKS THAT at first seem tiny? That's often how the great collapses start. They get ignored. Many scoff at predictions of their demise. The resources keep pouring in, so no one cares. The popularity is unshaken. The ratings beat everything else on television. The bond between product and consumer seems unbreakable. The empire looks imposing and unbeatable. Then something happens that signals a shift—a frightening moment inside the elevator of an insignificant casino, inside that elevator a declining player, once thought a good person, changing things forever. Or a 265-pound player being convicted for choking a petite woman. Or a star runner injuring his own four-year-old child. Is this how empires fall? Does it begin with the worst week in NFL history, in what was the worst year the sport has ever seen?

If the NFL's seemingly unbreakable stranglehold on the attention of American sports fans is indeed lost, then one week in particular—the week of September 8, 2014—and one season in particular—the 2014–2015 season—will be seen as the catalyst.

That week started when security video of Baltimore runner Ray Rice knocking his fiancée unconscious was leaked; continued when the story was broken of Minnesota Vikings player Adrian Peterson hitting his young son with a switch, causing deep abrasions in his son's leg; and ended with calls for Commissioner Roger Goodell to resign and the NFL to lose its invaluable antitrust exemption. That week would bleed into the most controversial season the league has ever seen. The New England Patriots, once punished for filming opponents' sidelines in an attempt to steal signals—the infamous Spygate scandal—being accused of underinflating footballs to gain a competitive advantage. The Cleveland Browns were involved in a sideline texting controversy. The Atlanta Falcons were accused of pumping fake crowd noise into their stadium to keep opponents from communicating at the line of scrimmage.

There have been ugly moments in football history before this year. The NFL once played games in the hours following the assassination of President John F. Kennedy, a decision that former commissioner Pete Rozelle would call his greatest regret. Recently, Patriots tight end Aaron Hernandez was accused of multiple murders. Michael Vick ran a cruel and brutal dogfighting enterprise, and Chiefs player Jovan Belcher killed his girlfriend and then shot himself. There have been NFL players who killed people while driving drunk. Maybe the most famous, and infamous, NFL alum is O.J. Simpson.

In 1909, 26 people were killed and 70 injured playing football. There was nearly a nationwide panic about the safety of the sport. The *New York Times* ran a lengthy story in 1909 that read in part:

> The State of Virginia will probably be the one which will give the heaviest blow to football. Following the death of one of the State University players and the injury of several of her youths within the State, a bill will be introduced into the Legislature at the next session to forbid all such contests in the future. It is expected that this bill will be passed. Already the City Council of Norfolk and Portsmouth have forbidden all contests within the city limits.
>
> The death which attracted the most attention throughout the country, and which revived to a large extent the movement for the suppression of football, was that of Cadet Byrne, a West Point cadet. Byrne was an upper classman, 22 years old, when he was fatally injured during the contest with Harvard University. His neck was broken during a mass play, and despite the fact that every attempt was made to save his life, he died soon after.
>
> The interest in this accident was so great that expressions of opinion were asked from the heads of nearly every institution of learning in the country. Some of them saw it in proof that the game should be abolished, while others urged changes in the rules. Some, however, looked upon it as an unfortunate accident and declared that the game as it is now played could not be

made less dangerous without taking away the exciting features.

The issue was so serious that it ultimately required intervention from President Theodore Roosevelt. Yet those deaths, while tragic, happened in another century, long before there was even an NFL, or even professional football. And the crimes committed by players like Vick and Simpson happened months or years apart. That week…it changed things because so many horrors happened in a span of days. The video of Rice attacking his fiancée, Janay, was a game-changer. It was no longer abstract; there it was, in living color. It was the same with images of the injured leg of Peterson's son. In the viral information age we live in, those images made it the worst year the league has ever seen.

There was no video of Vick killing and torturing dogs. There wasn't a camera mounted on the windshields of players who drove drunk and killed people. But there was video of Rice, and it was bad. The video first appeared on TMZ.com at 5:15 AM Eastern time on Monday morning. It clearly showed Rice hitting Janay once and knocking her unconscious. It became viral in just a matter of hours. One league executive who saw the video later that morning immediately texted home to his wife: "You may not see me for a few days. Armageddon is about to hit here."

At the NFL offices, there was widespread disbelief. The best way to describe the reaction, as one league executive put it, was panic. The NFL, especially its smart and highly effective public relations arm, knew instinctively the damage it would generate. One of the initial main concerns of the NFL were the racial implications of the video. With a player base that is approximately 70 percent African American, the NFL was worried that a general public would see a black man hitting a woman and assume that most of its black players were that way. One white NFL assistant coach remembers, after seeing the video on ESPN, sitting his young son down to explain, "You're going to hear from some whites that all blacks do this. It's not true."

Some of Rice's teammates were equally stunned. They stood by Rice after the initial incident became public, before any video of the incident was released. Rice had told players on the team that he struck Janay, but it wasn't with a fist, and she had hit her head against a railing inside the elevator. When the footage emerged, some on the team, according to players, felt Rice had misled them. Several players talked openly about how they no longer wanted Rice on the team. Rice would contend he always told the truth about that night.

The entire NFL was shaken. Perhaps the last time the league was this wholly disturbed was when Rae Carruth was accused of plotting to murder his pregnant girlfriend in 1999. He was convicted of the crime and sentenced to 18 to 24 years in prison. A close second may be Ray Lewis initially being charged with murder in 2000 before accepting a plea deal for misdemeanor obstruction of justice. Commissioner Paul Tagliabue later fined Lewis $250,000.

But, again, it was the pictures that changed everything. At 2:18 PM, still on that Monday, not even 12 hours after the video's release, the Ravens announced the termination of Rice's contract. Just 23 minutes later, Goodell announced in a statement that Rice would be suspended indefinitely due to the new video evidence. This was when the story shifted and it officially became one of the biggest threats the NFL ever faced. In the Rice case, the question became: What did the NFL know, and when did it know it?

Actually, there were two Rice videos. The first showed the aftermath of the Rice assault: an unconscious Janay being dragged out of the elevator by Rice as if she were a sack of potatoes. That led to Goodell suspending Rice on July 25, 2014, for two games. Then the second video was released, showing the assault. The NFL said it had never seen the second tape, but few believed that. Sentiment emerged among fans and media that the NFL was engaged in a cover-up. The redoubtable Keith Olbermann, longtime journalist of ESPN fame, called for Goodell's resignation after the commissioner gave an awkward press conference at the beginning of the 2014 season in Canton, Ohio, in which he defended Rice's initial suspension.

"We begin tonight with the pathetic performance of National Football League commissioner Roger Goodell in Canton, Ohio, today, in the wake of his insufficient suspension of the domestic violence perpetrator Ray Rice," Olbermann began on his Monday, September 8, 2014, show. "It was a performance distinguished only by a thorough, consistent, self-congratulatory tone-deafness to the realities of domestic violence, and the near-universal outrage at the NFL's weak, damaging, almost enabling reaction."

Olbermann later added, "It is necessary, Mr. Goodell, for you to now resign as commissioner."

The NFL's handling of the case was awkward at best and willfully ignorant at worst. One of the better examples of the latter came during the June 16, 2014, prediscipline meeting between Goodell and Rice at the NFL offices in New York. In addition to Goodell, a number of others were in attendance, including Jeff Pash, NFL general counsel; Adolpho Birch, NFL senior vice president of labor policy and government affairs; Kevin Manara, NFL senior labor relations counsel; Dick Cass, Baltimore Ravens president; Ozzie Newsome, the team's general manager; Heather McPhee, associate general counsel of the union; Ben Renzin, Rice's agent and friend; and Janay Palmer, Rice's then-fiancée.

As arbitrator Barbara S. Jones would later determine, the key principles from the Goodell side either didn't take notes or took extremely poor ones. "The Commissioner's notes are not detailed and do not contain any verbatim quotes of what Rice said happened in the elevator. They do not contain the word 'slap' anywhere," Jones wrote in her decision. "They do contain the word 'struck' at what appears to be the only entry relating to Rice's statements about what happened in the elevator."

"Birch's notes are even sparser, with the phrase 'bottle service' the only reference to the night of the assault," Jones continued. "Manara's notes are more detailed than those of the Commissioner and Birch, which is to be expected since he was the assigned note taker. In relevant part, Manara's notes read, in six successive lines: 'arguing while waiting for elevator / exchanging words / she hit him / got in elevator / she hit him again / he slapped her; fell; knocked herself out.'... While Manara was a credible witness, I am not persuaded that his notes reliably report that Rice used the words 'knocked herself out.' For example, although Manara's notes use 'slapped,' the majority of the witnesses, including Newsome and Birch [did not]," and Jones wrote that Manara's notes were "not verbatim."

My belief is that few of the NFL principals composed detailed notes because they wanted to be flexible in their recollections. It should be noted the arbitrator credited the union representative at the meeting, McPhee, with taking extensive and thorough notes. That's because the union likely wanted exact recollections because they would help its cause with an arbitrator.

Judge Jones also wrote this: "As soon as he arrived at the office [on the day the elevator video was released by TMZ], the Commissioner assembled all those who worked on the issue to a meeting, at which they looked back at the notes of the June 16 meeting, and 'made sure all of us had the same recollection.'" Of course, that is judge-speak for everyone got their stories straight. (It would not be the last time a judge, in the NFL's year from hell, would slam the league. Judge David Doty, a longtime NFL nemesis, in the winter of 2015 ruled against the NFL and ended Peterson's suspension. Doty said the NFL could not retroactively apply its new anticrime policies to Peterson's case.)

Then the arbitrator wrote something that devastated Goodell's credibility: "Following the release of the inside-the-elevator video, which prompted a new round of criticism," she wrote, "the League suspended Rice indefinitely. Now, the League argues that Commissioner Goodell was justified in imposing the second discipline because Rice had misled him and because the video demonstrated a level of violence that he had not understood.... I have found that Rice did not mislead the Commissioner. Moreover, any failure on the part of the League to understand the level of violence was not due to Rice's description of the event, but to the inadequacy of words to convey the seriousness of domestic violence. That the League did not realize the severity of the conduct without a visual record also speaks to their admitted failure in the past to sanction this type of conduct more severely."

Translation: the NFL had never cared about domestic violence before the Rice case, and the decision by Goodell to suspend Rice for just two games for such a serious offense showed that it didn't care about the issue of domestic violence. It only cared when such violence was caught on camera, showing not just how flawed the light suspension was but also the way the NFL hadn't evolved on the issue of domestic violence, while society at large—albeit slowly and by far not completely—had.

The NFL's uneven administration of discipline even caught the attention of President Obama. In an interview with the Colin Cowherd show on ESPN, the president said of Rice and the NFL's domestic violence policy, "I'm so glad we got more awareness about domestic violence. Obviously, the situation that happened in the Rice family was important, but it did lift up awareness that this is a real problem that we have to root out and men have to change their attitudes and their behavior.

"The way it was handled also indicates that the NFL was behind the curve, as a lot of institutions have been behind the curve, in sending a clear message," he continued. "You don't want to be winging it when something like this happens. You want to have clear policies in place. The fact that policies have now been established I think will be helpful in sending a message that there's no place for that kind of behavior in society, whether it's in sports or anyplace else."

Not since the deaths of dozens of players in the early 1900s had football been so widely and harshly criticized. Pash, the NFL's chief attorney, responded to the hammering Goodell and the NFL received from the arbitrator with a lengthy letter that was sent to each NFL owner. It was an attempt at doing damage control with Goodell's bosses, but the letter was also a tacit admission that the league's image was severely damaged. "No part of Judge Jones' decision questions the Commissioner's honesty or integrity," Pash wrote, "nor his good faith consideration of the issue when he imposed the indefinite suspension on Mr. Rice. Nor is there any suggestion that the Commissioner had seen the video from inside the elevator before it became public, or knew of the contents of the video."

One of the more stunning mistakes the NFL made in this case was that Goodell interviewed Janay Palmer with Rice present. It doesn't take a rocket scientist to understand the inappropriateness of having perp and victim in the same room together.

Goodell's mistakes were not just borne out of ignorance on the issue of domestic violence. They were also borne of arrogance. The NFL, up to this point, believed it was untouchable, and as a collective, the league thought it could never make serious errors. It was this same arrogance that led to the NFL's concussion crisis. Why it had seen player lockouts and strikes. And labor unrest with game officials. Why it put more and more football on television with no concerns about saturation. The NFL had never had to pay for making those errors because people kept watching. But now, arrogance has become one of the NFL's most potent forms of kryptonite.

"There are systemic issues in the league office much bigger than Roger Goodell," said longtime NFL veteran Scott Fujita, "and it's been that way for a very, very long time. So there have been plenty of reasons for people to question [its] credibility. But typically the NFL has been bulletproof. Why? Because we either have a short attention span or we're not paying attention or the games just keep coming. But I think [the Rice] case might be different. To me that videotape was a game-changer. Because that's imprinted in our minds now…the public is always going to have this perception there was foul play, and I don't know how the NFL escapes that." In other words, for the first time in its modern history, the NFL had a headwind. The Rice case could not be so easily neutered by what happened on the field.

Olbermann was not the only one to call for Goodell to step down. The Rice case would transcend sports and become one of the most talked-about news stories in the country. Never before in the history of the league had the NFL or its commissioner been talked about in such a brutally negative way. Much of the discussion in the media continued to center on accusations that Goodell and the league had covered up its knowledge of the Rice incident, specifically its knowledge of the contents of the second tape. It didn't matter that there was absolutely no proof of this. The narrative was set. It stuck. Even to this day.

Kyle Turley, a longtime NFL player, wrote for *Time* magazine, "The NFL knew. In my personal knowledge of the game of football and the inner workings of the league, I find it nearly impossible to believe that the top brass of the organization didn't know every bit of this Ray Rice situation from day one. It's pretty ridiculous to come out now and say, 'Oh, we just saw the tape.' The top guys know everything that goes on in their league. You can bet on it.

"Clearly, the NFL doesn't take domestic violence seriously. It certainly doesn't impose stiff penalties on players who are violent toward their wives or girlfriends. I don't think Ray Rice thought for one second that he'd have any problem getting away with knocking his then-fiancée unconscious."

The site Sidespin.com also called for Goodell to resign. It wrote: "There are 56 instances of domestic violence...since Roger Goodell became NFL Commissioner [September 2006 through that week]. Of those 56 instances, players were suspended for a combined 13 games (not including Rice's indefinite suspension, which cannot be quantified). Out of 56 instances, only 10 players were released by their team. Roger Goodell is a domestic violence enabler who must be stopped."

Writer Bill Simmons, who has three million followers on Twitter, excoriated Goodell on a podcast. "If he didn't know what was on that tape, he's a liar," Simmons said. "I'm just saying it. He is lying. If you put him up on a lie detector test, that guy would fail. For all these people to pretend they didn't know is such fucking bullshit. It really is, it's such fucking bullshit. For him to go into that press conference and pretend otherwise...I was so insulted." While Simmons was suspended for three weeks by then-employer ESPN for those comments, he was far from alone in those beliefs.

Wrote *New York Times* editorial columnist Maureen Dowd in a story called "Throw the Bums Out": "Goodell likes to present himself as a law-and-order sheriff bent on integrity, whose motto is: 'Protect the shield.' But that doesn't seem to include protecting the victims of violence or American Indians who see the Washington team's name as a slur. As with concussions, the league covered up until the public forced its hand. The commissioner, who has been a sanctimonious judge for eight years, suddenly got lenient. His claim that it was 'ambiguous about what actually happened' in the Atlantic City casino elevator between Ray Rice and his then-fiancée, Janay Palmer, during the Valentine's Day massacre was risible to start with. What did he think happened? The man was dragging out an unconscious woman like a sack of mulch."

Comedian Jon Stewart, speaking on *The Daily Show*, lambasted the league over its handling of the Rice case: "It's the kind of decision-making we've come to expect from people who don't know what the fuck they're doing." *Time* magazine ran a cover story that no mainstream media source had ever asked in previous decades: "Is Football Worth It?"

The National Organization for Women also asked Goodell to resign. The group said the NFL has a "violence against women problem...the only way to restore honor and integrity to the country's most lucrative and popular pastime." In the same letter they also demanded that his successor "appoint an independent investigator with full authority to gather factual data about domestic violence, dating violence, sexual assault, and stalking within the NFL community and to recommend real and lasting reforms." Later, a women's rights group, UltraViolet, hired an aircraft to fly over MetLife Stadium, home of the New York Jets and New York Giants, towing a banner that read #GoodellMustGo. The group did the same thing at a Saints-Browns game and later, at the AFC and NFC title games.

A staggering image went viral that week. It was a CoverGirl advertisement, featuring an attractive woman wearing a Ravens jersey, with the headline "Get Your Game Face On!" Except the picture had been Photoshopped by activists to make the model appear as if she had a black eye.

The NFL had caused such palpable and widespread anger over the course of a few days that it managed to do something almost impossible in America today: unite Republicans and Democrats. In a remarkable move, 12 Democrats on the House

Judiciary Committee wrote Goodell a letter calling for the NFL to be more transparent in how it handled the Rice case. Joining them in criticizing the league was Senator Dean Heller, a Republican from Nevada. "By waiting to act until it was made public you effectively condoned the action of the perpetrator himself," Heller wrote. "I cannot and will not tolerate that position by anybody, let alone the National Football League."

The White House released its own statement. A senior administration official told reporters in a briefing that "the NFL has an obligation not only to their fans but to the American people to properly discipline anyone involved in domestic violence or child abuse and more broadly, gain control of the situation. Many of these professional athletes are marketed as role models to young people and so their behavior does have the potential to influence these young people, and it's one of the many reasons it's important that the league get a handle on this and have a zero tolerance."

That same week, star Arizona Cardinals defenseman John Abraham simply walked away from the team, just 24 hours after enduring a concussion; he had been suffering from memory loss for more than a year. And Cowboys owner Jerry Jones was accused of assault.

That Tuesday, San Francisco 49ers owner Jed York announced that the team would not discipline player Ray McDonald. McDonald had been arrested on suspicion of domestic violence after police saw bruises on the neck and arms of his pregnant fiancée. Perhaps most interesting about the case was the fact McDonald called a San Jose police officer at approximately the same time a 911 call was made. That officer, who would later go to McDonald's home, worked security at 49ers games. This was of course a planet-sized conflict of interest. The officer should have told McDonald to call 911, but he didn't.

In response to the McDonald arrest, longtime NFL writer Tim Kawakami, who has covered the 49ers and Raiders for decades, tweeted, "Am I suggesting that [the San Jose Police Department] and the Santa Clara County sheriffs often work very, very closely with the 49ers? Yes, I am suggesting that."

The entire case shed light on the fact the NFL has at times been incredibly close, possibly too close, with law enforcement. The NFL has a large security arm consisting of former police officers, FBI, DEA, and Homeland Security agents. Individual teams also have their own security officials working for them. There have long been accusations that police and other law enforcement have, on more than a few occasions, looked the other way when it came to legal matters involving NFL players. The Pittsburgh Steelers, in a story detailed by ESPN, have a security chief who doubles as a high-ranking officer in the Allegheny County Sherriff's Office. That officer's nickname in some circles, according to ESPN, is "the Cleaner."

The 49ers would handle a second accusation of violence against McDonald, several months later, quite differently than the first. In December, a search warrant was issued for McDonald's home after a woman said she was sexually assaulted there. The first accusation against McDonald saw the 49ers adhere to due process and defend McDonald. The second accusation saw the 49ers immediately release him. The difference? McDonald isn't a good player, and the 49ers, at the time of his release, were eliminated from the playoff race. The entire due process argument, it turns out, was a sham.

Just five months before the McDonald arrest, the league was

rocked by an uglier domestic violence accusation against one of its players. Carolina Panthers defensive end Greg Hardy, who is 6'4" and weighs 265 pounds, was found guilty by a judge of assaulting ex-girlfriend Nicole Holder and threatening to kill her. Holder testified that Hardy dragged her by the hair through several rooms of Hardy's apartment before grabbing her by the throat. "He looked me in my eyes and he told me he was going to kill me," she testified. "I was so scared I wanted to die. When he loosened his grip slightly, I said, 'Just do it. Kill me.'" Due to the quirks of Carolina law, Hardy's appeal to the judge's decision was a jury trial. Yet Hardy reached a financial settlement with his accuser and the charges in that trial were dismissed after prosecutors were unable to find the accuser for the new trial.

What recent incidents of violence may have shown is a glimpse into the future. The connection between head trauma and off-the-field violence is strengthening to the point where a significant number of neurologists believe there is a connection between concussions and violent behavior. There could come a time when law enforcement and others will have to adapt laws to this frightening new reality. A recent *New York Times Magazine* story reported on a lawyer who represented concussed NFL players who sued the league. It also made the now-growing comparison between the NFL and the tobacco industry: "CTE and claims of football-induced brain damage are also likely to play a part in criminal trials, perhaps even some high-profile ones involving NFL stars." David Franklin, a clinical neuropsychologist at the University of California, Riverside, School of Medicine, said in the story, "'But you have to ask how the concussions issue changes the landscape from a law-enforcement perspective.

I think it has to over time, because we now know that players are suffering repeated insults to the parts of the brain that cause changes in behavior.'

"Rates of cigar smoking plunged and the industry declined because tobacco use could not be made safe. The NFL may be at a similar juncture now. It has instituted rules changes to make its own games less violent and is funding and promulgating supposedly less dangerous ways to play at the youth level. But there is no assurance that any of it will make football any more healthful than low-tar cigarettes made smoking. The burden will fall on the NFL to litigate the concussion issue in public and prove that its sport does not rob participants of their consciousness."

Even among professional athletes who played football at a younger age, and who have always loved the sport, there is an increasing awareness of the long-term dangers the NFL presents to the brain. Former longtime linebacker Brian Urlacher remembers playing against the Broncos in 2003 and getting hit in the head while attempting to tackle runner Clinton Portis. Urlacher was unconscious before he hit the ground. And yet he sat out just two plays before going back into the game. He later admitted that if he was playing today, he'd at least have gone through the league's concussion protocol and would consider the health implications of returning to play so soon after a potential concussion.

LeBron James was an outstanding high school football player, but he switched to basketball and he became, you know, pretty good at that. In November 2014 he said something telling to ESPN: that he won't allow his sons to play football because of the dangers. Instead, they could play only basketball, soccer, and baseball.

Still, it is clear that some in the NFL, despite proof to the contrary, don't believe there is a real concussion crisis. When Cincinnati Bengals linebacker Vontaze Burfict suffered his second concussion in two weeks early in the 2014 season, Marvin Lewis, head coach of the team, was asked a simple question: Did Lewis have concern for Burfict not just as a football player but a human being? "Well, he had a concussion against Atlanta," Lewis responded. "That's the biggest concern that way. You don't want him to have, you know, but again I coached defenses and linebackers for a long time and concussions didn't linger. Now we have found that because of the media and things they seem to linger longer. There's a lot of attention paid to it. I don't know why they linger longer. I don't remember them lingering like they do now." Lewis seems to allege that the media manufactured the crisis of head trauma in football.

Some both in and out of the league still don't understand the seriousness of getting concussed. If anyone ever doubts that seriousness, there are many examples to counter such ignorance. One example is that it was a concussion that sent Brett Favre into retirement. On literally the last play of his NFL career he was knocked out cold. He told interviewer Graham Bensinger in 2015:

"Our trainer had came out on the field: Eric Sugarman, we call him Sug. He is like 'Hey buddy, you all right?' I was kind of laying on my stomach with my head turned to my right a little bit. And I was snoring. I was taking a good nap…. And I got up and I kind of looked over and a couple a Bears, [Brian] Urlacher and Lance Briggs and a few of those guys were clapping, and I said, 'What are they doing here?' And I think I took one step towards the Bears sideline and Sug said, 'Oh, come over here with me buddy' and [I] went straight to the sideline and I said, 'Let's go on into the locker room.' I figured after 20 years I should be able to say what I want to do. Went right in and took a shower, put my street clothes on, got a jacket, got a hot chocolate and chili dog, and I never looked back. Never missed it since."

Perhaps most interesting is just how much science has known, for so long, how much concussions can damage the brain. Yet this knowledge never became anchored in the modern NFL.

Blogger Matt Cheney in 2015 uncovered an article that was written in 1928 about how concussions were wreaking havoc not just in boxing but in other sports. The headline, "'Punch Drunk' May Apply to Other Sports" was scary in its predictions. The story read:

> The 'punch drunk' condition of boxers has stepped into the medical field for determination whether others than boxers get it.
>
> The American Medical Association has issued in its Journal an appeal by Harrison S. Martland, M.D., of Newark, N.J., to find out the nature and extent of this state, which he says fight fans describe as "punch drunk, cuckoo, goofy, cutting paper dolls or slug nutty."
>
> The symptoms in slight cases are a "very slight flopping of one foot or leg in walking, noticeable only at intervals, or a slight unsteadiness in gait or uncertainty in equilibrium." In severe cases "there may develop a peculiar tilting of the head, a marked dragging of one or both legs, a staggering, propulsive gait."

Finally, marked mental deterioration may set in.

I am of the opinion that in punch drunk there is a very definite brain injury, due to single or repeated blows on the head or jaw. I realize that this theory, while alluring, is quite insusceptible of proof at the present time.

Dr. Martland suggests that if punch drunk exists in the form he suspects [then] it afflicts others than boxers and that establishment of the facts is important to courts and labor compensation boards in handling head injury cases. He foresees disadvantages in the field which may be opened for "so-called expert testimony" and says:

"While most of the evidence supporting the existence of this condition is based at this time on the observations of fight fans, promoters, and sporting writers, the fact that nearly one-half of the fighters who have stayed in the game long enough develop this condition, either in a mild form or a severe and progressive form, which often necessitates commitment to an asylum, warrants this report. The condition can no longer be ignored by the medical profession or the public."

Again, that was written *almost 100 years ago*. "If only the stakeholders in football would have heeded Dr. Martland's warnings in 1928," said Paul Anderson, a lawyer who has written extensively on NFL health and labor issues, "the science of football-related brain injuries would have been exponentially advanced and numerous lives could have been protected.

Instead, the stakeholders and guardians of football were willfully blind."

In 1979, Hall of Fame quarterback Roger Staubach, after one concussion in high school, one in college, and approximately eight in the NFL—six of which caused him to be knocked unconscious—went to an independent neurologist named Dr. Fred Plum. (Plum was the Cornell specialist who coined the term "persistent vegetative state.") Plum's examination of Staubach showed the quarterback wasn't suffering from any serious trauma. Still, there was something wrong. "He found a reflex on my right side that was a little different from the one on my left," Staubach told author Kevin Cook in the book *The Last Headbangers*. "That made me stop and think. If I'd been 32 or 33, I would have kept playing, but I had five kids and wanted to be a dad to them. So I said good-bye."

This, of course, raises a serious question. If the technology existed almost four decades ago to make the type of determination that Plum did for Staubach—too many concussions *should* lead to retirement—how was the NFL for decades, particularly as concussion awareness started to peak in the 1990s, able to convince players, and the public, that the opposite was true? The truth, as several team executives privately admitted to me for this book and as greatly detailed in the book and film *League of Denial*, is that the league misled everyone.

———

THE ACTS OF VIOLENCE COMMITTED BY NFL PLAYERS DURING THAT week in September were commented on by almost every aspect of American media. It also reached the NFL's de facto minor league system, Division I college football. South Carolina coach Steve Spurrier made a statement that should have been made policy in the NFL decades ago but was only then being discussed. "I've had a rule long as I've been here that if you hit a girl, you won't play. You're finished," Spurrier said. "We're not going to have any player on our team who has done that, and I can't understand why every coach doesn't have that rule, why every company doesn't have that rule for its employees. I think that would put a pretty good end to this stuff. It's amazing that America has sort of put up with it, compromised, but it's something that shouldn't ever happen."

If that week (and few months before and after) wasn't bad enough for the NFL, it would get worse. Early Friday morning, September 12, the *New York Times* and other media outlets reported that in court filings the NFL admitted that brain trauma will affect one in three retired players. The NFL had disputed for decades that its players had a high rate of brain damage. Not only was the NFL now admitting that their previous statements were false, but also that the number of players would be high, and the trauma would occur at much younger ages than expected.

"This statement clears up all the confusion and doubt manufactured over the years questioning the link between brain trauma and long-term neurological impairment," said Chris Nowinski to the *Times* in a September 12 story. Nowinski is the executive director of the Sports Legacy Institute and has pressured the league to acknowledge the connection between football and brain disease. "We have come a long way since the days of outright denial. The number of former players predicted to develop dementia is staggering, and that total does not even include former players who develop mood and behavior disorders and die prior to developing the cognitive symptoms associated with CTE."

Wrote *Washington Post* columnist Sally Jenkins: "Here's the deal: concussions are the black lung of the NFL. And the league knows it...If you want to be a mine owner, the price of doing business in that dark and hazardous industry is federal oversight and lifetime compensation for workers who are permanently disabled by your coal dust. The NFL is not coal, obviously; it's entertainment. But it has a dirty, dangerous problem that looks a lot like black dust. That black dust is spreading; it's impacting and sickening unconsenting people outside the league—such as wives and kids."

It didn't take long for author Malcolm Gladwell, who once compared professional football to dogfighting, to speak on the NFL's troubles. "Football is a moral abomination," he told Bloomberg News just a short time after that horrid week. He predicted that football would eventually "wither on the vine." Gladwell continued, "We're not just talking about people limping at the age of 50. We're talking about brain injuries that are causing horrible, protracted, premature death. This...is appalling. Can you point to another industry in America which, in the course of doing business, maims a third of its employees?"

Also that Friday, Minnesota Vikings superstar Adrian Peterson was arrested on one felony count of injury to a child. By 6:00 PM Eastern that day, photos of the injury started to appear on social media. Peterson had beat his son with a switch, causing multiple lacerations.

It was these moments—the video of Rice hitting his then fiancée, the pictures of the bruised, cut leg and back of Peterson's young son—that made this week so bad for the NFL. The pictures propagated across social media only incensed fans and others further. Peterson, like Rice, had been considered (mostly) to be one of the NFL's good guys. The arrest stunned the Vikings. While some Vikings players supported Peterson, others texted each other saying he should not only be gone from the Vikings but from the NFL. "AP is an animal," one text read. "He doesn't deserve to play in our league. We should stand for something. How does anyone treat a child that way?"

The week was so bad that veteran football writer Peter King asked his *Sports Illustrated* readers a simple question: Do you still like football? One reader had an interesting point. "Like you described in the introduction of this week's column, I've been growing more dissatisfied with NFL (and college) football in recent years. I'm still a Steelers and Penn State fan, but recent events in those organizations, as well as those mentioned from this season, have made my commitment to the sport wane slightly. I'm not going to stop watching just yet. The recent player misconduct, plus your mentioning of the apparent addiction people have to their phones, got me thinking. Is the recent spate of misbehavior among professional players truly a new trend? Or is the fact that people are essentially being monitored every minute of every day exposing behavior that has always existed, yet remained hidden? I doubt there's truly a way to quantify the effect of technology on athletes and society as a whole; the presence of a video camera in the hands of every person has to have an effect on what gets reported, though."

King's response was also interesting: "A couple of years ago, after Jovan Belcher of the Chiefs killed his girlfriend and then himself, Chiefs quarterback Brady Quinn talked the next day in a passionate way about how people on the team were too busy checking their phones all the time and not really conversing with each other. He wondered if that might have had something to do with the disconnect between Belcher and his teammates, who Quinn thought might have been so busy in their own little world that they didn't notice Belcher's life spinning out of control. That could well be wrong, of course, but I just think a lot of times in our culture now that we're so consumed by the machines that should be there to help us, that they end up controlling us instead."

Yet the week and further negative news involving player crimes and concussions was not stopping fans from watching football, at least anecdotally. Instead, the opposite was occurring. What was happening (again anecdotally) was that fans were looking for reasons to soothe their conscience about loving a sport that was causing so much pain and destruction to its players and the people around them.

The week was so bad that broadcasters, in pregame shows and during the games themselves, spoke critically about the league. Most television play-by-play types and color analysts rarely criticize the sport publicly, but this was different. The game was in crisis. On September 11, 2014, the classy James Brown, longtime broadcaster and host of CBS' *The NFL Today*, gave an impassioned speech prior to the Thursday night game between the Pittsburgh Steelers and Baltimore Ravens.

"Two years ago, I challenged the NFL community and all men to seriously confront the problem of domestic violence, especially coming on the heels of the suicide of Kansas City Chiefs player Jovan Belcher and [death of] girlfriend Kasandra Perkins, yet here we are again confronting the same issue of violence against women. Now, let's be clear, this problem is bigger than football. There has been, appropriately so, intense and widespread outrage following the release of the video showing what happened in the elevator at the casino. Now, wouldn't it be productive if this collective outrage could be channeled to truly hear and address the long-suffering cries for help from so many women, and as they said, do something about it?

"An ongoing, comprehensive education of men about what healthy, respectful manhood is all about. And it starts with how we view women. Our language is important, for example. When a guy says, 'You throw a ball like a girl' or 'You're a sissy,' it reflects an attitude that devalues women, and [negative] attitudes will eventually manifest in some fashion. Women have been at the forefront in the domestic violence awareness and prevention arena, and whether Janay Rice considers herself a victim or not, millions of women in this country are. Consider this, according to domestic violence experts, more than three women a day lose their lives at the hands of their partners. That means since the night of February 15 in Atlantic City [when the Rice crime occurred] more than 600 women have died, so this is yet another call to men to stand up and take responsibility for their thoughts, their words, their deeds and to get help, because our silence is deafening and deadly."

Later, during the game's broadcast, venerable announcer Jim Nantz called it "arguably the darkest week in the history of the league."

One longtime NFL executive quietly professed to me he thought Goodell, and many top executives, would be fired by the end of the month. He began to update his résumé. Outside of the NFL offices, numerous news trucks set up in the street. They stayed there for weeks.

ESPN writer Jane McManus wrote in 2013 about the perilous tightrope the NFL was walking when it came to its popularity, but her words apply now.

> There is something so Rome-before-the-fall about the league's approach. Boxing once ruled the sports landscape in the same way the NFL does now. At its heyday, boxing drew young men to gyms from across social classes and economic groups, but there aren't a lot of rings set up in high schools or gyms anymore. When the sports public was witness to some bouts in which men died from wounds sustained in the ring, it forced profound conscience examining from some corners, while others defended the brutality—a conversation that might seem familiar. Boxing never properly dealt with a number of corruption issues and an alphabet soup of authorities.... In football, there are already enough bodies in the pipeline to keep the NFL functioning for the next decade. But, beyond that, what parents want to set their fresh-faced kid up to succeed in a league that will require him to sign an agreement not to sue if he develops brain injuries as a byproduct of his employment?

It cannot be overstated just how popular the sport of boxing was in the early 1900s, and even decades later. In some ways, boxing then was more ingrained in the American psyche than football is now. Fighters, especially the heavyweights, were household names—much bigger stars than any football player today. In fact, the tradition of watching sports at bars may have actually started with boxing. Bar owners set up tickertape machines and did their own play-by-play of the fights. In his book *Harpo Speaks* the legendary Harpo Marx wrote, "Prize fighting itself in those days was not a sport, like baseball. It was show business. A heavyweight title bout was to me the biggest show of any year, greater than the St. Patrick's parade, the election bonfire, and the Watson Sisters all rolled into one.

"My supreme idol was [heavyweight champion] James J. Jeffries," Marx continued. "On the afternoon he fought Jack Munroe, in San Francisco, I sat on the sidewalk with 40 other kids in front of a saloon on 90th Street and Third Avenue. There was a ticker in the saloon. The bartender announced the fight blow by blow as it came off the ticker, and some kindly patron was thoughtful enough to relay the vital news to the kids on the street outside."

Later, boxers like Jack Johnson and Joe Louis would enthrall both whites and blacks, but African Americans in particular would gravitate to them (and later Muhammad Ali) in ways that eclipse any NFL player today. (Only Jim Brown came close to the same level of popularity.) Boxing dwarfed football then and would for many years. So anyone who says the NFL will never falter is unaware of history and how so-called unbeatable sports were indeed beaten.

The boxing comparison is appropriate, but the tobacco industry comparison is possibly even more apt. Michael Sokolove wrote a *New York Times Magazine* story about the connection. If the NFL were to falter, it might be this parallel that is the most accurate. He points out that smoking was once a central part of American culture, something that appeared deeply entrenched. The challenges came slowly, with doctors warnings slowly building and legal battles being waged.

> In 1998, [the tobacco companies] agreed to pay $206 billion to settle a lawsuit brought by the attorneys general of 46 states, who were seeking compensation for costs to the public related to smoking-related illnesses.
> It's worth noting the year that the first tobacco manufacturer acknowledged that cigarettes cause cancer: 1997. By then smoking was already in decline.... About 18 percent of American adults now smoke— fewer than one in five. Tobacco's shift from integral part of American life to its fringes took about half a century.

Like the tobacco industry, the NFL has spent exorbitant amounts of money in an attempt to prove its product is safe. According to a number of high-ranking NFL sources, football spent approximately $300 million over the past 10 years on various programs and public relations initiatives to combat imagery that football is harmful. A significant amount of this money, sources explained, was used to fund the NFL's Heads Up program.

The program purports to teach safe tackling techniques to youth football players, but one owner admitted in an interview that Heads Up is "more PR than practical." The program has been criticized because the tackling methodologies it teaches aren't truly safe or practical. Nate Jackson, who played six years for the Denver Broncos at tight end, told ESPN.com that Heads Up was formed to "create the illusion that the game is safe or can be made safe." He continued, "It's rather shameless. I think it's sad. I think it's indicative of what the league's motives are: profit, profit, profit."

The tobacco industry had the luxury of fighting to protect its product mostly before the social media age. Now, social media acts as an accelerant to controversy. As such, any near-fatal wounds to the NFL won't take 50 years to kill it. It'll happen much sooner because people's awareness is much more keen, information spreads more quickly, and cynicism about the NFL has never been higher.

Toward the end of that week in September 2014, ESPN.com published a story quoting a brand tracker who also doubles as a USC professor. Jeetendr Sehdev explained that he interviewed 3,000 people from ages 16 to 60 using polls, interviews and focus groups. Polling participants about brand trustworthiness, Sehdev found that in four of the seven most vital factors of trust, the NFL scored in the lowest 10 percent among 200 different brands. Those factors are openness, acceptance, compassion, and consistency. Sehdev told ESPN.com that if the NFL continued on that track, it would be one of America's least trusted brands within five years.

"It's surprising to hear people in the media say how durable the NFL brand is, that it can withstand a series of onslaughts and PR disasters, when the truth is the NFL has been crumbling," Sehdev explained. "Just because the NFL brings in a lot of revenue doesn't mean people can't perceive the league as incredibly untrustworthy," Sehdev said. "Exxon Mobil, Goldman Sachs, and Walmart all make a lot of money but have really low levels of trust among consumers." It's interesting to note that Sehdev's research was completed *before* September 2014.

Despite that worst week, despite the stunning level of violence against women—and a child—perpetrated by high-profile players, despite the extreme lack of understanding from the sport's commissioner of how domestic violence works, despite the arrogance, despite the ugliness, despite predictions of the league's imminent demise, despite a year of damaging headlines, despite a presidential tongue-lashing—despite it all, the NFL prospered. The top three most-watched television shows for that week were *Sunday Night Football*, *Thursday Night Football*, and *Monday Night Football*.

In 1980, the most-watched World Series games reached about 25 percent of America's population. Today the World Series reaches 3 to 4 percent. "Today, the World Series is like *The Ed Sullivan Show*, the Miss America pageant, Timex watches, and sitting in your favorite chair surrounded by a stack of daily newspapers," wrote *Boston Globe* columnist Dan Shaughnessy while covering the 2014 World Series. "It's like *Peanuts*. It was once the biggest event in sports. Now it's a relic of a simpler time before the Worldwide Leader and the World Wide Web.... I blame no one. It's evolution. Baseball is too long and slow for modern attention spans. The games drag, especially with late-inning pitching changes. The glut of games on television and the introduction of interleague play has blurred the identity of the respective leagues and taken away the mystery of star players in faraway lands."

Those are salient factors, but there is also another, an old-school motive: violence. Americans can't turn away because we like seeing other men, *on the field*, beat the hell out of each other. "The league is a microcosm," wrote Rich Cohen in the *Wall Street Journal*.

And football is violent—nothing but violence, controlled fury. This too is America. We live in a violent country, have violent impulses, love a violent game. Players must work themselves into a rage to succeed. Is it any wonder that some can't turn it off? They've keyed themselves up with Dexedrine and greenies from the start.

Football has never been more popular, but certain circles say the game is too brutal for modern America—that we've evolved away from it, or should have. Such people hold out soccer as an alternative, much the same way that, on cold days, my mom used to hold out a more sensible coat instead of the one with all the zippers. But America is still what it has always been: a tough country, made by violence, which the game compresses and presents in the course of an afternoon.

There was a strain of this reaction—though much more raw—from a segment of fans who felt that week and the criticism of the NFL was part of the "wussification" of America. While message boards are the sewer system of the Internet, one post on a Vikings message board typified the response of some hardcore football fans: "I want to take this moment to thank all the liberal progressive scum who have ruined the league that I once loved by injecting leftist propaganda into a sport that was an outlet away from political discourse. You have succeeded in your mission to emasculate this truly 'American' sport. None of you b@stards will be happy until every team changes their name and has a roster made up of women, trannies, and gays. First of all, Peterson's discipline went too far, no doubt... However in a time when black America is in crisis with absentee fathers, Adrian should be lauded for trying to have an impact in the rearing of his son. (no pun intended)... He is a good man, who despite his phenomenal talent (Arguably the most complete back in NFL history) has ran afoul of the Liberal elites that run the NFL with his Christian belief system and old fashioned viewpoints on marriage, etc... I have no doubt by this time tomorrow, AP will be without a team, and will be a pariah on the myriad 'talking head' sports shows. He will be relegated to the dustbin of NFL obscurity for doing nothing more that being a caring father. Lets take a moment, shall we to remember all of the great contributions other members of the NFL have made to the benefit of mankind." So, there's that.

The worst week in NFL history started the season, so it was only fitting the end of the season also ended in controversy. Fox's Jay Glazer reported the NFL was already planning to examine the Patriots' footballs after the Baltimore Ravens had tipped off the Colts and the Colts subsequently tipped off the NFL. Thus began Deflategate.

The Colts met the Patriots in the AFC title game for a second-straight year. It was again a Patriots blowout. But again, too, Brady was intercepted. And again, the Colts had suspicions the Patriots had deflated the football below NFL-mandated specifications. As every football fan now knows, an underinflated ball is easier for a quarterback to throw and a receiver to catch.

Each offense gets 12 footballs to use during the course of the game. They are inspected approximately two hours before kickoff by game officials who check the footballs' air pressure. When the NFL investigated midgame, they found that 11 of the 12 footballs used by New England had lower pressure. Belichick said he had no idea about any deflated footballs. In his press conference, Brady said the same.

Owner Robert Kraft, at the Super Bowl, offered a passionate defense of the team and said that if the Patriots were ultimately found not to have violated the rules, Goodell would owe the team an apology. Goodell, in his own Super Bowl press conference, scoffed at such a notion.

Some of the harshest comments about the Patriots came from Mike Pereira, the former NFL vice president of officiating and a current Fox rules analyst. His perception was similar to what many throughout football also felt. "Each game, 36 balls are brought into the officials' locker room," Pereira said on a January Fox broadcast. "Twelve from each team, and then the home team provides 12 backup balls, if needed. The referee has a pump and a needle, and with the help of the kicking ball coordinator, he checks them. And if they're between 12.5 and 13.5 pounds per square inch, he marks them and they're good to go. They leave the locker room before the game and go into the hands of the ball boys, and the extra balls are put at the replay monitor, where there is a guard standing by that monitor.

"Well, somebody got to somebody and took a couple of pounds out of those balls. It's an extension, to me, of the cheating that has gone on in the league. This is cheating and this is something that the league doesn't want. It's bad enough that rules get taken advantage of and you kind of work against the intent of the rule, but this is cheating." *Somebody got to somebody.* He made the NFL sound like organized crime. Pereira has quietly become one of the most powerful people in football. His interpretation of calls and explanation of them are usually marvelously on point and actually entertaining. I know NFL team executives that before filing an official complaint with the league over a call in a game, the day after the contest, will go back and see what Pereira said about the call.

Fox analyst Troy Aikman, a Hall of Fame quarterback, was equally blunt when it came to Brady. "I can't imagine anyone doing anything to the footballs without the quarterback having knowledge of it," he said. "I know, based on my experience, how much effort went in to trying to get the balls game-ready. Having them still fall within the guidelines of the NFL rules was challenging, and there is no way that anyone would have done anything with the game balls without discussing it with me first. I can't imagine that Tom Brady did not know that air had been taken out of the balls and my guess is that it was his request, it was the way he preferred to throw with them and that's why it was done."

Aikman wasn't the only Hall of Fame quarterback to effectively question Brady's integrity. Three days before Brady would play in the Super Bowl, his boyhood idol, Joe Montana, said he thought Brady was responsible for deflating the footballs. Footballs, Montana said, don't end up that way unless a quarterback wants them that way. "If I ever want a ball a certain way, I don't do it myself," said Montana. "So, somebody did it for him. But I don't know why everybody is making a big deal out of trying to figure out who did it. It's pretty simple. If it was done, it was done for a reason. I mean, it's easy to figure out who did it. Did Tom do it? No, but Tom likes the balls that way, obviously, or you wouldn't have 11 of them that way without him complaining, because as a quarterback, you know how you like the ball. If it doesn't feel like that, something is wrong. It's a stupid thing to even be talking about because they shouldn't have the rule anyway. If you want to see the game played at the best, everybody has a different grip, everybody likes a different feel."

One thing the controversy did was publicly expose a rift between the NFL elite and some others. Patriots owner Robert Kraft, one of the most decent men in football, has nonetheless engendered great jealousy. Part of the reason is that the Patriots beat everyone. Also, Kraft is extremely close to Goodell. This relationship has not gone unnoticed by other franchises and players that for years have privately complained to each other and members of the media that the commissioner and owner are too close. On the first day of media availability at the Pro Bowl, Seattle's Richard Sherman was asked by reporters if the Patriots were rule breakers. "Their résumé speaks for itself," Sherman said. "The past is what the past is. Their present is what their present is….Will [the Patriots] be punished? Probably not. Not as long as Robert Kraft and Roger Goodell are still taking pictures at their respective homes. I think he was just at Kraft's house [the week before] the AFC Championship. You talk about conflict of interest. As long as that happens, it won't affect them at all."

Sherman wasn't alone in those feelings. One of the things the investigation needed to do was act as a sort of cleansing. The perception that the Patriots could do whatever the hell they wanted because of that close relationship shared between Goodell and Kraft was a huge problem. A story that appeared Super Bowl week in *GQ* hit on this subject. The story was titled "The Season from Hell: Inside Roger Goodell's Ruthless Football Machine." The opening anecdote discussed the Rice case and hit on that perceived uber-close relationship between Kraft and Goodell.

> Goodell doesn't look the other way when it comes to the Patriots. That's simply false. If he did, there would have been no Spygate punishment or Deflategate investigation to begin with. There's no question, however, that is how things are seen. [Jay] Glazer discussed this when the controversy became public: "I will tell you this…it has been unanimous among owners, general managers, and head coaches I talk to and they're saying, 'We're sick of it, they always push the envelope. The league throws the book at us all the time'…a lot of people in the league look at it like, 'There's a double standard: We get in trouble, they don't get in trouble.'"

Amy Trask, the former Oakland Raiders executive, current CBS analyst, and one of the smartest people ever involved in the sport, hit on one of the most important points of all. "We have to be careful not to conflate practical issues with philosophical issues," said Trask. "From a practical perspective, the use of underinflated footballs is not the reason that New England won the AFC championship. From a practical perspective, the New England quarterback is not the only quarterback who wants (and who has communicated that he wants) his footballs 'just so.'

"From a philosophical perspective, the league can't trumpet the integrity of the game without protecting it. Belief in the integrity of the game is precious and to be cherished. From a philosophical perspective, the league can't enjoy the fruits of being the most popular game in the country without understanding the scrutiny and attention that come with being the most popular game in the country. Are these footballs the reason New England won? No. Is the New England quarterback the only quarterback who is particular about his footballs? No. But we must be careful not to conflate those practical issues with larger philosophical issues and the league must do what is in the best interests of the game and public trust in the integrity of the game. Those who love this game want that."

Wrote former NFL agent and Green Bay Packers executive Andrew Brandt in *Sports Illustrated*: "Most of the systematic issues in the NFL—the draft, salary cap, free-agency restrictions and revenue sharing—were established in the name of competitive balance. Owners have bought into a version of corporate socialism built on the notion that the league as a whole is only as strong as its weakest link. Skirting the playing rules flies in the face of this competitive fairness. Further, on a macro level, the NFL's credibility has been at issue all year, and the league has been in a reactive state on domestic violence since the TMZ drop of the Ray Rice elevator video on September 8. Now, with a new, more stringent personal-conduct policy and the soft reprimand of the Mueller Report behind them, the NFL had moved on from a crisis in integrity. Or so it thought."

Quarterbacks have always been weird about their balls. (Sorry for that—I'm 12 years old.) Several years ago, a group of quarterbacks, led by Peyton Manning and Brady, had a conference call with the league office about Super Bowl footballs. Quarterbacks hate their newness and slickness. But that's how they roll when it comes to footballs: they do push it to the limit of what the rules allow. Previously, the Patriots were warned about videotaping practices but did it anyway. They were severely punished by the NFL, and Spygate remains one of the most embarrassing moments in NFL history. Deflategate was not far behind, and it happened in a year of NFL controversy.

On January 22, 2015, all three of the broadcast networks led with the Deflatriots story. The *NBC Nightly News* started this way: "On our broadcast tonight, full denial from Patriots quarterback Tom Brady and from his coach, as a football inflation scandal remains bigger than the upcoming Super Bowl, as the question remains: Who or what was responsible?"

The *CBS Evening News*: "Tonight, caught in a pressure cooker: Is Tom Brady a cheater? Quarterback Tom Brady responds to reports that the Patriots used deflated footballs in the AFC Championship Game."

ABC World News Tonight: "On this Thursday night, the breaking news: the scandal before the Super Bowl. The star quarterback, Tom Brady, answering the question: Are you a cheater? Tonight, how Brady explains those deflated footballs, who handled them after they were handled by the refs, and what now for the football star with the supermodel wife?"

The Friday before the Super Bowl, the *New Yorker* magazine ran a cartoon mocking the Deflategate scandal. Yes, that *New Yorker*.

Indeed, the scandal had grown so big that the White House, yet again, was asked to comment. The spokesman, Josh Earnest, was asked about Brady's awkward press conference, in which both his statement and honesty were questioned. "For years it has been clear that there is no risk that I would take Tom Brady's job as quarterback of the New England Patriots," Earnest said.

"But I can tell you that, as of today, it is pretty clear that there is no risk of him taking my job either."

And what may have been the ultimate sign of the NFL's influence on pop culture, and how it was becoming targeted in almost all walks of life, is that during the Deflatriot scandal, *Sesame Street* reran an old episode in which the word of the day was "inflate." Yes, even *Sesame Street* trolled the NFL.

In a move that typified happenings in the sport over the past year—and beyond—the NFL conducted an independent investigation into the controversy. It appointed Ted Wells, who had expertly investigated the Dolphins' bullying scandal several years earlier.

In yet another unprecedented move in an unprecedented year, Kraft read a statement on the Monday of Super Bowl week, blasting critics. It was a remarkable document. He read it and took no questions; the only thing missing was a mic drop. "If the Wells investigation is not able to definitively determine that our organization tampered with the air pressure in the footballs, I would expect and hope the league would apologize to our entire team, and in particular to Coach Belichick and Tom Brady, for what they've had to endure this week," Kraft said. "I'm disappointed in the way this entire matter has been handled and reported upon. We expect hard facts rather than circumstantial leaked evidence to drive the conclusion of this investigation.

"I want to make it clear, I believe unconditionally that the New England Patriots have done nothing inappropriate in this process or are in violation of NFL rules," Kraft said. "Tom, Bill, and I have been together for 15 years. They are my guys. They are part of my family. Bill, Tom, and I have had many difficult discussions over the years. I've never known them to lie to me. That's why I'm confident in saying what I just said.

"It bothers me greatly their reputations and integrity—and by association that of our team—has been called into question this week."

The scandal opened old wounds across the sport. It was like ghosts making another appearance at a family's home after a long hiatus. These types of stories are also a threat to the NFL, putting the notion of competitive balance at stake. This idea is the cornerstone of football: everyone plays by the same rules (or mostly does). There is something bigger, though. If the NFL is viewed as wrestling—that what you see on the field can't be trusted—that is, well, a huge problem. How many of these types of scandals can the NFL endure? Or is the sport so bulletproof now that it can absorb any scandal and keep getting huge viewership? This is the intersection at which the league finds itself now.

For the first time in NFL history, a Super Bowl participant in the days before the game was being investigated for cheating. Nothing like that had ever happened before. Yes, worst year in NFL history, indeed.

Teams have always cheated, but in the past the attention given to the cheaters was minimal, and the media less abundant and probing. In fact, one of the biggest cheating scandals of all time is something few know about. This from Bill Parcells, Hall of Fame coach, in 2011: "I know from past history in two playoff games, one of these teams that was famous for using a script, which they rehearsed with their team prior to the game— they knew exactly what they wanted to do—mysteriously, two years in a row, when the game started, their phones went down, which mandates that the other side put their phones down.

Now, let me get this straight. You've got your script rehearsed, you know what you're going to do, the defense doesn't know what's coming, but they have to take their phones off?"

Parcells was referring to the playoffs after the 1985 and 1986 seasons and San Francisco 49ers coach Bill Walsh. Walsh scripted his plays, then twice cut the Giants' headsets, thus preventing the Giants coaches from coordinating their counterattack. It was a sneaky tactic by Walsh and clear cheating. Yet the totality of Walsh's actions didn't come to light for decades. Then, cheating was mostly ignored or unknown. Today, cheating would be diagrammed on Facebook within minutes. Today, cheating injures the league as a whole.

Some of the most critical comments of the Patriots—comments that could in some ways apply to the larger issue of the NFL's dilemma now, which is running a brilliant, high-profile business in a sport that doesn't always care or respect that glossiness—came from ESPN analyst and former Carolina general manager Marty Hurney. Hurney's Panthers lost to the Patriots in Super Bowl XXXVIII in February 2004 by three points. "There isn't a day that goes by since [then] that I haven't questioned...that there were some things done that might have been beyond the rules that may have given them a three-point advantage," Hurney said. "And I can't prove anything, and that's why I'm very angry. And the anger has come back over the last couple of days [after the revelation] that commissioner Roger Goodell decided to shred all of the evidence after Spygate, because I think there were a lot of things in there that would bring closure to a lot of people."

"This is about a culture," Hurney continued. "Is there a culture of cheating at probably what most people look at as the best franchise in the National Football League? There are people who swear to me that the Patriots taped our practice down in Houston during Super Bowl week. I can't prove it. I don't know. And I hate talking like this because I feel like a bad loser, but it just gnaws at you. And this latest incident brings it back up."

Hurney's words are interesting because he was the general manager of the team during another scandal, when Panthers players were busted for buying steroids from a South Carolina doctor. Among the players were three of the five starting offensive linemen. "That was wrong," Hurney said. "The organization didn't know anything about it, and we took steps and we addressed that. We weren't going to put up with that [Team owner] Jerry Richardson wasn't going to put up with that.

"To me, this isn't about deflating balls. It's about a continuing culture of alleged cheating, and to me, everybody's talking about Bill Belichick and Tom Brady. When is Robert Kraft going to come up and explain why, if they are found guilty of this, why do these things keep happening in this organization?...

"This is a bigger issue, and I think most people are missing the issue. It's an issue of if there is a culture of cheating at the organization that most people look at as the gold standard in this league. Is there a culture of cheating and breaking the rules?"

The Rice case. The missteps by Goodell. The cheating accusations against one of the league's premier franchises. The ugly Washington team name. There has never been a worse year for the NFL. Ever.

ESPN commentator Stephen A. Smith summed up one of the main undercurrents of the year and a belief many in the media had about the NFL's handling of them. Smith said the NFL mishandles some of these problems not because they aren't capable but because they are. He called it "purposeful incompetence."

"You can always spew ignorance," he said. "I don't know, I don't know, I don't know. We have, as a growing public, we have lost, lost the ability to trust the NFL at its word. They're just not thorough enough. They're just not thorough."

One of the last big-name critics to rip the NFL over its season from hell was Senator John McCain. McCain's criticism was extremely McCainsian: "I think these controversies would have gone away a lot easier if they had approached them from, 'How are the American people going to react to seeing the video of a professional football player knock out his wife?'" McCain told *USA TODAY* Sports, referring to the second Ray Rice elevator video, "If I were them, I would review my whole PR scheme. One thing we do in politics when there's an issue that arises, smart politicians have a rapid-response team. What is the reaction of Mr. Goodell in this latest one? He's MIA as far as I can tell.

"The whole scandal resonates very badly because just before the Super Bowl, which is the premier sporting event in America, the question is not about the contest. It's about the pressurization of the football. That's too bad."

If all of that, if all of what happened in that horrible year wasn't enough, more than enough, in January 2015 began the trial of former Patriots tight end Aaron Hernandez, who was accused of killing semi-professional football player Odin Lloyd. Lloyd was found shot to death near Hernandez's home, not far from Gillette Stadium.

Despite the controversy, the ugliness, the at times sheer insanity, there remains an element of football, beyond the violence and scandals, which still captures the attention of the public. It's this fact that keeps the NFL in its current dominant position: even Hollywood stars get captivated. In November 2014, the Broncos were staying in Providence, Rhode Island, before their game against the New England Patriots. The team's general manager, John Elway—and maybe the best quarterback of all time—was out at a restaurant when an unknown guest summoned Elway to a back room. When Elway walked into the room, the man who had asked for him smiled wide and welcomed him. It was William Shatner—Captain Kirk himself. The two had a few drinks together, one captain enjoying the company of another.

Also that November, at the halfway point of the season, NFL games accounted for the top 10—and 26 of the top 30—most-watched television shows since the season began on September 1. The only things that beat NFL football in that three-month stretch were Game 7 of the World Series and a few scant episodes of *NCIS* and *The Big Bang Theory*.

Through Week 15 of the 2014 season, NFL games averaged 17.9 million viewers. (A decade ago that number was 15.4 million.) In December 2014 the NFL Network broadcast the Jacksonville-Tennessee game, easily the worst Thursday night matchup of the year. It still drew a 3.4 rating—the same number as Game 1 of the World Series.

By the end of the 2014 regular season, the NFL had accounted for 45 of the top 50 shows that fall. NFL games reached 202 million people, according to Nielsen, which reached 80 percent of all television homes in the United States. In January 2014, about 42 million people tuned in to watch the Dallas Cowboys and Detroit Lions play on Wild Card weekend.

One of the more staggering statistics about the NFL's popularity is that in 2014 more than 45 million people watched the *NFL Draft*. To put that in perspective, that's almost twice the population of Australia. At the 2015 NFL Scouting Combine—an orgy of 40-yard dashes and measurements of prospects' hands and general eyeballing as potential draftees stand around in their underwear—the NFL issued 1,071 on-site media credentials, the most ever for the combine.

The top executive at PepsiCo, Indra Nooyi, told *Forbes* that while she "cringes" every time she sees a story about another player suffering from head trauma, her company won't be pulling any ad dollars from the sport. "We want to be associated with the right sport that sends the right message," she explained. "Having said that, the NFL is such a big part of American culture that to not be associated with it would be crazy." Pepsi has a 10-year deal with the NFL worth $1 billion, *Forbes* reports.

"The [number of] people tuning in [to watch the NFL] shows that even though, intellectually, people might think the NFL hasn't done a great job, and that some folks who play in the league are not particularly upstanding, it's not going to prevent them from watching the games," Ted Marzilli, CEO of YouGov BrandIndex, which tracks consumers' perceptions of brands, told the *Sporting News*. "As long as you have those eyeballs in front of the TV, you're going to have advertisers who are going to pay to reach them. I think the brand's been damaged a little bit. But viewership indicates it will bounce back."

The ultimate sign of the NFL's popularity came after the Super Bowl. Despite this awful season, with all its sordid and putrid storylines, the Super Bowl XLIX game between Seattle and New England garnered an overnight rating of 49.7, its highest ever. Indeed, he Nielsen company announced on February 2 that Super Bowl XLIX was the most watched television program in American history with 114.4 million people tuning in. According to Facebook, the game generated 265 million posts. Twitter reported 28.4 million global tweets.

Then, the day after the Super Bowl and those fabulous ratings, it was announced that No. 1 draft pick Johnny Manziel had entered a rehab facility. And at approximately 7:00 in the morning, again the day after the Super Bowl, Hall of Famer Warren Sapp was arrested for soliciting a prostitute. Just hours after the news was first reported by TMZ, his contract with the NFL Network was terminated. (Sapp is one of the more high-profile former players in the ex-jock analyst industrial complex.)

The bad news didn't stop there. The Ravens officially terminated the contract of Terrence Cody, a defensive tackle, before he was indicted on grand jury charges of animal cruelty. From *USA TODAY*: "Cody faces 15 charges, including two felony counts of aggravated animal cruelty, related to the death of his dog, a Bullmastiff from Spain. Cody also is facing a misdemeanor charge of illegal possession of an alligator and five misdemeanor counts of animal abuse or neglect of the alligator. And, he was charged with misdemeanor possession of drug paraphernalia and possession of marijuana."

Sports Illustrated once wrote a story about the demise of football. Writer John Underwood described how many in and around the sport predicted its doom. In the story, former Penn State president Dr. Eric Walker told the late (and now infamous) Joe Paterno: "If football doesn't do something about the injuries, soccer will be our national sport in 10 years."

That story was written in 1978.

So we've heard it before: the NFL is about to fall. Thus, the NFL can't be beat. Right?

Right?

2 ROME

SCENES FROM A LEAGUE SIMULTANEOUSLY AT THE HEIGHT OF ITS power, and perhaps closest to the precipice than it's ever been and maybe ever will be...

At an NFL league meeting in the spring of 2013, Goodell was chatting casually with a small group of owners, when one of them had a question. "What's the biggest threat to our dominance in sports?" the owner asked, according to another present at the time. Goodell didn't hesitate. "Everything," he said. "Everyone is going after the big boy on the block." Goodell had no idea at the time how right he was.

One owner, following that horrible week, and after other scandals, was asked by me about the NFL's mortality. "This is the most vulnerable the league has ever been," he told me. "Can the NFL as we know it die? I'd say probably not, but a year ago I would have said, 'Impossible.' Now I say, 'It's possible.' The dinosaurs died. Presidents have died. Great people, great institutions…great civilizations died. Rome died. Yes, we can be Rome. We can die."

———

THE NFL IS RARELY STUNNED, BUT IN MARCH 2015 SHOCK WAVES ran through the entire sport when a star young player named Chris Borland retired; he played in the NFL for a total of one year before leaving it behind. Borland came from a football family, and was just 24 years old and a key cog on the San Francisco 49ers when he made the announcement. In doing so, he became the most prominent player to leave the game because of concern over brain trauma. "I just honestly want to do what's best for my health," Borland told *Outside the Lines*. "From what I've researched and what I've experienced, I don't think it's worth the risk."

"I feel largely the same, as sharp as I've ever been. For me, it's wanting to be proactive," Borland later said. "I'm concerned that if you wait till you have symptoms, it's too late.... There are a lot of unknowns. I can't claim that X will happen. I just want to live a long, healthy life, and I don't want to have any neurological diseases or [to] die younger than I would otherwise. I just thought to myself, *What am I doing? Is this how I'm going to live my adult life, banging my head, especially with what I've learned and know about the dangers?*"

Borland was raised in a family that was completely educated about the dangers of the sport. In fact, his father wouldn't let him play football until he reached high school because of those dangers, and Borland, according to players who know him, long studied the potential problems football posed to the mind.

In April 2015, Borland was at a film premiere about football and brain injuries, when he was asked about the future of the NFL. Borland spoke of a key issue the league faces. "It's such a part of our culture...it'll continue to be played," he said. "That's for sure. I don't know for how long and in what capacity. It's a catch-22. It's so violent that improvements need to be made, but improving it creates something other than what we know as football."

The Borland case also fits squarely with what many team officials have told me privately—and consistently—and it's a recurring theme for football's future: that the sport will become more classist. That future is not so distant, and in many ways it is starting even now.

Borland grew up middle class. Went to a private school and was raised in a two-parent family. His brothers played football and have postfootball careers outside of the sport. So Borland can afford to not have football in his life. He can afford to walk away. He has a financial cushion and familial safety net. There are others, though, who won't walk away because they can't. Or they—or their parents—will see football as a way out. Football could become manned solely by the poor and disadvantaged.

Green Bay Packers president and CEO Mark Murphy was asked by ESPN in 2014 if he thought the demographics of football were changing due to concussion awareness. Murphy is one of the most honest executives in all of sports, and he was again forthright in answering the question. In the ESPN article he brought up the drop in youth football participation and also brought up an issue discussed by writer Malcolm Gladwell.

"I think the league and USA Football is really doing a great job of breaking through a little bit of the hysteria," Murphy said. "But there's no question that it's an issue. Whether that trend reverses, I don't know.

"But there is an argument that you've probably heard, that eventually all football players are going to come from poorer backgrounds. It's that way a little bit now, for whatever reason."

Gladwell, as ESPN noted, called it the "ghettoization of football." In the documentary *United States of Football*, Gladwell compared a future NFL to the current armed forces. This is an analogy I've heard several NFL team executives make. People who join the army know the serious risks involved. In the future, people who play football will know the risks and play anyway—if they are poor, that is. The middle class, guys like Borland, and the wealthy won't play.

"If I'm spending $30,000 to send my kid to a private high school," Gladwell said in the movie, "am I going to let my kid participate in a sport with some unknown percent chance of permanently impairing him cognitively? No way. It's just not going to happen. That's over. So from there it's going to go slowly down the line."

Gladwell, a football doomsayer, is one thing. But Kirk Herbstreit is another entity entirely. You have to understand who Herbstreit is. Herbstreit is a former college quarterback and an unabashed cheerleader for football (particularly college football). He rarely criticizes anything football does. Ever. He rarely sees flaws. Ever.

So when after the Borland news broke and Herbstreit expressed dire concerns about football's future via social media, it was shocking. "I think it absolutely will impact the sport," he tweeted. "I'm not sure I would do it over again."

"Obviously guys will continue to play Fball, but I guarantee the Borland early retirement gets the attn of a lot of Moms and youth fball," Herbstreit continued.

"I'm just tellin ya head trauma & concussions are very common & with the attention & responses now to them this is uncharted waters for Fball," he added.

Herbstreit also added: "Sad to see Borland retire after just 1 yr, but I get his concerns-Will this be the beginning of a trend for this sport? Is Fball in trouble?"

———

HOURS BEFORE HIS NEW ENGLAND PATRIOTS WOULD TAKE THE field, the owner of the team, Robert Kraft, had a question for analyst Cris Collinsworth. Collinsworth is the notoriously blunt, and talented, analyst for NBC's *Sunday Night Football*. He played from 1981 to 1988 for the Cincinnati Bengals. Also present in the group were several top executives from NBC. At the time, NBC was in the process of bidding for the Thursday night package, which would eventually go to CBS.

Kraft's question was simple: "What do you think of the Thursday night games?"

Collinsworth looked at the NBC executives, then looked at Kraft. "Do you want the real answer, Bob, or the bullshit one?"

Kraft said he wanted the real one, and Collinsworth gave it to him: "When the players sue the owners a second time over concussions, exhibit A will be Thursday night games. Having players play again so soon after a Sunday game will destroy their health. It's criminal, Bob."

Kraft was stunned. Despite asking for bluntness, he didn't expect it to that degree. Kraft would later recount the story to Collinsworth's booth partner, Al Michaels, perhaps the greatest sports voice ever. "Did you ask Cris to be blunt?" Michaels implored. Kraft acknowledged he did. "Then that's what you get with Cris: total honesty," Michaels responded.

Collinsworth was saying what almost every player in the NFL feels: Thursday night games are a money grab. Players get part of that cash, of course, but several dozen of them told me that the vast majority of the league's players despise playing Thursday night. And most of them feel that way because their bodies don't get sufficient time to rest from Sunday's game to Thursday.

"No one wants to play Thursdays," said future Hall of Fame defensive lineman Dwight Freeney, "because while football is violent enough, playing another game just a few days after a first one is the type of thing that seems like it can damage your mind and body for the long-term."

———

UNITED STATES DISTRICT COURT, EASTERN DISTRICT OF PENNSYLVANIA: *Turner and Wooden v. the National Football League.*

Kevin Turner's first NFL concussion came when he was playing for the New England Patriots, a brutal hit that ended when his head smashed into the turf. The second came when Turner was part of a wedge—a sort of human battering ram— while running on special teams. At some point after the violent collision, the only thing he remembered was looking around the stadium and wondering where he was. He looked into the face of the team's backup quarterback, Bobby Hoying. "You're going to think I'm crazy," Turner told Hoying, "but are we in Green Bay or are we in Philly?" They were in Cincinnati.

Several plays later, Turner was back in the game. This is simply how it was in the late 1990s. Before that it was even worse. Your brain was damaged and you kept on playing. This practice created a legion of damaged minds—men who would go on to hurt themselves, hurt their loved ones. A new phrase would soon enter the NFL lexicon: CTE or chronic traumatic encephalopathy, a degenerative brain disease that has been diagnosed in people who've sustained multiple concussions or head injuries.

Turner believes football gave him amyotrophic lateral sclerosis, or ALS, commonly known as Lou Gehrig's disease. There is no known cure. Turner sued the NFL. It wasn't a baseless suit. Indeed, one of the people who testified on his behalf was neurologist Robert A. Stern. Stern is a professor of neurology, neurosurgery, anatomy, and neurobiology at Boston University School of Medicine. He's considered one of the foremost brain experts in the world.

According to court documents, during Turner's deposition, Stern provided one of the more defining quotes about football, then and now (and maybe for decades to come):

> Individuals with impairments in mood and behavior
> but without significant cognitive impairment can still
> experience devastating changes in their lives. Based on
> my review of the medical and scientific literature and

on my interviews of living research participants, informal discussions with former players and/or their family members, and formal interviews with family members of deceased former players with neuropathologically confirmed CTE, it is my scientific opinion that many former NFL players have significant changes in mood and behavior (e.g., depression, hopelessness, impulsivity, explosiveness, rage, aggression), resulting, in part, from their repetitive head impacts in the NFL, that have, in turn, led to significant financial, personal, and medical changes, including, but not limited to: the inability to maintain employment, homelessness, social isolation, domestic abuse, divorce, substance abuse, excessive gambling, poor financial decision-making, and death from accidental drug overdose or suicide.

The significant changes in mood and behavior relatively early in life can lead to significant distress for the individual with CTE as well as their family, friends, and other loved ones. I have learned about the tremendous pain and suffering the family members experienced while their loved one's life was destroyed by the progressive destruction of the brain. I have interviewed the adult children of former professional and college football and rugby players whose fathers had dramatic changes in personality, the development of aggressive and out-of-control behavior, and suicidal thoughts. And, I have spoken with the parents of young athletes in their twenties and thirties who impulsively took their own lives.

———

THE WHITE HOUSE. DECEMBER 2013. PRESIDENT OBAMA SPEAKING
on an issue seemingly unrelated as a threat to professional football. The topic? income inequality. "We know that people's
frustrations run deeper than these most recent political battles.
Their frustration is rooted in their own daily battles—to make
ends meet, to pay for college, buy a home, save for retirement.
It's rooted in the nagging sense that no matter how hard they
work, the deck is stacked against them. And it's rooted in the
fear that their kids won't be better off than they were. They
may not follow the constant back-and-forth in Washington or
all the policy details, but they experience in a very personal way
the relentless, decades-long trend that I want to spend some
time talking about today. And that is a dangerous and growing
inequality and lack of upward mobility that has jeopardized
middle-class America's basic bargain—that if you work hard,
you have a chance to get ahead. I believe this is the defining
challenge of our time: Making sure our economy works for every working American."

Income inequality has become one of the most discussed
topics among average Americans. Researchers at the University
of California at Berkeley and the London School of Economics
said in new data released in 2014 the middle class is the poorest
it's been since the 1940s. Meanwhile, they write (as documented
in a CBS News story) the wealth of the rich has reached "dizzying heights only seen during the era of *The Great Gatsby* and
the Gilded Age of the robber barons."

One of the greater examples of the disparity between the
wealthy and middle class is football. The median salary of an

NFL player in 1980 was $50,000. (Half of the incomes are above the median and half below.) The median player salary in 1985 was $160,00, in 1990 $275,000, in 1995 it was $301,000, in 2000 it was $441,000. Then from 2001 through 2007 it was $501,000, $525,000, $534,000, $537,000, $569,000, $772,000, and $772,000. The median NFL salary today is about $1.9 million.

In 1980, the median income for the average American was $16,354—or about $33,000 less than the typical NFL player. In 1990, the median income for Americans was $28,149—or about $250,000 less than the median NFL player's income. In 2012, the median salary was $49,486—or about $950,000 less than the NFL player median.

That disparity has led to a gradually increasing sentiment from some fans about the salaries players earn. It's understandable. The salaries of average Americans have remained relatively stagnant while those of the athletes have skyrocketed. The cost to attend a game has also increased dramatically. In 2013, the average ticket price for a Dallas Cowboys game was $110.20, while the average premium seat was $340. A beer was $8.50, a soda $5.00, a hot dog $5.50, parking $75 (though I have personally seen parking at the Cowboys' stadium at as much as $150), a program $10, and a hat about $20.

Overall, the average NFL ticket price has increased by 30 percent in less than a decade. The NFL increases its ticket prices for one reason and one reason alone: because it can. But how long will fans put up with ballooning prices for a product that doesn't drastically improve?

The disparity between player and fan is big, but the disparity between owner and fan is staggering. In many ways, there is no better example of the gap between ordinary and wealthy Americans than the exponential rise in the value of NFL teams.

In 1976, two cities bought their way into the NFL: Seattle and Tampa Bay. Each franchise cost $16 million. To put that into modern-day terms, that was the salary cap figure for Ravens defensive tackle Haloti Ngata in 2014. In 1995, owners of Carolina and Jacksonville paid $140 million. And then three years after that, football returned to Cleveland for a price tag of $530 million. The Texans were purchased in 2002 for $700 million. *Forbes* magazine reported in 2014 that the average NFL team is worth $1.43 billion. That's the highest figure, the magazine says, in the 17 years it's tracked the values of NFL franchises.

There is a number—a remarkable number—that perhaps illustrates even more the gap between the fan and the sport. Goodell took the job as commissioner in 2006. Between then and 2014, Goodell has earned $210 million, according to former union candidate Sean Gilbert. *That is 5,000 times the median salary of the average American worker.* Goodell's own tax returns show he made $44.2 million in 2012.

None of these figures, these examples of massive wealth, have injured the NFL's popularity thus far. But how long will NFL fans simply eat cake?

———

A POLITICAL FUND-RAISER. INSIDE THE HOME OF JETS OWNER Woody Johnson. Fund-raisers make for interesting meetings, and interesting is what happened on this fall night in 2014. Johnson's accidental encounter was with one of the NFL's most bitter enemies, a man who in many ways is an American hero.

That man is Ray Halbritter, the Nation Representative and CEO of the Oneida Indian Nation. The Oneida were among America's first allies during the Revolutionary War; centuries later, they are fighting another great power: the NFL. Halbritter and the Oneida have been among the leaders in what has been a noble fight against what a significant number of Native Americans consider the highly racist Washington team nickname "Redskins." Halbritter was one of the leaders of a massive protest that took place before the Washington-Minnesota game on November 2, 2014. Approximately 5,000 people from all walks of life (not just Native Americans) showed up to protest the name. It was thought to be the largest protest to ever take place outside of a football stadium in the modern history of the sport.

But before that, a small protest of sorts took place at the political fund-raiser. The NFL—and particularly the owner, Dan Snyder—has remained vehemently opposed to changing the name. No one knows for certain why the NFL is so entrenched. The theories are endless, and almost pointless, because the end result is the same: the NFL refuses to change it.

Woody Johnson has also been outspoken in his opposition to the change, for whatever unknown reason. So when Halbritter got an invite to the fund-raiser, he saw it as an opportunity to ask him why. The two were introduced.

"Hi, I'm Ray Halbritter," he said, "very nice to meet you. I'm working on the Washington team mascot issue."

"You mean, to keep it?" asked Johnson.

It was in that moment the insular nature of a man who *Forbes* estimates is worth $3.5 billion comes into play. It seems he couldn't imagine that a Native American would be opposed to being stereotyped as an angry savage.

"No, I'm actually working to change it," said Halbritter.

Johnson suddenly became highly agitated, almost angry. "To what? To what?" Then, Johnson said, "Dan is never going to change it. Ever," before walking away. There was no conversation. No discussion. Just a billionaire telling another man what he should be called.

Not long after that, in December 2014, Halbritter's organization published what it believes should be a racial code of conduct for the NFL to follow. The opening part of that conduct asked that "NFL team owners will not be permitted to employ the use of dictionary-defined racial slurs as the name and mascot of their teams."

As of press time, Snyder has not changed the Redskins name. Nor, perhaps, will he—ever

———

AGAIN, BACK TO THE NATION'S CAPITAL AND AGAIN, BACK TO THE president. This time, doing something no American president had done in more than 100 years: criticize football.

President Obama told *The New Republic* that if he had a son, he would think long and hard before letting him play football. It was a stunning moment. Not since president Teddy Roosevelt was credited with saving football in the early 1900s had a sitting president spoken so harshly about the game.

In 1905, 19 college players were killed while playing football. A newspaper, the San Francisco Call, listed each of the deaths that year: "Body blows, producing internal injuries, were responsible for four deaths, concussions of the brain claimed six victims, injuries to the spine resulted fatally in three cases, blood poisoning carried off two gridiron warriors, and other injuries caused four deaths.”

In a story titled “How Teddy Roosevelt Saved Football,” History.com wrote, “With little protective equipment, players sustained gruesome injuries—wrenched spinal cords, crushed skulls and broken ribs that pierced their hearts. The *Chicago Tribune* reported that in 1904 alone, there were 18 football deaths and 159 serious injuries, mostly among prep school players. Obituaries of young pigskin players ran on a nearly weekly basis during the football season. The carnage appalled America. Newspaper editorials called on colleges and high schools to banish football outright. ‘The once athletic sport has degenerated into a contest that for brutality is little better than the gladiatorial combats in the arena in ancient Rome,’ opined the *Beaumont Express*. The sport reached such a crisis that one of its biggest boosters—President Theodore Roosevelt—got involved.”

But even Roosevelt didn’t openly question the validity of the sport, and that is what makes Obama’s statement so staggering. In many ways, what he said was one of the stronger signals of the dangers the NFL faces in terms of how it’s perceived.

What Obama said next was equally interesting. The rules changes, the president explained, will make football “a bit less exciting,” but in the future, with those changes that could make football safer “those of us who are fans maybe won’t have to examine our consciences quite as much.”

———

AFTER THOUSANDS OF PLAYERS SUED THE NFL, CLAIMING THE LEAGUE knew of the dangers of concussions but hid that information from the players, the NFL settled the case. The league agreed to pay retired players for their concussion-related injuries, absorb the expenses for medical exams, and fund concussion-related research. The cost to the NFL: $765 million.

"This is a significant amount of money [and] the plaintiffs also believed it was an appropriate amount," Goodell said in September 2013. "The mediator felt it was an appropriate amount. It's a tremendous amount of money that we think is going to go to the right purpose, which is helping players and their families. So $765 million is a lot of money."

Actually, to the NFL, it wasn't. It was a pittance. As of the spring of 2015, senior US district judge Anita B. Brody in Philadelphia was nudging both sides toward a plan that could pay $1 billion over 65 years. And while a cool billion is a lot of money to you and me, it is *still* not much to the NFL.

In many ways, the NFL got off incredibly easy. There was no admission of wrongdoing. No owner was deposed. None of the NFL's top executives were either. What the NFL may have done was buy itself (for a relative pittance) a free pass from being held accountable for what attorneys and players were saying was the borderline criminal act of hiding pertinent concussion-related medical information from its players. There's also the fact that some part of the settlement won't even be paid by the NFL but by its insurance carriers.

Is $765 million a lot of money to the NFL? ESPN pays the NFL $1.9 billion a year for the rights to broadcast the 17 regular-season Monday night games. That comes out to $111 million per game. So, the cost for the NFL to settle the lawsuit was what is earned *for television alone* for approximately seven football games. Seven. That's it.

The settlement for the case lasts for 65 years. That means—and the site Vice.com did the math—that unless an asteroid destroys the Earth, there will be at least 1,105 Monday night games. Or other ways to think of it, as Vice wrote: the settlement money the NFL paid is two seasons' worth of Thursday night football profits, four regular seasons worth of hot dog and beer profits, 3½ years of profits from the league's on-field apparel deal with Nike, and 96 minutes of Super Bowl ads.

———

THE GOOD GUYS IN FOOTBALL...THEY ARE THERE. THERE ARE PLENTY. One is Menelik Watson from the Oakland Raiders. What he did late in 2014 was a naked act of giving. Jay Glazer, the Fox correspondent, had arranged for a young Raiders fan to visit the team using Glazer's Touchdown Dreams program. The Raiders made her captain for the day. She got signed footballs and shirts and was able to hang out in the team's locker room. At the time, Ava Urrea was just four years old. She was born with hypoplastic left heart syndrome. It's a birth defect that prevents normal blood flow. Her first open-heart surgery happened when she was only five days old, and she's had two more since then. All told, she's had more than 20 different surgical procedures. Yet there she was, thanks to Glazer and the Raiders.

Then came the best part. At the end of her visit, Watson approached Ava's family, and handed the family his game check. His *whole* game check. Union records show that Watson's base salary for 2014 was $622,948. So his salary for that game was $36,944. Subtracting federal and state taxes, Watson gave the family about $18,000. No, Watson won't be hurting for cash, but that's still $18,000. More importantly, Watson was so moved by the story, and meeting Ava, his charitable act was completely spontaneous. Moments like that can go a long way toward saving the obliterated public image of a league.

———

PERHAPS SURPRISINGLY, ONE OF THE BEST DEBATES ABOUT THE future of the NFL happened in March 2013 on ESPN2's *First Take*. It's a show that catches a great deal of heat for its occasional buffoonery, but that particular episode featured one of the most intelligent discussions about the league's long-term future ever televised. Airing after one of the original lawsuits from a group of players claiming the NFL hid information about concussions, the segment was called "What Will the NFL Be Like in 20 Years?" with Hall of Famer Cris Carter and commentators Stephen A. Smith and Skip Bayless debating.

Bayless said, "Because of the hysteria surrounding concussions right now, that because of the mom factor in this country, that 20 years from today, the NFL's talent pool will be much smaller than it is today. Just because mothers everywhere, and fathers for that matter, are saying, 'Oh my God. You really can't protect the head…' I think parents everywhere are scared to death right now for their children…Is there a chance that 20 years, 40 years from today, we wind up with sort of an elite warrior class in the NFL? Almost like Roman gladiators. These are the ones who said, 'I'll take that risk. This is what I'll do with my life. High risk, high reward.'"

What Bayless said is not an uncommon belief among current and former team executives (and even some in the league office). They take it even a step further, saying that not only could there be a narrower talent pool but that pool will be nearly one color. The NFL is currently approximately 70 percent African American, and some NFL executives, agreeing with Bayless, see an NFL future where wealthier white families abandon the sport (as well as wealthier families of color) and the sport will be played almost exclusively by African Americans and Latinos from underprivileged backgrounds. What football could see, as one NFL general manager told me, is white flight—or, more generally, *wealth* flight.

Said Smith, "When you come from nothing, and you see a light at the end of the rainbow [sic], that says you can have something, you don't care what the risk is."

In a strange way, Smith and Bayless were making the same point. Bayless was saying the talent pool will be reduced due to fear of what the sport could do to the brain. Smith was stating there will always be a talent pool because the poor will see the sport as a viable option. Both things can be true. Both things could easily happen.

———

HE IS A COMPETITOR OF THE NFL. IN MANY WAYS, HIS LEAGUE IS THE NFL's biggest enemy. So his words may be biased—no, they are biased. But they are also truthful, and I have learned to listen to every word Mark Cuban ever says. He's one of the most intelligent people in professional sports. He's also rarely wrong. I asked Cuban a simple question: What are the threats to the NFL's dominance?

"In any business, it's one type of challenge to get to the top,"

Cuban said. "It's a completely different challenge to stay at the top. It was about 20 years ago that the NFL had teams leaving basically in the middle of the night. [He's referring to the infamous event when the Baltimore Colts loaded up Mayflower moving vans and bolted to Indianapolis in 1984.] They have done an amazing job of leveraging TV and its popularity on TV. But I get the sense that rather than focusing on cementing their customer base, they think it's inevitable that things could never decline. When you think things can't go wrong, they always do."

Cuban isn't the only one who sees the NFL's troubles as an opportunity for other sports leagues. Former NBA player and current analyst Charles Barkley was extraordinarily blunt in speaking to the *Sporting News* in December 2014 about how basketball could rise to dominance. "I hate to say this: We got an opportunity with the concussion thing," Barkley explained. "I think all the sports now are going to start getting some better players. No disrespect. I'm a big football fan. Boxing and football are my two favorite sports, because I think it takes tremendous courage to play those sports. But as a parent, I'm not letting my kid play football. I think, in that aspect, we can gain ground."

Barkley added that if the NBA shortened its regular season from 82 to 70 games and started its season at Christmas, it could gain ground on football. "I know everybody's greedy and they want money," said Barkley, "but if we started at Christmas, then we'd have a period where we didn't have any competition. College and pro football are pretty much off the radar then, except on the weekends. We'd have a very nice window where we control the sports market. I think we should consider that."

Cuban isn't the only billionaire genius to wonder about the NFL's future. The *New York Times* in May 2014 asked several leading thinkers across all aspects of society to look at future trends. One of the questions the *Times* asked was: "What is the next issue to undergo a sea change in social acceptance?" Peter Thiel, a venture capitalist and hedge fund manager who co-founded PayPal, said his answer was football. "We realize it is very harmful for you," Thiel said, "but we haven't yet reached the tipping point where it becomes broadly unacceptable to condone."

The challenge to the NFL is also less theoretical. It was epitomized bluntly by NBA commissioner Adam Silver to reporters not long after he took the job. "As much as we talk about international…I still think there's an enormous opportunity in the United States," Silver said. "I think this game should be a rival to football. In the United States, it's the No. 1 participatory sport. We've all played it. I want to focus on the game. The business is going well, but this is a beautiful game."

In his interview with me, Cuban wasn't finished. "Here are the nuts and bolts of the risk," he said. "They keep on adding TV nights. Every night they add creates the risk that they may not be the dominant show on TV that night. It also adds the risk that it dilutes the product to the point that some, not all, but some portion of the audience has had enough and turns away. That's risk one. Risk two is all the concussion stuff. There is a growing concern about letting young kids play football…. This could lead to far less participation and impact fandom."

Both of those risks are actually conflated with the NFL's Thursday night package. On October 30, just four days after playing on a Sunday, the New Orleans Saints traveled to North

Carolina to play the Panthers. The Saints won, but coaches and players on the team were so angered by having to play so soon after a Sunday game—and they were also infuriated over the NFL's stance that Thursday games do not add to concussion risks—that the team boycotted the league-owned NFL Network's postgame show.

Saints coach Sean Peyton told reporters that Thursday night games are "Crazy...silly. Shouldn't happen."

The injuries are such a concern that some in and around the sport believe they could cause a shift in demographics. Former Pro Bowler Bart Scott, now an analyst for CBS, said high-caliber black athletes will pursue baseball instead of football. "You'll see a resurgence of African American athletes back in baseball," he said. "[Baseball has] less injury concerns and guaranteed contracts."

Cuban isn't done. "Third risk is school finances." He believes some high schools may drop tackle football for insurance reasons due to the increasing awareness of what head trauma does to the brain. This would reduce the available pool of talent for college and, subsequently, the NFL.

"Fourth, the game is becoming more compelling on TV than in stadiums." Cuban added, "That could cause the brand to be impacted and make people think its not as popular as it was.

"Fifth, there is some level of dependence on fantasy football on the margins. Meaning that if something else captured the imagination of guys who play [it], it could reduce their interest.

"Lump all these together and the NFL risk profile increases. If it continues to increase for 10 to 15 years, they are fucked."

3   HEAVY IS THE CROWN

I SPOKE TO GOODELL IN DECEMBER 2014, AFTER MUCH OF THE NFL'S tumultuous season had calmed. Or, call it a calm between cri-ses. He didn't sound like a man who was too worried about the future of the league.

Does Goodell believe the NFL is in trouble? No, he doesn't. Though even if Goodell did, he'd never say it publicly. No commissioner would. And, again, there are numerous indicators the NFL will continue to be excessively wealthy and pop-ular. Maybe forever. But I can also say, with certainty, that privately, Goodell has expressed to some owners and other top league officials concern about the league's long-term future. I'm told Goodell believes that week from hell, and other events that negatively affected the NFL, such as the concussion crisis, gravely concern him. That was the phrase one person close to Goodell used—"gravely concerned."

The concern Goodell has, I'm told, is the same as other high-ranking officials, as well as some owners: that negative PR can topple a giant. The analogy one owner said Goodell has used is the NFL as a fast, thoroughbred horse—all it takes to stop that horse is a slightly injured leg.

Many in the NFL media think Goodell is full of shit. Personally, I do not. I believe almost everyone is full of shit, to some degree, but Goodell is no more full of shit than your average player, coach, or reporter is full of shit. The larger question isn't if Goodell is full of shit; it's whether he's the right man to lead the NFL in its time of prosperity and its time of crisis. I believe he is.

Personally, I like Goodell. There, I said it.

What I can say is that Goodell is not who many believe he is. I believe Goodell is a good man who made mistakes but then corrected them. I believe his heart is good. I believe he's a convenient target, a symbol of a league that has become massive, partly because of its mishandling of issues, partly because the big boys on the block always get targeted. I'm not a Goodell apologist; I'm a Goodell realist. I just know that he cares deeply. I also know he has screwed up. Both things can be true.

It may seem strange to say that a man in charge of a league that continues to be the most popular sport in America, a league that is making more money than any league ever has, is under fire. But Goodell has been under the microscope considerably, and where the league goes from here, in part, will be determined by him. And this is where it gets interesting for him and the league. Did the worst week in NFL history, and the poor handling of the Rice case, damage Goodell irreparably? Or can Goodell recover? Those are the central questions.

There's no question that some people—the union specifically and some in the media generally—attempted to paint Goodell as controversial. Some tried to attach every negative story in the NFL to Goodell specifically. His own actions, at times, didn't help. But the portrayal by some of Goodell as a football devil is totally inaccurate.

One thing is certain: no commissioner has ever faced the questions that are posed about the NFL now. From *GQ*:

> And then there is Goodell's most fundamental challenge of all: the long-term prospects for the NFL in an increasingly anti-football world. From 2010 to 2013, the league's under-50 audience declined 10 percent; this season, *The Walking Dead* repeatedly trounced the NFL on Sunday night. In a recent Bloomberg Politics poll, fully half of Americans said they wouldn't let their sons play football (in similar polls, the numbers skewed even higher in left-leaning demographics), and only 17 percent said they believed the game will grow in popularity over the next twenty years. Could football, an institution as American as Thanksgiving, wind up just another wedge issue in the country's red-blue divide? The new NASCAR? Fred Nance, an adviser to the Cleveland Browns and a former candidate for NFL commissioner, puts it like this: "A cultural IED is exploding in the middle of the business of the NFL."

The concussion crisis became (and is) so vast and deep that it created a moral dilemma: is it wrong to enjoy football? Such a question had not been asked about a sports league in modern times. This dilemma was perfectly epitomized by the *Huffington Post* blog "All Together," which explores religious and ethical issues. Its December 2014 edition examined football and asked if audiences were "contributing to the harm of [college and NFL players] by tuning in on the television or showing up at these sporting events that bring in billions of dollars for colleges and the National Football League? By our presence, are we aiding and abetting the harm of other human beings? Is watching football a sin?"

Former Giants linebacker Harry Carson was asked by the *Huffington Post* what he would tell young high school and college players. Carson, a Hall of Famer who has suffered from debilitating brain trauma after dozens of concussions during his playing career, explained that playing football, no matter how safe you try to make it, is like "playing Russian roulette… the point [players] have to come to grips with [is] is it worth it or not." When asked if he would play in the NFL again, Carson said succinctly, "No."

Also, no commissioner before Goodell has had to deal with emerging technology that shows playing football causes long-term brain damage. There were no MRI scans of the brain in the 1940s. There are now. Dr. Annegret Dettwiler, a researcher at Princeton University's Neuroscience Institute, is working with Princeton athletes to see how concussions impact the brain both functionally and structurally. Her findings are frightening and show why this issue is such a threat to the sport's future. Her work shows that a concussed player, days and even weeks after the injury, takes far greater effort to complete cognitive tasks than individuals in the non-concussed control group. The brains of the concussed players, in other words, have to work harder, even long after a concussion.

The information regarding the structural change in the brain chemistry, according to Dettwiler, is even scarier. She said "cautiously emerging evidence" shows that concussions compromise the fiber tracts that connect different parts of the brain. In the two weeks the concussed athlete would sit out, the brain would start to heal itself. Then the athlete would go back to playing, get exposed to more concussions, and the brain structure would literally change again. But she has only studied what happens to athletes in a two-month span. It's still unknown what happens to the structure of the brain in a year or two or ten.

What has helped football is the same thing that once helped climate change deniers, and that's confusion. There was a time when climate talk sounded mystifying and was laced with strange-sounding phrases like "greenhouse gases" and "carbon footprints." But as people became accustomed to the language, and the science more mainstream, most began to see that climate change was real. The impending problem for Goodell is that the science of CTE and concussions is starting to coalesce into something that people can grasp more easily. It's not there yet, but it's getting there. And once parents recognize that football can lead to possibly irreversible damage to the brain, support of the sport could wane. In fact, it could wane dramatically.

And this is where the ethics also come in. Professor Eric Gregory, an ethicist who teaches in the religion department at Princeton University, spoke eloquently about the dilemma football presents. A former high school football player in his own right, he told the *Huffington Post*, "I used to watch without reservation. It was a moment of joy without concerns about the violence. But I'm one of those who's in the midst perhaps of a shift. Now we know, especially about concussions and the links to depression, dementia, even domestic violence.

So that is stealing my joy. I'm wondering about [my] complicity in watching it."

Gregory said that since he doesn't go to games and pay money directly to the NFL in doing so, his complicity would be what Roman Catholics call "remote." Still, he wondered, "'Should I not enjoy watching it, should I stop watching it?' I think it's a question many people are starting to ask."

It is, perhaps, the most dangerous question the sport—and Goodell—faces.

———

THE THING THAT HAS ALWAYS BEEN LOST WHEN IT COMES TO Goodell is that people—media, players, and fans—fail to understand what his role is: it is to be a heat shield for the team owners. Now, Goodell is paid handsomely for it. He earned well over $100 million in the past four years. "Why does he get paid what he does?" Miami Dolphins owner Stephen Ross, a member of the compensation committee, asked *GQ* in February 2015. "Because you try herding thirty-two cats. He does a great job of it."

One of the more crucial moments in Goodell's tenure came in early January 2015. Go back to the horrid Rice case. The question arose if Goodell (or anyone in the NFL league office) knew of the second tape, the one that showed Rice attacking his then fiancée, before the tape became public, and possibly ignored it. Former FBI director Robert Mueller led an independent investigation into the matter, and the report was released just after the new year. Mueller found that no one from the NFL had knowledge of the tape in question, including Goodell.

The Mueller report, said an NFL source familiar with it, cost approximately $4 million. One of Mueller's main charges was to ascertain if there was truth to the Associated Press story that claimed an unnamed law-enforcement official had sent a DVD with in-elevator video footage of the Rice assault to the NFL. The AP story claimed an unnamed person at the league acknowledged receiving that video by leaving a voice mail on the official's cell phone on April 9, 2014. "The League asked that I conduct an independent inquiry into two questions: whether anyone at the League had received or seen the in-elevator video prior to its public release on September 8; and what other evidence was obtained by, provided to, or available to the League in the course of its investigation," wrote Muller in the report.

> As to the first question, despite extensive investigation, we have found no evidence that anyone at the League received or viewed the in-elevator video prior to its public release. Likewise, we have found no evidence of a woman at the League acknowledging receipt of that video in a voicemail message left on April 9, 2014. With respect to the second question, we have identified the investigative steps that the League took in the wake of the Rice incident, steps that reflect the League's longstanding practice of deferring to law enforcement—a practice that can foster an environment in which it is less important to understand precisely what a player did than to understand how and when the criminal justice system addresses the event. In this case, that deference led to deficiencies in the League's collection and analysis of information during its

investigation. We conclude that there was substantial information about the incident that should have put the League on notice of a need to undertake a more thorough investigation to obtain available evidence of precisely what occurred inside the elevator. Had the League done so, it may have uncovered additional information about the incident, possibly including the in-elevator video prior to its public release.

Mueller's report states that his team of investigators interviewed "every female employee, contractor, vendor, or intern whose electronic badge recorded that she was in the League's main office on April 9, the date the alleged call was made. Each of the 188 women denied making the April 9 call—or even hearing a rumor that an in-elevator video of the Rice incident had been received." Mueller put more blame on Rice's team, the Baltimore Ravens, than he did Goodell and the league office.

I am one of the few who actually believes in the veracity of the report. I do not believe Mueller, a former marine officer who served in Vietnam and was awarded, among other commendations, a Bronze Star and a Purple Heart, and who then would go on to head the FBI, would simply want to be a kiss-ass for a bunch of owners so he could get free tickets to football games. No, I don't believe the NFL knew of the second video before its public release. But they should have known.

If there was any doubt whether Goodell's future was in trouble with the owners, it was removed when John Mara, co-owner of the New York Giants, and Steelers owner Art Rooney II released a joint statement that was basically a "we trust in Roger" pledge. The statement is long, but run in its entirety to demonstrate just how much ownership trusts Goodell. The note also shows why that trust will likely not be broken any time soon.

On behalf of the owners of the thirty-two National Football League teams, we would like to thank Director Mueller and his staff for the work they have put into this investigation. Mr. Mueller's report is detailed, extensive and thorough. His investigators reviewed millions of documents, emails and text messages. Investigators searched the computers and phones of Commissioner Goodell, senior NFL executives, people in the mailroom, and others who might have information about the in-elevator video.

After interviewing more than two hundred people, including every woman who worked at the NFL at the time the alleged call was made acknowledging receipt of the in-elevator video, and after an exhaustive forensic search of all electronic records, the investigators found no evidence that anyone in the League received or viewed the in-elevator video prior to its release. The investigators also found no evidence of a woman at the League acknowledging receipt of the video in a voicemail message.

The investigators also identified a "weakness"—as they call it—in the League's longstanding practice of deferring to the criminal justice system when matters like this arise. Mr. Mueller concludes that the League should have conducted a more substantial independent investigation of this matter and he has made six recommendations. This morning, we spoke to Commissioner Goodell about these recommendations. We want to review them and understand them in greater detail. We look forward to moving forward on this.

The report also states that the Associated Press declined to cooperate with the investigation.

As owners, we are the first to agree that the NFL did not have a sufficient policy in place to deal with players or other personnel accused of domestic violence. As leaders of this sport, it is our responsibility to recognize the pain domestic violence causes to families in our league and in our society. We were slow to react, and in the case of Ray Rice, the original punishment was insufficient. In addition, the steps taken by the NFL to investigate this matter were inadequate. Since then, a new policy concerning domestic violence and other rules for conduct violations have been put into place. We believe these new policies are tough and appropriate.

This matter has tarnished the reputation of the NFL due to our failure to hand out proper punishments. It has been a wake-up call to all involved and we expect the changes that have been made will lead to improvements in how any similar issues are handled in the future.

It is clear to us that Commissioner Goodell was forthright in the statements he made to the owners about this matter, and we have every confidence that Roger Goodell is the right person to lead the league as we move forward.

Not everyone was satisfied with the report. Olbermann obliterated it. "Wow! You said all that?" Olbermann said the day the report was released. "What a guy! So you concluded, you know, what everybody else in America figured out by about September 1st? Or some of us had figured out by August 1st? That the NFL pursued that videotape with the tenacity of a snail? A sleepy, unfocused snail? A sleepy unfocused snail with attention deficit issues? And you wrote it up in a way that made it look like there shouldn't be firings or any kind of accountability on the NFL because of its extraordinary malfeasance in this Rice case."

Olbermann made a highly intelligent criticism of one aspect of the report. Investigators asked every woman if they got a call or saw the tape. Of course all the women asked said no. Saying yes would mean the end of their NFL careers and possible future careers as well. So while I believe Mueller conducted an honest investigation, it was also an impossible investigation unless the Associated Press source came forward and revealed its source—and no way was that happening.

After the report was released, Goodell sent a memo to all NFL staff highlighting the finer points of Mueller's findings and issuing a rallying cry to his staff for the future.

———

July 2, 1981
Mr. Pete Rozelle
410 Park Avenue
New York, NY 10022

Dear Mr. Rozelle:

I am writing to you in reference to any job opening you may have in your offices.

Having just finished my undergraduate education at Washington and Jefferson College this past May, I am presently looking for a position in the management of professional sports. Being an avid football fan, I have always desired a career in the NFL. Consequently, as a great admirer of you, it would be both an honor and a pleasure to work for you in any position that may be available.

Thank you for your consideration. I look forward to hearing from you.

Respectfully,

Roger S. Goodell

———

MY INTERVIEW WITH GOODELL STARTED WITH A SIMPLE QUESTION. When he took the job in 2006, did he envision all of...this? The controversies? The ugliness? The misreads? The good reads? The bad decisions? The smart ones? Goodell laughed. "No. I have to admit, I couldn't have imagined some of the things that have happened over the nine seasons," he said. "I don't know if there was anyone who had a better insight having been in the league for over 25 years. But you never know until you're in that seat. You have that responsibility and you feel that responsibility to everyone. It's challenging, it's exciting, it's an opportunity to really have an impact on something that we know so many millions of fans care about. And we have that opportunity, and that's the inspiration for all of us," he told me.

As popular as the league was when Goodell first became a part of it decades ago, and as popular as it had become a decade ago when he was named commissioner, it's gotten even more so. Insanely so. People care so much about the NFL that the bar has been raised to an almost unrealistic place. Athletes are asked to be moral role models and Goodell to be flawless. "But we like that and we embrace that," Goodell said. "That's an opportunity. I'd rather have it that way than they don't expect a lot from you or they have lower standards for our organization. I think we've helped establish that and we have to meet that. That's a good thing, to me."

I asked Goodell if he's ever seen a time when fans cared more about the NFL than they do now. He answered the question knowing what I meant to ask, which was, has he ever seen the NFL held to a higher standard than now? "No, I haven't," he said. "But that is what I meant when I said people hold the NFL to a higher standard. Yes, maybe that [is] a negative when you don't hit that bar. But we embrace that. We don't want to have it any other way. People expect a lot from us, and we have to deliver on it. That drives us. That inspires us. That is why we continuously look to see how we can improve the experience for our fans and improve the game for our players and coaches. And do everything we can to get better."

The league and some owners staunchly defend Goodell. They point to a number of positive things that occurred under his commissionership:

- The personal conduct policy was revised and improved in 2014.
- Television viewership continues to grow. (No, this isn't directly because of Goodell. This is due to the very nature of

what's happening in the sport now. But conversely, if ratings were dropping significantly, Goodell would be blamed.)

- The DirecTV Sunday Ticket contract was extended in September 2014, and *Thursday Night Football* on CBS—even with the crappy games—checked in as one of the 10 highest-rated shows on television in 2014. (No Goodell credit, but again, if ratings fell, he'd be faulted.)
- In 2014, there were no local TV blackouts of games for the first time ever.
- There were three games in London for the first time ever; all were sold out. (Again, not directly tied to Goodell actions, but if they were a flop, writers like me would be critical of him.)
- Officiating has improved (13 new zebras, wireless communication, replay control in New York).
- The technology is advancing, with tablets for coaches, better headsets, and testing of NextGen stats.
- The pace of games has improved, and the average game time has decreased.
- Following the death of owner Ralph Wilson Jr., the Buffalo Bills organization has been restabilized with the sale of the team to the Pegula family.
- Over 1 billion dollars has been spent in stadium improvements and new stadium construction.
- The league adopted HGH testing, along with other improvements to both drug programs.
- The draft was held in Chicago in 2015 (one of the best moves the NFL has made recently).
- The playoff ticket policy has improved, so fans pay as teams play.

- The game is slightly cleaner: unnecessary roughness penalties, hits to defenseless players, and possibly even concussions have decreased.

What's more, Goodell has made some fascinating personnel
changes. The NFL has diversified its upper echelons with powerful women. Dawn Hudson was brought in as head of marketing, and Cynthia Hogan as head of its government affairs
department. And Lisa Friel was hired as outside advisor on domestic violence issues. I also believe Troy Vincent (the former
player who is now the league's vice president of football operations) was one of the best hires of the Goodell era.

I asked Goodell what would be his biggest takeaway from
the year from hell.

"It's a learning year," he said. "We stress that in our organization all the time, about learning and getting better. That's a focus that we always have. As I look back at this year, I continue
to see the game get better, get stronger, get safer. We're protecting our players from unnecessary injuries. We like the way we're
integrating technology into the game. We saw it with instant replay this year, and we saw it with tablets on the sidelines, and I
think that will continue to accelerate and bring technology into
the game and innovate further.

"I think the way we engage our fans and the passion of our
fans. Every one of our metrics is up again this year as far as fan
engagement is concerned. More and more people are watching,
whether it's on television or on alternative devices and platforms.
And we're delivering on that experience. The last thing I would
focus on is our organization and how we take that opportunity
to learn and get better. While we've had challenges, we've learned

from them and we are a better organization for it."

Was there something from the year Goodell wishes he had done better?

"Sure. You always do that," he said. "I look back and I wish I did everything better. That's how we operate. I can't isolate it to one thing. Some of the things that we always have taken great pride in is having the right people at the table, having the right voices, having the expertise, having the kinds of discussions that are necessary to make sure we're staying ahead of the curve and we're looking to see what the next issues addressing us [are]. Whether it's innovation, whether it's policies, whether it's technology, whether it's the game and how we deal with it, how we deal with the medical side of the game.

"We think we are making enormous progress on all of those fronts, but you can't let down on any particular area. I wouldn't call it learning, but it's something we've talked an awful lot about. The general public expects a lot from the NFL, and we have to deliver on that. We have embraced that. We don't run from that. We embrace it. And we have to deliver on that. When we fall short, we acknowledge it and we go and try to do better."

The one thing Goodell has to do now, in his estimation, is communicate better with the union. Repair that relationship. These days, the union and NFL exchange drone strikes; that's the nature of their relationship.

———

GOODELL HELD HIS STATE OF THE LEAGUE PRESS CONFERENCE ON January 30, 2015. It was, easily, the most anticipated presser of his tenure. It was met with both curiosity and cynicism from some in the media. Goodell handled himself well (mostly), even when a reporter asked if there was any circumstance Goodell could see where he might resign or lose his job. "No, I can't," he said. "Does that surprise you?"

At one point, Goodell was asked if he deserved a pay cut. "That's up to the owners," he said. "They evaluate my performance and compensation and I don't argue."

In some ways, the press conference saw a change in Goodell. In a September 2014 press conference about Ray Rice, Goodell displayed, at times, a lack of humility. This press conference was different. He was humbler and reestablished himself as a leader. To me, at least. To others, not so much. On ESPN's *NFL Live*, hosted by Trey Wingo, former players Mark Schlereth and Tedy Bruschi—both multiple Super Bowl winners—excoriated Goodell as being out of touch, particularly with the players.

Tom Curran, a veteran journalist who has covered the Patriots for decades and now works for Comcast Sports in New England, blasted Goodell as a buffoon. In his column, he quoted union president Eric Winston saying: "Hey, even the worst bartender at spring break does pretty well. Think about it, a two-year-old could [be NFL commissioner] and still make money."

Winston later tweeted an apology to Goodell, saying the comment he made to Curran was off the record, but he never denied that he felt that way. "In a casual conversation with a reporter about the success of the NFL and how nothing seems to get in its way, I inappropriately and flippantly made a remark about the job of Commissioner Goodell," Winston said in the statement. "We often disagree on the issues but I want to apologize to Roger for being unprofessional. I am disappointed that my comment was taken out of context and inserted into a column without any knowledge that the conversation was 'on-the-record.' I am disappointed that this reporter chose to burn me, but this is an important lesson that I will learn going forward. This is my fault and again, I apologize." (I believe Winston is off-base; it was disingenuous to blame Curran when all Curran did was ask Winston a question.)

One of the best journalists alive is CNN's Rachel Nichols. At the press conference, she asked a smart and pertinent question. It was about the independent investigators used by the league to examine the various scandals that had occurred in 2014. "Roger, you guys have faced a lot of problems over this year that have a really wide range, but a lot of the issues have in common the conflict of interest," Nichols asked. "When you do something like hire an outside investigator like Ted Wells into the Patriots investigation, you're still paying him and Robert Kraft who owns the Patriots is paying you. So even when you do everything right in one of those situations, it opens you guys up to a credibility gap with some of the public and even with some of your most high-profile players. What steps can you guys take in the future to mitigate some of those conflict of interest issues?"

Goodell's answer wasn't helpful. "I don't agree with you on a lot of the assumptions you make in your question," he responded. "I think we have had people that have uncompromising integrity. Robert Mueller is an example of who—I think you asked me the same question last fall about a conflict of interest—their integrity is impeccable. Ted Wells' integrity is impeccable. These are professionals that bring an outside expertise and an outside perspective, and their conclusions are drawn only by the evidence and only by the attempt to try and identify that truth. So, I think we have done an excellent job of bringing outside consultants in. Somebody has to pay them, Rachel. Unless you're volunteering, which I don't think you are, we will do that. But, we have the responsibility to protect the integrity of the league, [and] whether we have an owner that's being investigated, whether we have a commissioner that's being investigated, they're being done at the highest level of integrity and quality."

It was this comment—"somebody has to pay them, Rachel. Unless you're volunteering, which I don't think you are"—that was a sort of "mansplaining." It provided ammunition to critics who say he just doesn't get it when the truth is he does.

Goodell was also hurt by the optics of a situation that happened several hours before the Super Bowl. Goodell declined to speak with NBC for their pregame show. Yet President Obama did talk to NBC as part of the network's pregame extravaganza. The visual of the president of the United States talking to the media but the commissioner not doing so just looks awkward. And it looked even worse when the NFL threatened to fine Marshawn Lynch for not speaking to the press on Media Day. In fact, it was during his press conference just 48 hours earlier that Goodell chastised Lynch for his approach with the media. "When you're in the NFL, you have an obligation to the fans," Goodell told hundreds of members of the media. "It is part of your job, and there are things in all of our jobs that we have to do that we necessarily don't want to do."

The NFL faces major threats, but these mini-tremors, sometimes self-inflicted, are also problematic.

In some cases, there is nothing Goodell can do to satisfy people. There is a level of Goodell Derangement Syndrome at work. It's the same illness that targets some people when it comes to President Obama. Goodell could cure cancer and some people would say he didn't do it fast enough. Yet there are times such as moments in that press conference—particularly that arrogant moment with Nichols—when Goodell does make things worse for himself.

Those awkward Goodell moments sometimes overshadow the brilliant ones. There were several of those in the press conference, too. Goodell was asked his thoughts on the fact that Kraft, in a moment of extreme hubris, expressed that Goodell owed the Patriots an apology. "My thoughts are that this is my job," the commissioner said. "This is my responsibility: to protect the integrity of the game. I represent 32 teams. All of us want to make sure that the rules are being followed, and if we have any information where the potential is that those rules were violated, I have to pursue that and I have to pursue that aggressively. This is my job. This is a job of the league office. It is what all 32 clubs expect and what I believe our partners, our fans expect. We will do so vigorously, and it is important for it to be fair."

Goodell later added: "It has been a tough year. It's been a tough year on me personally. It's been a year of what I would say is humility and learning. We, obviously as an organization, have gone through adversity. More importantly, it's been adversity for me. We take that seriously…. It's an opportunity for us, for our organization, to get better. We've all done a lot of soul searching, starting with yours truly.

"We have taken action. A lot of the concerns that we had

back in August where we didn't have a policy that addressed a very complex issue, we didn't have answers for that. We didn't fully understand those issues. Now we have experts in the field. They're in our office. They're helping us understand this. Advisors have given us a better understanding of the issues and how to deal with these complex issues. We went on the road. We have spoken to, last count I had was well over 150 experts, whether they are former players, college and university presidents, law enforcement officials. How can we do a better job of managing these complex issues? We set out to create a new personal conduct policy, which was unanimously approved by our 32 owners in December. We made enormous progress. The things we didn't know and where we were in August, are not where we are today. We're in a good place in knowing and learning and having a lot more humility."

Goodell has been accused of being arrogant, but he's been no more arrogant, in my experience, than any other commissioner I've encountered—and I've interviewed several of them, from former NFL commissioner Paul Tagliabue to ex-NBA commissioner David Stern. Any perceived arrogance of Goodell isn't the problem. It's the arrogance of some of the men who *really* run football: the owners. And among them, there is one man who epitomizes that arrogance. His name is Dan Snyder.

4   ARROGANCE

AS FRANCHISE VALUES HAVE RISEN DRAMATICALLY, A SENSE OF invulnerability has increased exponentially, to the point where some owners (not all, there are humble ones such as the Mara and Rooney families, among others) have come to believe they are infallible. No owner epitomizes this arrogance like Dan Snyder, owner of the Washington team. His arrogance even extended to his treatment of fellow owners.

There is a scene that illustrates why Snyder is feared, liked, despised, admired, and admonished. Why he is seen as a bully, a genius, a constant threat to litigate, an unabashed defender of a slur, a money maker, and maybe the most important and most hated owner in football. That scene begins with a threat.

It was the 2012 NFL's owners meetings, not long after Washington and Dallas were penalized by the NFL for $36 million and $10 million in salary cap room, respectively. The NFL—specifically the league's management council, which is the business arm of the NFL—accused both clubs of frontloading contracts during the 2010 season, when there was no salary cap. Teams had been warned not to do this because it could destroy the central lifeblood of the NFL, competitive balance. The owners' meetings, where all 32 were present, along with high-ranking league and team executives, was the first opportunity for Dallas and Washington to address the top of the NFL's hierarchy at once.

Jerry Jones, owner of the Cowboys, spoke first. He expressed his annoyance and anger over the cap penalties but he was succinct, taking only a handful of minutes and making it clear there would be no lawsuit against his fellow owners.

Then Bruce Allen, Washington's general manager and Snyder's most trusted lieutenant, addressed the room. According to a longtime NFL team executive who was present, it wasn't long into his speech before Allen threatened to sue every owner in the NFL. He would go on to get more fiery, personal, and ugly from there, as he began pacing furiously around the hotel ballroom. There were more threats of a lawsuit. Allen grew angrier. He began screaming.

He wasn't done. He then pointed at each member of the management council, saying Washington and Dallas should have never been penalized because the council had approved the very contracts that would cause the teams to be punished. He saved some of his harshest remarks for John Mara, co-owner of the Giants and one of the most respected men in all of sports, a key cog who has been with the team for decades. Mara was furious.

Everyone in the room was stunned. Owners and executives, sitting just several feet from one another, began texting each other, incredulous at what they were witnessing. In some of the texts, Allen was facetiously called Clarence Darrow, the legendary litigator known for his bombastic courtroom speeches. Owners and executives say they had never seen anything like it. Nobody had ever gotten so personal or made such threats. (It wasn't Allen's finest moment, and there are others that rival it. Some years later, he would make one of the dumbest comments any team executive ever has. After yet another losing season, at his year-end press conference, Allen told reporters: "We're winning off the field, but we've got to start winning on the field." (What in the hell does that even mean?)

They also say Allen was acting as proxy for Snyder, which would seem evident given the owner's behavior. The chairs at the owners' meetings are usually oversized. They can swallow up a smaller person. (Snyder is approximately 5'6".) As Allen spoke, a high-ranking team executive who was there remembered, Snyder gleefully swiveled back and forth in a chair that practically enveloped him. At times, as Allen spoke, Snyder smiled widely.

When a fellow owner or league official threatens to sue, per league rules, they are forbidden to take part in certain aspects of the meetings. So when Allen's speech ended, because it included a threat to litigate, both Allen and Snyder were told to leave the room. They did.

So ended one of the most notorious (and mostly unknown until now) chapters in NFL history.

———

THE EPISODE WAS INSTRUCTIVE IN THAT IT OPENED A WINDOW INTO Snyder, who has emerged as one of the most important—and notorious—owners in the NFL. His decision to fiercely defend the Redskins nickname, an act that has inspired congressional condemnation as well as vocal backing from fans of the team, has spotlighted him as a central figure in all of sports. His stance, in many ways, has opened another front in America's culture wars.

"I will never believe that Dan Snyder does not want to win," former *Washington Post* columnist Mike Wise, who has written about Snyder extensively, once told me. "Now, you could argue that winning to him isn't winning in a classic sense. Winning doesn't just mean winning a Super Bowl to him, I believe; it means winning the off-season, making prospective luxury-box purchasers believe you have made the right moves to contend again; it means winning the fan base that thinks he's the worst owner ever over. If that means putting failure at the coach's feet or on someone else's, fine. But don't blame Dan. He's trying so hard.

"Finally, winning for Dan Snyder means being right. Damned if he's going to let some politically correct mad libs take his name away from him. That's how he sees it. He has no idea of [how] the hundreds of thousands that want the team name gone really feel. He thinks it's a media conspiracy, and by getting a couple of hundred letters from Native Americans who like the name he can solve it. The name issue is a major window into who he is as an owner."

There are several questions regarding Snyder, but one is the most pertinent of all, and it is a question few have been able to successfully answer: who is Dan Snyder?

———

IN NOVEMBER 2014 *ROLLING STONE* NAMED ITS 15 WORST OWNERS in sports. Snyder was No. 1. Its reasoning was one of the most scathing things ever written about an NFL owner in any sport at any time in recent history:

Snyder has marshaled every resource of the rich white asshole invoking tradition to defend the indefensible.... There's Snyder co-opting any local media going knives-out on the name or the fact that his team is stupendously mismanaged. There's Snyder trying to buy silence from Indian tribes.... You could go on for pages about the paranoid, Hitler-in-the-bunker mentality of the team, or the blithe unconcern with a shredded field and player health that already nearly Cuisinarted RG III's knee.... Dave McKenna of the *Washington City Paper* wrote a devastatingly hysterical A-to-Z guide to every contemptuous, miserly, greed-headed, soul-dead move Snyder has pulled in D.C., every bit of it true. Snyder sued McKenna and the paper anyway, because he wanted to see if the size of his war chest would back them down. Because he could. Because he's Daniel Snyder, and because fuck you. Fuck your access to a true narrative, fuck your local pride, fuck your fandom, fuck your pocketbook, fuck your fun and fuck a genocide.

How do you really feel?

There is more than this to Snyder, of course. It is also impossible for Snyder to be the despicable human, almost a caricature, the way he is often portrayed. For one thing, he has donated millions of dollars to charity, notably to fight breast cancer (his wife beat the disease). But it is also true that Snyder epitomizes what is wrong with some elements of NFL ownership.

The NFL owners are an interesting group. There are a handful of high-profile owners, but most stay in the background.

Ownership meetings are among the most secretive aspects of professional football. Some owners (and management person-nel, including general managers) are genuinely decent people who want the best for their players. Some other owners see their teams simply as ATM machines, and the players as interchange-able parts. They don't see the players as true partners. If they did, they would care more about them, and definitely not say what the owner of the Texans said to *GQ* magazine in February 2015.

In the story, Texans owner Bob McNair was quoted as being dismissive of the NFL's concussion crisis saying, unbelievably, that most head trauma of NFL players didn't happen in profes-sional football. Wrote the magazine:

> By the summer of 2013, Goodell was determined to put Bountygate and the broader concussion issue behind him. He held a series of meetings with team owners in New York and persuaded them to settle the class-action lawsuit brought by more than 5,000 play-ers who were seeking financial payouts for concus-sion-related conditions such as Alzheimer's, dementia, and depression. Goodell argued that while the league could fight in court and likely prevail, the litigation would be a festering wound on the league's image.
>
> "It was about protecting the brand," recalled Bob McNair, who attended the sessions. "Do we want the brand attacked on this for the next ten years? Or do we want to go ahead and take the high road? In ef-fect, we don't think most of these concussions refer-enced even occurred in the NFL, but we're not going to complain about it."

It wasn't about protecting the players, it was about protecting the brand. McNair might as well have called the players cattle.

Indianapolis Colts vice chair and co-owner Carlie Irsay-Goron, who is 33 years old, didn't do much to dispel the stereotype of owner as out-of-touch millionaire. Talking to *Glamour* magazine in January 2014 about her confidence in the Colts, this was how she responded: "You don't ever want to become one of those doubters.... These [late-season] games can be really, really rough because everyone's tired. You'll see the strains. A lot of it is just fatigue-related...[and] they don't take care [of themselves]. A lot of these guys are younger and they're less educated and...you'd be amazed at what some of them eat.... Some of them, all they eat is McDonald's."

And they're less educated.

On concussions: "At the end of the day I think [these athletes] are adults and they're getting paid large sums of money.... A lot of these guys that are claiming they're having these concussion issues, they have alcohol or drug problems that are just going to compound it. A lot of them—if they weren't coached properly and they weren't coached in a smart way—they're going to lead with their head and they've been having concussions since they were playing Peewee football.... There are so many different things that [could contribute].... I mean, that's kind of what my dad will say, because he was a walk-on linebacker in college, and he'll say, 'You know, am I going to go sue Southern Methodist University for the fact that I've had a back surgery and now my shoulder's being repaired and now I'm having a hip replacement?'...There's no secret there are risks associated with this game."

No player who has talked about CTE or concussions—or were members of the lawsuit against the NFL over concussion issues—ever said he didn't know there were risks. They say that the NFL has covered up the extent of its knowledge about concussions for several decades. That's why there was a massive lawsuit and an entire book published on the subject. Also, the hip bone is different from the brain bone.

One of the more interesting aspects of covering ownership is the perception of owners by fans and even many in the media that the owners are pseudo-gods—men of industry, world conquerors—when in fact they are ordinary, flawed human beings like the rest of us. Their blemishes are hidden by money and power. Perhaps most interestingly, in some cases, the reins of a franchise are simply handed to a son after a father passes. Some of them, like John Mara, son of the late Wellington Mara, who ran the Giants for decades, work hard (and intelligently) to make the franchise better. They have the drive and smarts to do it.

They also do not flaunt their privilege. Late in 2014, a sixth grader named Cade Pope, who is from Yukon, Oklahoma, wrote all 32 NFL owners, telling them he was looking to become a fan of a team, and asking each why he should support them. Only one owner wrote back: Jerry Richardson, owner of the Carolina Panthers. Richardson sent Pope a replica team helmet signed by star linebacker Luke Kuechly and a handwritten note. "Cade, we would be honored if our Carolina Panthers became your team, we would make you proud by the classy way we would represent you," Richardson wrote.

Yet some of the league's owners reflect the current state of the league and how it acts as if it can do no wrong. Or whatever it wants. Snyder exemplifies that attitude. Also unlike Mara or Kraft, the teams under Snyder have been horrible. In 2014, Washington finished in last place in the NFC East for the sixth time in seven years. It was the eighth last-place finish in the past 11 years. Also in 2014, Washington's nine double-digit losses tied for most in the NFL, with the Tennessee Titans.

There are many ways to begin to understand Snyder and his almost pathological stubbornness in refusing to change his NFL team's nickname, even though many in the American Indian community and others find it offensive. There are many ways, yes, but the most important is understanding two vital facts about him: Snyder is a Marylander and a lifelong fan of the team. Those two facts drive him, his philosophy, and his inability to see the other side of the nickname issue.

Sure, there are other reasons why Snyder remains immovable on the nickname. But I believe it is his fandom that drives him the most. Snyder's stance on the nickname has been consistent. "We'll never change the name. It's that simple. NEVER," Snyder told *USA TODAY* in May 2013. "You can use caps," he added.

The issue of what is offensive to American Indians has become a contentious one, even opening another front in the culture war. It has been argued in sports bars and living rooms, from the nation's capital to Indian reservations. People like Snyder who grew up fans of the team protect the nickname because it has become a part of their identity. It's part of who they are, how they see themselves. And though deep in their core they know the nickname is wrong and offensive, some fight to protect it because they see it as a part of history, *their* history.

I know all this because I lived it myself. I was born in Washington, D.C., but raised in one of the great social experiments of the 20th century, a planned community called Columbia, in Maryland. The city's goal was to eliminate racial, religious, and financial segregation. At the time of Columbia's founding in the mid-1960s, nearby Virginia had just banned interracial marriage. D.C. was highly segregated, as was most of the state of Maryland. As time went on, in the years after my family moved there, I grew up with people of every conceivable race—including American Indians—had friends of various ethnicities and dated girls from different racial backgrounds. I was arrogant in my belief there wasn't a single bigoted bone in my body—and completely unaware I loved a team that racially insulted an entire people.

Worse, the only time I thought of the nickname as a slur while growing up was during Catholic high school. A Colts fan and I got into a fight when he called my team the "Niggerskins." We scrapped and both got detention or "JUG" (Justice Under God). I was offended at the use of the N-word but not at "Skins." Somehow, my love of the team allowed me to be angry over one slur but fail to recognize the other.

Marylanders are among the most insecure and proud people in the country. They straddle the line between genteel Southernness and hearty East Coast abruptness. But mostly, it's insecurity that defines us. We're good, decent people...but insecure. Maryland is the little brother standing in the wings while New York struts on the red carpet for a movie premiere. Philly possesses a greater sense of historic greatness, which is also shared by Delaware. And while many Americans view Washington as a symbol of political gridlock, it is the nation's capital. All of this makes Marylanders, particularly the ones closer to D.C., feel like second-class citizens, and we grab on to any sense of pride we can. That's where Washington's football team comes in.

Growing up, I followed the Colts and Washington, gravitating toward the Washington team, long before the Colts moved to Indiana in the dead of night. And when Baltimore stole a team from Cleveland, that cemented my Washington allegiance for good.

The Washington team made us feel relevant. Washington fandom has long been extremely underrated. Everyone around me—family and friends, neighbors, the postman, the babysitter, everyone—cherished the team. When it played, time stopped. A football team placated our insecurity.

Snyder grew up in Silver Spring, Maryland, about 25 minutes from Columbia and minutes from the Washington, D.C., border. He grew up adoring the team, particularly during the Joe Gibbs era. Snyder and I have talked about this—the strangeness of how a football team, a game, can have so much significance in your life. Snyder grew up a Marylander with those same Marylander insecurities, and I believe he uses the nickname issue as a rallying cry to solidify his football base. To Snyder, the critics are not attacking a name. Rather, they are attacking all of us...Maryland and D.C. folks who love this team. I can't say I speak for all Marylanders, of course. Some will say this notion is insane. Yet I can say that every Marylander I know has a deep and personal connection to the team.

The irony is that a significant number of fans are African American. If there is any group that should be sensitive to a slur, it is us. Yet it seems many black fans support the name, and this remains the most tragic part of the Washington team nickname story.

In my family, I was raised to be aware of my roots and history. My family's Maryland ties go back to the 1600s and an Irish woman named Eleanor Butler (her nickname was Irish Nell), who came to America as an indentured servant to Charles Calvert, or Lord Baltimore. Calvert preached religious tolerance, and Butler would eventually fall in love with a slave, marry him, and produce a family.

My D.C. roots trace back to a woman named Elizabeth Proctor Thomas, my mom's great, great aunt, a freewoman and civil rights activist who once met Abraham Lincoln. So I'm related to an Irish freedom fighter from Maryland and a black activist from D.C. I was always socially aware of race, studied my history extensively, and yet I was totally ambivalent regarding my favorite football team's questionable nickname. I was part of a racially conscious family in a racially tolerant community with racially diverse friends and family, yet we never once discussed that "Redskin" is a Webster-defined racial slur. None of my black friends and I did either. *Ever.* That is the power of growing up a Washington football team fan in Maryland.

Why is it so powerful? Because thinking seriously about the nickname ruined our football utopia. It was our insecurities at work. Yes, it's a racist, flawed nickname, but it's *our* racist, flawed nickname. So even though we were all being extremely hypocritical, we ignored the Redskins slur. Yet if after purchasing the team, Snyder renamed them the Washington Niggers, we wouldn't have stood for it. There'd be a million blacks marching on Washington, and we fans would've been among them.

Joel Barkin, a spokesman for the Oneida Nation, which opposes the Redskins nickname, told me, "I think what a lot of [Native Americans] that oppose the nickname see with Snyder is that so much of him is wrapped up in that team. In many ways it defines who he is. To him, giving it up means giving up a piece of himself. That's how we see it.

"With Snyder, that brand, even though the name is racist, that brand means everything to him. I think Snyder feels, 'This team meant something to me as a child. My connection to this team is worth more than you, an American Indian, being offended.'"

To Snyder and the NFL, the nickname isn't racist. It is a point of pride—particularly to someone like Snyder. Remember those Maryland roots. He watched his heroes, guys like Joe Gibbs and Joe Theismann and Doug Williams and Art Monk and John Riggins, all wear that helmet with pride. Preserving the history of the team is paramount. If it offends a significant number of people, so be it. And if Snyder has to pay a bunch of suits to take PR bullets for him, so be it.

———

I LIKED SNYDER A GREAT DEAL UPON FIRST GETTING TO KNOW HIM after he purchased the team in 1999 because he was a Maryland guy. He was one of us. We got along well when we met and talked. I interviewed him several times in his office at the team's complex and spoke with him more than a few times on the phone. He was always smart and helpful. I likely interviewed Snyder dozens of times during the first few years of his tenure as owner. Snyder was to me, initially, brilliant, a new-wave owner in the mold of Jerry Jones, who would spend money on the team. My team. Almost everyone I knew in my old neighborhood who was a fan felt the same way.

Then, I started to see things. It began with little things. When at the complex, I saw how he occasionally mistreated people around him—secretaries, assistant coaches—and began to hear stories from those coaches about how Snyder would scream at them over a play call. At first, the stories were just a trickle. They'd eventually become a flood.

Then there was the overpayment for free agents. Two of the more notable examples were Bruce Smith, the longtime Buffalo Bills defensive end, and Deion Sanders, long past his "prime-time" days. But it was more than just paying through the nose for guys who turned out to be absolute busts. Snyder's teams have made the playoffs just four times in the 16 years he's owned the club. Meanwhile, he has gone through seven head coaches, a staggering number. (There are good sides to Snyder, to be sure. He donates millions to charity, including $600,000 to victims of Hurricane Katrina. So perhaps there is a warm and generous heart inside of him.)

For me, everything changed when my mother began tracing our roots and officially documented what was generally known in our family: that we had American Indian ancestry. That's when I began to rethink my support of the Redskins nickname. There was no steady evolution. As a child, I rooted for the team and didn't care about the nickname. As a teen, the same. In my twenties, the same. Then, after the DNA test in my thirties, the change was sudden and transformational. I was related to the people who were being caricatured. The moment was instructive in many ways. It showed, to me, the hypocrisy of a black man ignoring a slur his entire life just because a football team meant so much to him.

It showed me something else. I looked around at the diversity in my life, which was extensive, and noticed something:

long into my adulthood, there were few American Indians in my life. There was no one around to express his or her displeasure. And this is a key point in my change, and I think central to the argument overall. Since the American Indian population is around 1 percent of the total US population, it's safe to assume most of the people in support of the nickname have never had a face-to-face discussion with someone of American Indian heritage who disagrees with it.

It's one thing to read in a newspaper the objections of American Indians, or see it on television. It is quite another to have someone voice his or her displeasure to your face. Maybe the nickname did or didn't start as a slur, but it doesn't matter. At the very least, it evolved into one.

It was also clear an unrepentant bigot had founded the team I rooted for my entire childhood, something I was unaware of until my research began later. George Preston Marshall was the last NFL owner to racially integrate his team, and he only did so after threats from the federal government. "We'll start signing Negroes," Marshall once famously said, "when the Harlem Globetrotters start signing whites." Why would a white supremacist owner use "Redskins" to honor Native Americans when he despised non-white races? This is a question none of the backers of the nickname has ever been able to answer satisfactorily.

There is another question. Would non–American Indian backers of the nickname call an American Indian a "Redskin" to that person's face? Goodell was asked that very question at his Super Bowl press conference in 2014; he declined to answer. Of course, that non-answer said a great deal.

———

AT THE END OF YET ANOTHER LOSING SEASON IN WASHINGTON, ON New Years Day 2015, Sally Jenkins, a highly skilled columnist for the *Washington Post*, absolutely atomized Snyder in a column. It was hard to argue with anything Jenkins wrote: "If you had to sum up Snyder's organizational philosophy it would be this: Stability is for wimps. Year after year, he commits one dictatorial error after the next, piling self-deceit on self-deceit as he tells fans that success is close. His style is a cross between a cat caught in a yarn and a moth banging at a windowpane."

Then Jenkins hit on one of the main problems with Washington's team. It is incredibly expensive to attend a game for the privilege of watching one of the worst-run franchises in all of sports. "Over the course of an execrable 4–12 season, the game-day experience at FedEx Field was the fourth-most expensive in the NFL, according to the annual Team Marketing Report," wrote Jenkins. "Parking prices were second highest ($57.50) in the entire NFL. A team hat cost $30—10 bucks more than a Dallas Cowboys hat. The average price for a premium seat was $375, which was $50 more than a premium seat for the Baltimore Ravens, and $60 more than for the Philadelphia Eagles."

Snyder may have gotten something right. In January 2015 Snyder hired Scot McCloughan, a sort of super scout who built teams in San Francisco and Seattle, as the team's general manager. Few are better at evaluating talent than McCloughan. He wrote this in his report on then college player Russell Wilson: "Obviously we are really interested in passers with better height, but this guy may just be the exception to the rule. He has the 'it' factor."

I think, despite his shrewdness and ineptitude, a part of me still likes Snyder. Our Maryland connection is strong. I want to root for Snyder, but the nickname issue is like an anchor, pulling the franchise toward the depths. So how does this nickname problem end?

There is a good chance that the fight will go on for years, as Snyder and the NFL continue to assert that the name isn't a slur, until they are forced to change that position by either government edict or an overwhelming number of Americans speaking out against the name. But neither of those is on the immediate horizon.

I know other owners want Snyder to give up the nickname fight. I also know some owners have not asked Snyder, or forced the issue, because they fear him. I believe this could be why Goodell has publicly backed Snyder. The notion of Snyder threatening to sue his fellow owners? Well, I think he would, in a second.

There is also the belief that Snyder wants something in return. Some owners believe, for instance, that Snyder might give up the nickname in exchange for a Super Bowl in Washington. Or, perhaps, just a vault full of cash. Another dynamic could also come into play: Snyder may weaken on his stance if his teams continue to be pathetic on the field. Changing the name may distract from that fact. In other words, change the name to an inoffensive one, and he would get a temporary reprieve from criticism of how poorly he's managed the team.

Snyder's desire to keep the nickname is strong, but the opposition is increasing drastically. In 2015, the powerful Fritz Pollard Alliance, one of the key groups that helped to force the NFL better its hiring practices when it came to African

Americans, came out publicly against the nickname. That move is one of the most monumental in the nickname fight. "As the NFL continues to move in the direction of respect and dignity, one of its teams carrying this name cuts glaringly against the grain," read a letter cosigned by the group's chairman, John Wooten, who played for Washington in the 1960s. "It hurts the League and it hurts us all."

The likely outcome, however, is that Snyder keeps the name as long as he can. The racist nickname will have to be pried—to borrow a phrase—from his cold, dead hands. He likely will refuse to change, no matter what evidence contradicts his worldview, because that's what arrogant men do.

———

THESE QUOTES FROM WISCONSIN PLAYER BRONSON KOENIG, A member of the Ho-Chunk Nation, to the *Milwaukee Journal-Sentinel*, epitomized the feelings of many Native Americans. He spoke passionately about both the mascot issue and specifically the Washington team nickname.

"When a Native American kid sees that growing up and sees the disrespect, it lowers their self-esteem and puts them in a lower place in society. It's just not a good feeling," Koenig told the newspaper in 2015. "It's honoring them? It's not racist? How are you going to say that when you're not a Native American?" On the Redskins nickname, he said: "That term comes from when we were skinned and our flesh was red. I don't see how that is honoring us in any way. Is our skin red? Would it be OK for the Kansas City Negroes or the Blackskins? That's not OK at all."

Ray Halbritter has been fighting this nickname issue for years, decades even. He wrote an opinion piece in January 2015 and provided it to me. I found it one of the more compelling pieces ever written on the subject (which is why I'm putting it here in its entirety below). I also believe it is sad that in the 21st century, a man has to plead for people—namely Snyder and the NFL—to show respect for his race. He has to plead for people not to caricature an entire ethnicity. Maybe *sad* isn't the word. Maybe *tragic* is.

A Change Will Come

From one perspective, the campaign to force the Washington football team to stop promoting a dictionary-defined racial slur has already won its most significant battles. The campaign has sparked national discussion concerning the NFL and the Washington team's refusal to openly confront the issue.

In the past two years alone, the campaign to change the Washington team name has garnered support from a broad coalition of civil rights groups, sports figures, media organizations and political leaders, including a majority of the U.S. Senate and the President of the United States. Tens of thousands of people joined our campaign, and the United States government has rescinded trademark protections for the team's continued use of the racial slur. Polls show a sharp rise in the number of Americans who now say they oppose the NFL's continued use of the R-word, which was the term screamed at Native Americans as we were dragged at gunpoint from our lands.

As an educational effort for the hearts and minds of a fast-changing America, this campaign has been an unmitigated success. With Washington team owner Dan Snyder now ranked as one of the most loathed figures in professional sports, the NFL's intransigence has become a stain on the league's history—one that future generations will look back upon with disbelief and disgust.

However, it is clear that the campaign has yet to fully succeed. The Washington franchise is still using the slur, and the NFL has so far refused to take any action to right this historic wrong. In his stadium, Mr. Snyder still proudly honors the memory of George Preston Marshall, the infamous segregationist who originally gave the team the name.

The obvious question this raises, then, is why have all of the aforementioned successes still not brought about the ultimate objective of seeing the team end its use of a racial slur as its mascot? What accounts for the gap between the remarkable and indisputable progress and the continued use of this offensive moniker? The answer lies with fans.

While Americans like to ascribe all sorts of emotional and moral meaning to their favorite teams, the NFL has proven itself to be an emotionless, amoral corporation. The league seems to react only when it fears fan revolts may jeopardize its $9 billion annual revenue. So far such a revolt has not happened. Indeed, while many fans have expressed their displeasure with the league's use of the R-word, not enough have been willing to match that displeasure with actions that put a real price tag on the league for its continued bigotry.

The good news, of course, is that a league so singularly focused on profit probably does not need much of an economic nudge from fans to finally do the right thing. A few Washington games with diminished attendance might be all that is required (and let's be frank: that's not so far-fetched a possibility considering how consistently horrible and mismanaged a football team Mr. Snyder has put on the field over the last many years).

The bad news, though, is that many fans still want to see sports not as a modifiable reflection of reality, but as a frivolous escape from reality—one that should not be disturbed, even by the most moral of causes.

That impulse is certainly understandable—at a moment of economic, political and environmental crises, we all need a periodic escape. But there is a difference between a rejuvenating escape into entertainment and a destructive retreat from a moral imperative. The campaign to get Roger Goodell and the other owners to support ending the use of the name is most certainly the latter.

No doubt, the NFL does not want fans to see it that way. The billionaire owners and their minions want fans to continue reflexively forking over their money to be entertained, and to do so without any thought about the league's inaction on domestic violence, player suicides, astoundingly high rates of traumatic brain injuries, racism or other catastrophes in its midst. In other words, the NFL wants football enthusiasts to believe that being a loyal fan means joining the league in turning a blind eye to moral crises.

The moment more fans reject that paradigm and hold the league accountable will be the moment things will finally change for the better. In a more diverse and tolerant America that increasingly rejects for-profit bigotry, that moment is coming sooner rather than later—but it cannot come soon enough.

5   THE SAVIOR

"Success isn't owned. It's leased—and rent is due every day."
—J.J. Watt

HIS STORY IS A TRUE TALL TALE, HISTORY LIKE NOTHING WE'VE EVER seen before, or may ever see again.

Enter a Houston hospital. It's November 2014 and J.J. Watt, unannounced, is there to visit a mother dying of cancer and her children. It was typical Watt: a genuine act of kindness done anonymously. Except that nurses and others caught wind that he was in the building and swarmed the hospital wing. Soon, the crush of people became so large Watt had to leave to prevent the scene from becoming unsafe for patients and others.

Watt is Elvis in Houston. In fact, he is Elvis almost everywhere. He can date, but it has to be clandestine. "There's a lot of cloak and dagger," Watt said. "Security, back entrances, roped off parts of a restaurant."

On Halloween, neighbors asked him not to hand out candy at his house, afraid that traffic would flood their block. Because he didn't want to be rude, Watt obliged. "J.J. loves Halloween because of the kids," said Watt's mother, Connie, "but if he handed out candy, it would be mayhem."

His story is about remolding the barbarism of football into a tradable commodity that can change the lives of those less fortunate. He does all of this while navigating the tumultuous waters of celebrity.

At a time in the NFL's history when public trust in players and the league might be at an all-time low, there is an antidote, and its name is J.J. Watt. On the field, his story is pure dominance. The obliteration of offensive lines. The strip sacks. The speed. The aggression. The touchdown catches. Watt is a basketball player in a footballer's body who sees every play as an opportunity to dunk.

"He's a crazy good athlete," said offensive lineman Marshall Newhouse, who played against Watt this season. "For that position, there [aren't] a lot of guys who are as good of an athlete." In fact, there are none. And Watt's athleticism and commitment, as Newhouse explained, "makes you honest and makes you play every snap with great technique."

Consider Cleveland, where in a game on November 16, 2014, Watt shifted up and down the defensive line, beating every single Browns lineman at least once. In that game, Watt scored a touchdown, had a strip sack, made five tackles (three of them for a loss), recovered a fumble, and hurried Browns quarterback Brian Hoyer, forcing the QB to make several bad throws.

Watt's story is Houston lore. In January 2012, he intercepted Cincinnati Bengals quarterback Andy Dalton and returned the pass for a touchdown, helping to give the franchise its first-ever playoff win. Watt was a rookie. "One of the best moments of my life," he says now.

His story is one of historic proportions. Watt is the first NFL player with two touchdown catches, an interception return for a TD, and a fumble return for a TD in a single season. No one had done that in 76 years, according to ESPN's statistical arm. Actually, in the modern history of the NFL, *no one* has done what Watt is doing now—on or off the field. It is not unusual for Watt to appear at a hospital or a fund-raiser or kid's birthday party unannounced. He's engaged in dozens of charitable acts, Texans players tell me, that no one will ever know about.

In the hour or so before the Texans played the Cincinnati Bengals on November 23, 2014, it was Watt who, while standing on the field, played catch with a group of soldiers who were seated in the stands' front row. Then he shook the hands of each soldier—nine from the army and four from the air force. Each one smiled as if they had shaken the hand of a Hollywood movie star.

Watt's story is inescapable. Part of the Watt tale remains an unvarnished, unmitigated, unabashed sense of genuineness. There is nothing phony about him. It comes across in his interviews and commercials. The Texas grocery chain H E B two years ago created a Houston Texans Tackle Crunch ice cream. The ice cream sold fine until Watt did a commercial for the store; after that, it became their best-selling ice cream.

"He could run for Congress right now and win by a landslide," said former Texans player Chester Pitts, who is now a sports anchor and analyst on KPRC Local 2 in Houston. One NFL scout, who had watched Watt in college extensively, wrote this in his notes on Watt prior to the player's entrance in the draft. It was, in many ways, highly prophetic: "I see a player who gets it and has gotten it for a long time. He has surrounded himself with good people and has a level head. He could be a star on the field and then *a governor once his career ends.*" A governor once his career ends. That was actually written years ago—and by a scout! If that is what Watt wanted…but for now it isn't. More on that in a moment.

Watt's story has become so large, it ripples across time, careening from the NFL's past to its future. The comparisons for Watt are not to today's linemen. Too mundane. Instead, they are to names like Deacon Jones and Michael Strahan and Alan Page. And to players who will be in the game 100 years from now.

Everyone has been watching Watt's story, including a woman many miles away, in North Carolina. Her name is Sara White. She is the widow of Reggie White, the player many consider the best defensive lineman of all time, and one of the best football players the sport has ever seen. "J.J. is the closest thing to Reggie that I've ever seen," she said in an interview.

————

WATT AND I MEET IN THE STADIUM BEFORE PRACTICE. THE FIRST thing you notice about him—besides his striking height and the fact he's built like LeBron—is the lack of bullshit he spouts. Watt speaks the way he plays. There is no filter. An example of this is the expression on his face when I inform him of what Sara White said. He's rarely stumped by the media—heard it, seen it, done it—but her words cause genuine surprise. "I mean, to hear that, that means a lot. He's the greatest defensive lineman to play this game. To have her compare him to me is a great honor.

"I think one of the things with Reggie was his work ethic, and he was very humble," Watt continued. "I try to be the same way. My dad was a firefighter for almost 30 years. My mom worked her way up from a secretary to vice president of her own company. They taught me to work hard for everything and take nothing for granted. That's how I play.

"I think that's why you won't see me be one of these guys [to] spend 15 or 20 years in the NFL. I don't want to play forever. I want to give everything I can now and then walk away knowing I gave everything. The example I think of is Barry Sanders. He was such a great player and he left when he was still on top. I want that to be me."

Watt added: "I think one of the things Reggie did was use football to try and make change. That's always been my goal."

Sara White keyed in on this as well. "The first thing with J.J. is that I know Reggie would first look at him as a man and see what kind of man he was," she said. "The way J.J. handles himself in the community is something Reggie would be proud of. I really think Reggie would be proud to have him as a son."

To understand how far Watt has come since his rookie season just two years ago, you have to go back in time, to when White dominated the sport as a player with the Eagles and Packers. No defensive lineman in history could annihilate an offensive line like the 300-pound White. (Until Watt.) The comparison isn't perfect because White didn't shift up and down the line the way Watt does. But the dominance…their dominance is the same.

"What I love is he has desire to excel in every facet of the game," Hall of Fame defensive lineman Michael Strahan told me recently. "He plays the run like a champ and can line up and rush the passer unlike anyone else on the field. He plays as if it's an insult if the opponent only blocks him with one person.

"He plays with max effort every play and never leaves the field after the game with any regrets. I feel he makes all these incredible plays not because he's the most physically gifted lineman in the league but because he plays every play at a pace that puts him in the right place to make the spectacular play. You can tell that it's not about anything but being the best, and most of all being respected."

White did the same. He was also the first superstar NFL player to use his prowess on the field for extensive charitable endeavors off of it. What Watt has done is even more impressive, and in many ways what we are seeing with Watt is unprecedented because of three things.

First, Watt is already the player White was. This is not hyperbole. It is accurate. We don't know if Watt will have White's longevity, but he is already having the impact. Second, like White, the Texans defensive end understands that his football skills are a hypergenerator for changing the lives of ordinary people for the better.

Third, unlike White (and other superstars who met that second criteria noted above), Watt is without blemish. There are no controversies. No attacks on women. No beaten children. No accusations of deflating footballs or otherwise cheating. Nothing but production and selflessness on the field.

Watt doesn't play dirty. That is not an easy accomplishment, even in today's safety-obsessed NFL. Many players aren't dirty, but a significant number are. They twist ankles in the bottom of piles, slyly punch to the groin, elbow under the face mask. It's all still done, but only occasionally caught by cameras. One of the few times it was happened during the Cincinnati-Carolina game in October 2014. Bengals linebacker Vontaze Burfict clearly attempted to damage some Panthers' ankles during the tackle by severely twisting them at the end of the play.

"It's pretty obvious that's not what this league is all about," Panthers tight end Greg Olsen said of Burfict. "You understand that sometimes there's penalties and guys kind of go above and beyond the lines with some hits, and helmet-to-helmet. That's all in the flow of the game, and it's hard to avoid at times. But I think instances like that, that are so clearly premeditated that he had in his mind if those opportunities, that he was going to try to attack not only guys' legs, but guys who were coming off ankle problems specifically, there's no room for it. At some point, if the NFL wants to really say they care about guys' safety, they have to start putting guys [who commit dirty plays] out for weeks cause me and Cam are lucky we weren't out for weeks. Or Kelvin's out for weeks. If you're going to start putting guys on other teams out, then the ramifications need to equal that."

Watt isn't dirty because he thinks dirty play is, well, dirty. But he also realizes that dirty play would not just tarnish him as a player but also his team and the sport itself. This is a significant part of who Watt is. He's always cognizant of the bigger picture.

What Watt has avoided is controversy of any kind, something even the superhuman White could not do. In 1998, six years before his death, White drew massive, and legitimate, criticism for racist and homophobic remarks. He would be seen as a legendary player, but to some he was also a bigot.

Watt, speaking of himself, said something fairly interesting about the potential for missteps. "I know I can't mess up," he said. Translation: Watt is seen as a sincere, good man, doing sincere good things. He is currently in a cynicism-free zone. But so was Ray Rice. So was, in some ways, Adrian Peterson. So was NFL player Darren Sharper, who was viewed as one of the

NFL's most charitable players but then was accused of raping numerous women in different states. One mistake, or several, changed everything for all of them. Watt is keenly aware of this. "If I mess up," Watt said, "then people will doubt everything. I know that."

One Texans player told me that Watt has even studied what happened to some of those players who found themselves in trouble. "I think J.J. sees it as arrogance can get you in hot water," the player explained. "J.J. doesn't see himself as infallible. He doesn't think that because he's a football player he can't make mistakes. He's not arrogant. That is why I don't think you'll see him in any beefs."

To Watt, it's simple. He won't make a catastrophic mistake. That is, in many ways, an inhuman standard Watt must live up to, because people are fallible. It is our nature. But he is used to being super. To Watt, that is just another challenge, like beating a double team, and he will succeed.

In many ways, what's happened with Watt is that he gets it. He gets the job and the optics of the job. Historically, some players, quite simply, have not; to them, optics are something you get at LensCrafters. Once, former Rams quarterback Tony Banks brought a puppy to training camp. A puppy. To training camp. The best part of the story was the name of the dog: Felony. He named his dog Felony. The team's general manager ripped Banks for bringing the pooch to camp.

Last season, NFL playboy Johnny Manziel was fined by the Browns for being late to receive treatment for his various injuries. Several reports said Manziel was tardy because he had been partying the night before and team security officials had to be sent to find Manziel. But Manziel shouldn't feel too ashamed. Another player once had security sent in search of him, and they walked into a hotel room to find the player in bed with multiple women.

Former NFL player Roman Oben, one of the most intelligent people I ever covered, was relentlessly teased in the Giants locker room for driving a Toyota Land Cruiser with 68,000 miles on it (instead of purchasing a high-end car). Oben understood why some players went broke: by making multiple expensive purchases only to see their careers end just a few years into playing.

What Watt has become, both on-field and off, is the NFL's savior. That may sound outrageous. That may seem ridiculous. It may even be bigoted to call a white player—in a 70 percent black league where the majority of players do the right thing—its savior. But that's the truth of the matter.

These are extraordinary times in the NFL. In the past, controversies were spaced apart by months and years. No more. And there was a time, not so long ago, NFL executives believed the league was in a renaissance era that could last decades. Now, team and league executives believe the NFL's popularity is in danger of becoming diluted by the criminal conduct of players *and* owners, like a battery drained by frigid temperatures. "I can tell you," says Sara, "Reggie's heart would be broken with so many of the bad decisions some of the players are making today. He would be devastated."

What the NFL needs now, more than ever, is a hero. Watt is stepping into that role. It fits him perfectly. More importantly, he wants the responsibility. Again, there are hundreds of NFL players who do the right thing. None, however, is like Watt. Maybe no one in NFL history is like him.

Several days before Thanksgiving, a group of Houston firefighters and police officers received a special delivery. It was pizzas sent by Watt. That act itself was thoughtful, but it was the handwritten note Watt sent that was, well, very Watt:

HFD & HFP

I just wanted to send y'all a small token of my appreciation for everything you do. My Dad and Uncle were both firefighters, so I spent a lot of time around the firehouse when I was younger and gained a great deal of respect for both firefighters and the police along the way.

Y'all show up day in and day out, never knowing what the day might hold and never getting enough thanks for what you do, yet you continue to put others before yourselves and save lives because of it.

As athletes, we often get the headlines and big crowds, but just like the men and women in our military, y'all are the ones who truly deserve the credit, appreciation and admiration. I know it's not much, but please enjoy lunch on me today. Thank you for all that you do!

JJ Watt 99

———

HERE'S AN ADMISSION: I TRIED. I TRIED TO FIND DIRT ON WATT. MOST journalists either don't admit they've done this (with Watt or other players on whom they are writing profiles) or keep it quiet, but many of us do. It's for protection. We're cynical. You don't want to write a story declaring a guy is a good dude when he's secretly out robbing banks. Some of us have been fooled by polished smiles and publicists before. We have written about athletes spending time with the kids at the YMCA only to find out later they had enough kids with a mistress to populate that YMCA. So I had to ask myself: is everyone being played by Watt?

"What you see with J.J. is no phoniness in any way," said longtime NFL writer John McClain, who has covered Houston football for decades and is one of the most knowledgeable and savvy writers I have ever known. McClain then ticked off names of legends who have come through Houston. Names like Hall of Famers Warren Moon and Earl Campbell and great players like Bruce Matthews. "J.J. has worked harder than any of them off the field," McClain said.

"There is nothing phony about him in any way," echoed former Texans wide receiver Andre Johnson, adding, "Players would know."

"What makes him so good is his work ethic," he continued. "The reason you see him succeed so well on the field is because of what he does in practice and in the weight room and in the film room. First guy here, last one to leave."

I wondered, is there resentment in the Texans locker room toward the attention Watt is getting? I've seen that before, once in particular, in Detroit in the 1990s. Linebacker Chris Spielman became one of the most popular players with fans and the media. He was a friendly and charismatic guy who never turned away an interview (which is why I liked him). I remember black players telling me specifically that they felt Spielman was overrated by the media because he was white.

Marcellus Wiley feels differently. The former NFL player who is now an NFL analyst, called Spielman the toughest teammate he ever played with. Know those powerful, vile-smelling capsules used to help wake unconscious people? One, waved under the nose, is like getting punched in the face. Wiley remembers Spielman taking two of the capsules and sticking one up each nostril. Players do what they need to get ready. Another case in point: former Giants receiver Plaxico Burress, at the NFC title game at Lambeau Field in 2008 where the wind-chill was sub-freezing, covered his entire body with Vaseline to help keep himself warm. He finished with 11 catches and 154 yards in the game.

Hard as I tried to find it, no one seems to have resentment about Watt. Sure, there are some in and around football who believe that Watt is talented, but not as talented as everyone else does. Hall of Fame defensive tackle Warren Sapp says Watt rarely attracts two blockers simultaneously. Sapp also said that Watt doesn't always draw the full attention of offensive coordinators. When Sapp played, by contrast, he was routinely doubled—I believe there were multiple occasions when I covered his games there were three offensive players blocking him. To players like Sapp, you aren't elite unless you consistently draw that kind of attention. It's not an unfair point, except that in the games I personally covered Watt, he was indeed double-blocked, often. I can also say offensive coordinators are obsessed with him, though as one told me, perhaps not as much as we in the media like to believe.

In my five days with the Texans, I saw Watt interact with almost everyone on the team. I mean, just about everyone. I can tell you, that is highly unusual for a superstar. Many superstars, in all sports, often stick to themselves or a small circle of teammates. In that locker room, and outside of it, Watt is everyman.

"I haven't seen any resentment I think because my play matches the hype," Watt said.

"If you're jealous of him," Johnson said, "you need to look in the mirror."

———

ONE OF THE THINGS WATT DOES MOST OFTEN IS VISIT HOSPITALS. Many instances, if not all of the time, he does this secretly. It's only later that news of his visits (and photos) occasionally leak. Watt's mother, Connie, believes this impulse in her son to visit the extremely sick stems from when he was younger. He went into the doctor to see if he had mononucleosis, but initial indications were that Watt had leukemia. He didn't, but that moment changed everything for Watt. "I think he took to heart what it might have meant had that leukemia diagnosis been true," she said. "I don't think he ever forgot."

That became apparent as Watt befriended the Berry family. Aaron, Peter, and Willa Berry were orphaned in July 2011 after their parents were killed in a horrific car accident in the Houston area. The kids survived, but two of them, now eight and nine years old, were paralyzed from the waist down. The family received donations from many, including athletes, but Watt would becomes friends with them and remains so to this day. "I didn't want to be one of these guys who dropped in and they never heard from me again," he said. Yet all of the work Watt does to generate goodwill presents a significant challenge to the man himself. "The challenge J.J. is running into now," says Connie, is that "he is asked to help people all the time, but there is just one J.J."

There are pitfalls awaiting Watt. White faced them, dodged all of them for a good chunk of his career before several chased him down the way he pursued quarterbacks. Those moments have stuck to him even beyond his death.

Sara said Reggie would give Watt three pieces of advice. "One or two mistakes can damage your legacy," she said. "That would be first. On the field, be consistent. Then lastly, be careful with your money." Sara said Reggie's first contract was worth a total of $125,000.

"The one thing with Reggie was that he loved to speak to kids, help people, and help fellow players," said Sara. "But people used to try and take advantage of his popularity. I would not be surprised if the same thing is happening with J.J. Reggie would always feel guilty about not being able to help someone or make it to an event, [even] after he had already done so many things to help people. I used to say, 'You can't be in two places at once.' I think Reggie would tell J.J. to be careful. Make sure you find time for yourself."

Watt did just that not so long ago. He planned a trip to Europe for himself and his two brothers. They visited France, England, and Ireland. "That meant the world to me that J.J. did that," Connie said. "Taking time for himself and being with his brothers."

Watt and players like him, guys like Richard Sherman, are saviors in another way. While the NFL emphasizes making cash, players like Watt and Sherman humanize the sport. They show the NFL isn't just a money-making machine; human beings play it. The NFL sometimes forgets this, but players do not.

At the end of the 2014 season, Watt was named Defensive Player of the Year for a second time. He received 13 votes for league MVP, losing to Aaron Rodgers—but it was the first time this century that a defensive player received more than three MVP votes.

Watt joined Reggie White, Bruce Smith, Lawrence Taylor, Mike Singletary, and Joe Greene as a multiple Defensive Player of the Year honoree (and he was the first player ever to win the award unanimously). That's pretty good company—and remember, Watt's only been in the NFL four years.

There was another good moment for Watt, at the January 2015 Pro Bowl in Arizona. I saw Watt before the game, interacting with fans, excited for a contest that most people generally mock. But that is Watt: if he's playing football, he's happy. After the game began, during a commercial, Watt danced on the sideline. At the end of the game, he was named the Pro Bowl's defensive MVP. Watt timed a pass, jumped into the air, and plucked the football out of the sky for an interception. The play only added to his lore. He had fun in a game that many players dread. But that, too, is Watt.

Watt was undoubtedly also the star all week leading up to the Super Bowl. I followed him briefly as he did media interviews and he gave each one the same amount of attention, whether it was ESPN or a small radio station. Every person was greeted with a sincere smile and a handshake. That, too, is Watt.

"One of the things I have to do, and I'm working on it," said Watt, "is making sure I enjoy the ride along the way. I have to remind myself, 'Take a look around, look at things, and enjoy it.'

"What I want to do now," he said, "is use the power of football to help people. But when I retire, I want to be normal. I will always do what I can to help others, but when I retire I want to be a dad and a husband. I want a house and a dog in the yard. I want to have barbecues."

That, too, is Watt.

6   THE THREE HORSEMEN

THE GREATEST

I asked Joe Montana a simple question: Who is the quarterback who most reminds you of yourself. Montana didn't hesitate: "It's Aaron."

That would be Aaron Rodgers, of course. In high school, Rodgers sent out his game tape to colleges. One assistant on the Purdue staff sent him a note back. Rodgers recounted that part of it read, "Good luck with your attempt at a college football career."

Now, years after so many college coaches got it wrong about Rodgers—and so many in the NFL after that—on December 28, 2014, with a few snowflakes falling at Lambeau Field, Rodgers would make one of many demonstrations as to why no one is playing the position better than him. It was the first half in the team's regular-season finale, against Detroit. That day was the start of a brilliant run in the 2014 season. Really, it was the exclamation point on what has been a remarkable career so far, a career that I believe will end with most people thinking of Rodgers as the best to ever play the position.

On one play, Rodgers was scrambling right. At about the 5-yard line, the left calf he had injured the week before, against Tampa Bay, seized. Rodgers flicked the pass sidearm, throwing the football with both great force and accuracy, as he fell to the ground. The ball traveled at warp speed and landed into the arms of Randall Cobb. The Packers led 14–0, but everyone at Lambeau Field collectively pooped themselves. Rodgers was taken off the field on a cart.

"I just remember thinking, *This feels like it could be really, really bad*," Rodgers said in an interview with me. "I thought I tore my Achilles'…I wondered if my season was over."

There was numbness in the calf, but it didn't feel catastrophic. Rodgers left the locker room and went to the sideline. He began to toss the football lightly. Things felt better. Then better. Then even more so. The score was tied at 14 when Rodgers put his helmet on, and the crowd erupted. Soon after, he hit Cobb again for a score. The Packers went on to win. Along the way, Rodgers would even endure a cheap shot from the dirtiest player in football, Ndamukong Suh, who stepped on Rodgers' injured leg. "He was just trying to show affection for me," Rodgers later joked.

Beating the Lions on an injured leg was impressive. What he would do the following week against Dallas, again at Lambeau, was almost historic. It turns out Rodgers had a torn calf muscle (or a strain, but strain and tear are almost tomato/tomahto). Rodgers had what amounted to a Willis Reed moment. He was sluggish in the first half, but in the third quarter, with Dallas leading 21–13, vintage Rodgers appeared. Throwing on basically one leg, he completed a 46-yard touchdown pass to Davante Adams. Then, on a crucial fourth-quarter drive, Rodgers went

7-for-7 for 95 yards, capped off by a 13-yard touchdown pass to Richard Rodgers. "That is the best throw that I've seen this season," said Hall of Famer Deion Sanders at the time on the NFL Network.

I remember speaking to a Cowboys player after that game and he said something that stuck with me. He studied Rodgers on film and thought, *Yeah, he's good, but maybe people are making him out to be too good. No one can be that good.* "And the game came, and he was running around back there hurt, still making huge plays," the player remembered, "and I wasn't intimidated but he does wear a defense down. He wore us down because in the back of our minds he was killing us, even when he was hurt, and that sort of thing hurts your mentality. It makes you give up a little."

The Cowboys would still almost win with a circuslike catch/non-catch from star receiver Dez Bryant, but Rodgers' destiny continued. That win gave Rodgers a 9-0 home record, 28 touchdowns, and no interceptions. None. Zero.

Entering the playoffs in the 2014–15 season, nine times Rodgers ran for first downs on third down, and eight times he succeeded. Rodgers is also the only player in NFL history with a 100-plus passer rating in six consecutive seasons. "Aaron Rodgers right now is in a whole elite category by himself," said former NFL player Jamie Dukes on the NFL Network at the time. "[With] all due respect to Tom Brady, all due respect to Peyton Manning and anybody else…Aaron is in a class all by himself."

"Playing with Aaron Rodgers, every time I went into a game you always felt like no matter what happens, he was going to bail you out somehow," said defensive back and future Hall of Famer Charles Woodson.

None of this means Rodgers has been immune from the brutal life that is being an NFL quarterback. The Packers' playoff loss to Seattle in January 2015 was one of the toughest losses in Packers history, and maybe the most pain Rodgers will ever feel when it comes to football.

He was also treated horribly by Brett Favre while his understudy. Favre defended his treatment of Rodgers in a 2015 interview with Graham Bensinger. "I don't owe him or anyone else anything other than, in my opinion, being a nice guy and being thoughtful. You know, I don't have to give him any insights to what I do or don't do," Favre said. "Nowhere does it say that you have to take that guy under your wing and teach him the ropes. You don't have to do anything but win ballgames for whoever it is you're the starting quarterback for."

To my mind, the top five quarterbacks in football are Rodgers, Tom Brady, Russell Wilson, Andrew Luck, and Ben Roethlisberger—in that order. Lists like these fluctuate and often cause people to throw things at one another at the dinner table but the commonality of this list is struggle and perseverance over those struggles. This is particularly true with Rodgers, Wilson, and Luck. Rodgers overcame doubt that he could play college football, let alone become a professional, and became the best at what he does. Wilson fights doubters about his size, or who don't believe he is an elite thrower. Luck has numerous believers, yet a poor performance in the AFC title game at the end of the 2014 season led to some in the sport wondering if Luck is further from winning a title than many originally thought. More on those two in a moment.

Rodgers hit another rough spot in the NFC Championship Game in January 2015. Playing on that still-injured leg, Rodgers was brilliant early in the game, throwing with accuracy, and along with the play of his defense, led the Packers to a 19–7 lead with just more than five minutes to play. At that point, the Packers, according to ESPN statisticians, had a 96 percent chance to win. And they lost. They lost. It would go down as one of the most traumatic losses in Packers history. Still, does the loss injure Rodgers' legacy? No, not really. There is still no one in the sport who is better. One loss doesn't change that.

After the game, Seahawks cornerback Byron Maxwell was asked about Rodgers. "He's a great quarterback," Maxwell said. "You remember the throw? It was in the first quarter and he was on the other hash and threw it all the way back to the other side. I was like, 'Okay man, what is this, a robot?'"

————

WHAT HAS PROPELLED THE POPULARITY OF THE NFL IS THE COMBUS-tible combination of television, gambling, social media, violence, and star power. In Rodgers' case, he has become the best in the sport at a time when its popularity has never been higher. It is a symbiotic relationship for the QB and the NFL. Rodgers' uber-skill is seen and appreciated by more fans (except in Chicago) while that uber-skill helps to boost the league (except in Chicago). It also helps to cover the sport's blemishes and stave off any notion perpetuated by negative jerks like me who believe football is in long-term trouble. Some players like Rodgers are so good, so eternal in some ways, that they act as counteragents to the NFL's missteps and public-relations debacles.

It's long been thought that the NBA is a player's league. You can see their faces during games clearly, unlike in football, where face masks hide smiles and expressions, and rules prevent celebratory outbursts. But now, social media has transformed the NFL in which coaching personalities dominated to one in which coaches take a backseat to players. Once, Bill Parcells or Bill Walsh were stars as big as Montana and Phil Simms. Gone are the days of *Saturday Night Live*'s "Ditka"; Packers head coach Mike McCarthy can venture into parts of this country and still not be recognized. (The only exception to this rule is Bill Belichick, whose popularity is equal to almost any player.) Rodgers, on the other hand, is a household name and face.

One measure of Rodgers' dominance was the Associated Press All-Pro voting. The AP vote is among the least political—though, like all sports voting mechanisms, still has its flaws. Of the 50 total votes for quarterback, Rodgers had 44, Tony Romo 3, Tom Brady 2, and Andrew Luck 1.

Some of the best comments about Rodgers came during the debate in December leading to the league's MVP announcement. Several of those comments were documented in Peter King's *Monday Morning Quarterback* column. "I went with Rodgers over Watt merely because Rodgers played as flawlessly at his position over a 10-week stretch as I've ever seen," NFL analyst Rich Eisen told King. "Plus, for a quarterback to directly address his fan base in this social-media-driven, long-time-listener-first-time-caller-laden day and age and [tell] them to relax, it makes his play the greatest walking of the walk I've ever seen."

Said Tom Pelissero from *USA TODAY*: "We can debate the definition of 'valuable,' but in considering J.J. Watt for MVP, I keep coming back to this question: Would Aaron Rodgers be under consideration if the Packers missed the playoffs at 9–7 'because his team didn't have a defensive lineman?' Any argument for Watt leans on his ability to keep the Texans in the hunt amidst their quarterback issues. But that's the problem with voting for him over Rodgers or, in my opinion, several other quarterbacks this season. That position controls everything, and not even the best defensive player of a generation can supersede it. Watt seems to make two or three high-impact plays every game—which is incredible—but the QB has a chance to impact the game every play he's on the field, both before and after the snap. My vote is for Rodgers, who played the most important position at the highest level over the course of this season."

Montana says it's easy for the trained eye—meaning a Hall of Fame quarterback like himself—to see why Rodgers is so good. "You can see a work ethic," he said. "It translates on the field. I had some natural talent, but throwing routes—throwing hundreds of them and thousands and more—combined with talent, helps a good quarterback become a great one like Aaron."

This point cannot be emphasized enough. The reason Michael Vick—despite unbelievable natural ability (maybe the best the NFL has ever seen)—never developed much beyond that ability is because he never seriously studied his trade. (He's admitted this—twice.) The reason Russell Wilson has become so good so fast is because he constantly studies. Many times the differences between a Rodgers and a Jeff George are practice routes and film study. Rodgers will one day enter the Hall of Fame because of his work ethic. George, on the other hand, has entered infamy.

———

THIS IS ONE OF THE DEFINING QUOTES FROM RODGERS. IT CAME in Bruce Feldman's book *The QB: The Making of Modern Quarterbacks*. Rodgers talked about his journey. "You really need to remember where you came from and have appreciation for the journey that you went on," Rodgers said. "I think a lot of kids these days, especially with the outlets we have, the exposure that we have, where a lot of these young guys are 'blue-chippers' from the time they're in high school to the time they get drafted, there's not a ton of adversity that they go through. I dealt with adversity on every level, from not getting recruited out of high school to going to junior college, to being a backup in D-I, to falling farther than I thought I would in the draft. For me, it was great, because I got to sit and learn and be with the disappointment. Those experiences can either strengthen your character or make you really bitter. Thankfully for me, it really strengthened my character and gave me a good resolve."

This in many ways is the essence of Rodgers. It's not that Rodgers plays with a chip on his shoulder; I think he's moved beyond that. It's something simpler, something that's even cornball. It's what all of the greats like Montana or Johnny Unitas or Lawrence Taylor or Dick Butkus or Jim Brown and now Rodgers all have in common. They want to be better than anyone else, and all of the elite ones will do what it takes to get there. (Just look at J.J. Watt.) In an interview with me, Rodgers recalled one of the more interesting stories from early in his rookie season with the Packers when he was backing up Brett Favre. Then–head coach Mike Sherman instituted a practice some other teams used, which the Packers called "Feel-Good

Friday." Friday practices on most teams are fairly relaxed, but the Packers took it to another level. Rodgers was on the scout team, and coaches asked him to throw an interception on certain plays. "To me," Rodgers said, "you never purposefully throw interceptions. Competitors don't do that." The defensive coaches complained when Rodgers refused to throw the interception, but he didn't care. He wouldn't do it. The great ones despise failure. Even practicing it makes them twitch.

Quarterbacks, perhaps more than any other players, can recall a moment when everything falls into place. Rodgers, during his interview with me, remembered that moment for him. It was 2007, and the Packers were at Dallas. Rodgers came into the game, replacing Favre, in the second quarter, and with 38 seconds left in the half threw an 11-yard touchdown pass to Greg Jennings. "For me, it was that game where something clicked," he said. "It was actually maybe more of a feeling, a feeling of settling in. I hadn't really felt it before. The confidence [overtook] the nerves." Rodgers would finish that game 18 of 26 for 201 yards and a score. He also rushed five times for 30 yards. In many ways, it was the game when the Rodgers we know now was born.

"The thing I love about football is when I step on that field, it's the competition," he said. "I live for it. I think people from all walks of life who want to be the best live for that competition. I want to play at the highest levels because that's what the best in this game do. The challenge is to stay at those highest levels."

I asked Rodgers how long he thinks he can play in the NFL. "I heard Tom Brady once say he wants to play forever. Sounds good to me."

———

ONE OF MY FAVORITE RODGERS MOMENTS CAME NOT ON THE FIELD but off of it. It was Rodgers sharing his story with a group of young quarterbacks at the 2004 Elite 11. The Elite 11 is a combination of a competition to determine the best high school quarterbacks and also serves as a teaching tool. Professional players like Rodgers are invited as counselors to share their stories. Rodgers, as he often is as a speaker and leader, was electric.

He told the room he had wanted to be a quarterback since he was three and that Montana was his idol. "The thing I would tell you guys is come in and be humble," he said. "Go out of your way to be nice to guys. Don't come in with a cocky attitude. Guys want to see what you're like. Are you a cool guy? Are you an arrogant guy? Are you a humble, hard worker?"

Then Rodgers discussed his first year at Cal and a three-way battle at quarterback. He was beaten out. "I was thinking, *It's my job. I got this*," he said, "and he beat me out. It was really a shot to my self-esteem, you know, because I had never really been a backup at anything in my life."

So what did Rodgers do? He did what would become a hallmark of his career. He studied. Rodgers took mental reps while sitting on the bench. He studied everything he could get his hands on. He learned from the mistakes of the quarterback ahead of him. He did that at Cal and then he did it again in Green Bay while sitting behind Brett Favre.

And here he is now. A guy on his way to being the best of all time.

#MAKETHEMNOTICE

I watched Rodgers walk off the field of that January 2015 NFC title game. He looked like a man who didn't know what had just happened. He wasn't alone. The Seahawks players were stunned as well. So were some of the Seattle fans. Thousands of them had left the game early, thinking the Packers had won. They tried unsuccessfully to get back into the stadium.

Rodgers walked off the field like a zombie, practically stumbling into the locker room. Wilson, on the other side of the field, momentarily took a knee as cameras surrounded him. Then he began to cry uncontrollably. Watching Wilson closely as he walked off the field I saw a man who wasn't simply ecstatic about reaching the Super Bowl—again. It was that he had once again proven people wrong. Those people who had said he was too short to play in the NFL. Or couldn't throw from the pocket.

As it happened, Wilson threw four interceptions against the Packers that day. He looked positively buried...until Wilson did what he always does. He stayed mentally sturdy. Two plays made by Wilson changed the game. One was a 35-yard pass that was a perfect throw and the second was a 35-yard pass that was a perfect throw to win the game in overtime. Two throws. Two displays of accuracy that some people say Wilson doesn't possess.

"He's a phenomenal player, a phenomenal leader for his team," said Tom Brady about Wilson leading up to the Super Bowl. "Every quarterback has a different way to get things done. It's all your skill set and what your ability is—to either throw it, run it—and the ability to move the ball down the field through creating first downs and ultimately scoring points.

A lot of teams do that different ways. You try to play to the strengths of your players. Russell has a lot of strengths. You can see it on the field. I think he's obviously a great competitor. A couple of those overtime games, where they've gone right down the field and scored, I think that's all you really need to know about a guy like that."

Wilson is an enigma to some but not people who know the game well. They know who Wilson is and that's an evolution at the position. He doesn't fit into a neat box because he is the 21st-century quarterback—and in some ways the 21st-century human being. He violates the comfort zone of the old-school NFL that likes its passers to stay in the pocket and stand tall as a redwood. Yes, he confuses some—even some of his own teammates.

———

THE RESTAURANT IS BUSY BUT NOT CROWDED. THERE ARE THREE of us on this particular night, eating six different dishes spread across our table: two Seahawks players I've gotten to know well over the past several years and me. (Later, we'd go to dinner again, and one more player would join us.) The only ground rules set by the players: no pictures and everything was off the record unless I got permission from the players to publish it. My goal was fairly simple: I wanted to know what one of the most secretive locker rooms in the NFL was like. The conversation would cover numerous aspects of life not just as a Seahawks player but also across the NFL. Eventually, the conversation turned to Russell Wilson.

"Fuck that dude," one player said.

Thus began a weird odyssey for me about a player whom I believe to be one of the great players—and role models—in the sport, a guy who just might end up being the best quarterback of his generation.

———

MY GOAL IN WRITING THE STORY FOR BLEACHER REPORT AT THE time was simply to find out what the true dynamics were inside a Seattle locker room that is quite hard to penetrate. The Seahawks have given us the best quotes in the NFL of late, and maybe ever. (Even with the occasionally verbally challenged Marshawn Lynch.) Yet what I had been told, in bits and pieces, by several Seahawks players was that the team was quietly in turmoil. The trade of wide receiver Percy Harvin opened wounds that had already existed and then became exacerbated when the Seahawks struggled early in the season.

I had no intention, or notion, to write a story critical of Wilson, but after several different dinners with a handful of Seattle players—and not just bench players, either—it was clear some players viewed Wilson as being behind the trade of Percy Harvin, who was one of the most popular players on the team. These players viewed Wilson as too close to management. One wondered aloud if Wilson was black enough. That caused quite the tempest. It was a statement I didn't agree with and I argued with the player who said it, but it was clear it was how these players felt. (Not one or two players, either, but more than a few.) The statements, when published, caused a fair amount of controversy. And for reporting the feelings of some Seahawks players, a Seattle radio troll called me a "race baiter."

Wilson isn't an Uncle Tom, but it's clear some of the players believed he was. There was also an element of jealousy at work with some of the guys since Wilson had quickly become one of the most popular on the team. "I think one of the problems some guys had with him," explained a Seattle player, "was how he acted like he was this great player, and some of us were beneath him."

What makes Wilson even more impressive was he fought through some of his own teammates' dissatisfaction—and there *was* dissatisfaction, despite some of the public denials from Seahawks players that ensued following my story. ESPN's Kenny Mayne went on ESPN and quoted two Seahawks sources who said my story was essentially correct. Most interesting, perhaps, is that Wilson faced issues someone like Luck or Rodgers did not. The fact that Wilson overcame them, while also proving to be one of the best young stars in the sport, says a great deal about him.

Seahawks head coach Pete Carroll called a meeting with a small group of team leaders. Everyone in the meeting was asked to air their grievances. I'm told things got extremely heated—not *over*heated but heated. After that meeting, the Seahawks would put their issues behind them and again reach the Super Bowl.

———

WILSON'S CONFIDENCE HAS ALWAYS BEEN THERE. THE PATRIOTS saw it at the NFL's scouting combine in 2012. An excellent story on Wilson written by Robert Klemko in *Sports Illustrated* tells the story of when Wilson met with Belichick during combine meetings. As Klemko wrote, Belichick was looking for a quarterback to groom once the indefatigable Brady retired. One member of the Patriots contingent said the team already had a pretty good player in Brady. What did Wilson think of that? "Yes, I understand who he is, but I've competed against everyone," Wilson told the Patriots, "so if you choose to bring me in here, I'm coming to compete and coming to win the job."

"It wasn't arrogance," Wilson's uncle, Ben, told Klemko. "That's just his makeup. He loves competition, and it doesn't matter to him what he's up against."

Five hours before the NFC Championship Game, Wilson tweeted the hashtag #makethemnotice. He was perhaps talking about the Seahawks as a team (though that is partly silly since the Seahawks were favored and, um, extremely noticed), but the hashtag also applies to him personally. Wilson has still had to shake people by the shoulders and make them see what he truly is: an outstanding talent who plays the position in a new way.

The Seahawks are an eclectic group of guys with bold personalities who give scrumptious sound bites. At one of the Super Bowl media events in late January, Michael Bennett was talking about how their defense may be the best of all time. Then he added, "I think I'm the greatest lover of all time, too. Ask my wife."

By contrast, Wilson suffers because he is extremely straightforward, even boring, in his dealings with the media. He doesn't brag. He doesn't take credit. He gives it all to others. He is, at times, extremely dull. This hurts him with some in the media.

Yet on occasion, Wilson lowers his shields and shows real emotion, as he did after the NFC title game. Or he gives a brilliant answer, as he did during Super Bowl week when he was asked why he was so calm on this big stage. "Growing up, my dad and my mom used to always ask me questions, especially my dad," Wilson said in response. "He used to always ask me questions. 'Russell, you just got to the Super Bowl' or 'You just won Super Bowl MVP.' All these questions as I was growing up—7, 10, 15 years old. So those questions prepared me. I went to a great school in Collegiate School growing up in high school. I went to NC State for communications/broadcasting, then I went to grad school for business...I've just been around great people and great education. My parents taught me about education, how important that was."

One thing Wilson likes to do before a game is find a solitary spot in the stadium to stand there alone and decompress. "I always have the same spot in CenturyLink. I'm not going to tell anybody where it is, but it's a good one. It just worked for me. It lets me relax. It lets me focus on the moment more than anything else."

In 2015, Wilson became the youngest quarterback to start in two Super Bowls. His first Super Bowl was a success; his second was not. The game, like Wilson's career—like the entire NFL season—wasn't a simple matter. Wilson played solidly. Not spectacularly, but well. The problem for Wilson was that on basically the last play of the game he was intercepted by Patriot Malcolm Butler. For whatever strange reason, the Seahawks decided to pass on the pivotal play instead of running the football from the half-yard line. The decision spurned talk of a conspiracy—with first-and-goal from the 5-yard line, unleashing Beast Mode had seemed a certainty facing short yardage. Some in the media harkened back to my story on turmoil in the Seahawks locker room centering on Wilson.

Dave Zirin, the thoughtful and thorough writer for *The Nation*, penned a story the morning after the Super Bowl called "The Conspiracy Theory Surrounding the Seahawks' Last Play." Zirin wrote of a text message he received from a Seahawks player: "I contacted someone inside that locker room and they said to me as if on repeat. 'CAN'T BELIEVE IT. WE ALL SAW IT. THEY WANTED IT TO BE RUSS. THEY DIDN'T WANT MARSHAWN TO BE THE HERO.'" Mike Silver, another talented writer, who works for the NFL Network, wrote that he wanted to "refrain from lending any legitimacy to the conspiracy theory [that] one anonymous player was willing to broach: That Carroll somehow had a vested interest in making Wilson, rather than Lynch, the hero, and thus insisted on putting the ball in the quarterback's hands with an entire season on the line. 'That's what it looked like,' the unnamed player said, 'but I'd be willing to bet that he merely muttered it out of frustration, and that it was a fleeting thought.'"

Despite the Super Bowl loss and despite the drama that might still surround Wilson—he remains one of the league's brightest stars. He's definitely made them notice.

ALL LUCK

Luck would experience his own brutal loss in the 2015 playoff season. It was against the Patriots in the AFC Championship Game. As has happened to many quarterbacks, young and old, against Belichick and his defenses, Luck struggled. In fact, against New England, Luck has always struggled. Luck has lost each of his four games against the Patriots by at least 21 points. In that AFC championship he was intercepted twice and completed just 12 of 33 passes for 126 yards.

I rank Wilson ahead of Luck because Wilson—the NFC title game aside—usually makes far fewer mistakes. It is true that Wilson throws fewer passes and has a far better team surrounding him, but I think he could do the same if he was asked to throw the football 40 times a game on a less talented squad. I think he would still be terrific.

"Russell is very smart and adaptive," said Rodgers to me. "I think he is a very special player. I think he can do anything in this league. I think with Russell you see with him some of the same doubters I saw when I was coming [up]. There are always doubters. The great thing about doubters is that they usually are proven wrong."

Then Rodgers switched to Luck. "I think when his career is over we are going to be talking about him as one of the very special quarterbacks to ever play in this league."

Who is Andrew Luck?

"I remember Andrew's rookie year…second practice, and the defense was just blitzing the hell out of him," Colts quarterbacks coach Clyde Christensen said. "The defense brought all these exotic blitzes. I think Andrew threw some picks and was sacked a bunch. We were walking off the field, and Andrew looked at me and said, 'Coach, what the hell just happened?' The next day, the defense blitzes again. Different kinds of blitzes, but a lot of them. The passes were flying out. *Bing, bing, bing.* I think he had one incompletion. That was Andrew in a nutshell. You get to him once. You don't get to him a second time."

"We played Jacksonville [in 2013] and had a sluggish first half," remembered offensive lineman and Luck's close friend Anthony Castonzo. "We were in the locker room, and Andrew was pacing up and down the room talking to all the players, saying, 'Keep working, keep working, keep working!' I grabbed him and said, 'Andrew, do you think we're going to stop working?' He smiled, and we laughed.

"Here we were at halftime of this tough game, and we were laughing like a bunch of kids. That's one of the many great things about him. He's so smart and tough, but he makes football fun again. He has this way of taking us back to our childhood, when we played football because we loved it. In the second half of that game, we blew them out."

Who is Andrew Luck?

In 2013, Luck addressed the entire Colts team. "The thing I like most about football is it's a meritocracy," Luck told the players. There was a long silence in the room. Then Luck spent the next several minutes explaining what a meritocracy was. "He explained it well," said Luck's backup, Matt Hasselbeck. "If you didn't know what a meritocracy was, you did then."

Luck rarely goes out partying, but when he does, he hangs at a few restaurants and bars in downtown Indianapolis, where he lives. He rarely strays far from that area. "He goes into these bars, and it's very low-key," said Hasselbeck. "When he goes to these places, he's not the Colts quarterback. He's Norm from Cheers."

"When we hang out, we hang at his house and play board games," Castonzo said.

"If I had to guess what would be one of Andrew's ideal nights out," said Hasselbeck, "it would be hanging with a small group of friends and playing Settlers of Catan." (Yes, that would be the D&D-like board game Settlers of Catan.)

Amazon describes the game this way: "The board consists of 19 terrain hexes surrounded by the ocean. Each type of terrain produces a different type of resource: brick, wool, ore, grain or lumber. There's also a desert hex that produces no resources. As the game progresses, players use resources to build roads along the edges of these hexes and settlements or cities on the intersections where three hexes meet. Each player begins the game with two settlements and two roads." Brett Favre probably never played Settlers of Catan.

Who is Andrew Luck?

We know who Luck was when he played at Stanford, but he's changed rapidly in his short time in the NFL, so the question becomes "Who is he now?" The answer is like Luck himself: complex. He isn't just a dork. He isn't just an intellectual. He's not just tough or athletic or a leader. Luck is all of these things. He is, in fact, one of the most unique talents in all of sports. It is the total package of Luck, his uniqueness and calmness, that allowed him to step into the cleats of Peyton Manning, as tough an act to follow as there ever was. Then, Luck beat Manning, prompting the original question: Just who exactly is this man?

"I'm here [at the practice facility] at 6:45 in the morning," said linebacker Jerrell Freeman. "I walk in, and his bag is already there." Freeman points to Luck's locker across the room. "No one beats him in here."

"The team will start stretching for practice at 1:40," Hasselbeck said. "The quarterbacks go out at 1:15. Andrew wants us to beat everyone else out there. It's a competitive thing."

"I played with Tom Brady," Darius Butler said. "[Luck] has the same kind of presence as Tom. He commands that kind of respect in the locker room, and this is only his second year," Butler said in 2013.

"I think my favorite Andrew Luck story is the one that hasn't been written yet," linebacker Pat Angerer said. "His future is so big. He's just beginning to show us what he's capable of."

Who is Andrew Luck?

He is the guy who bemuses his teammates. "I laugh all the time," said Butler, "because he still rocks the flip phone."

"Condoleezza Rice came to practice one day," Hasselbeck remembered. "Andrew was absolutely giddy. They talked about leadership."

"The laugh he has is something else," Christensen said. "He's so smart, and he tells these jokes that sometimes you can't tell if he's serious or not. Then you hear that laugh, and you know he's joking."

"He loves northern Indian food," said Hasselbeck, "not southern Indian food. There's a difference."

"Andrew is a soccer nut," Castonzo said.

"Books and soccer," Christensen said. "Two of his favorite things."

"When we play on the road, I'll go to dinner with him," Hasselbeck said, "and we'll get a car service and sometimes the driver will be a huge soccer fan. The conversation will invariably go to soccer. So you'll have this kid from Stanford and a guy from Egypt talking soccer. I don't know how he knows all the rosters."

One of the common themes in speaking to Colts personnel about Luck is the quarterback's physical and mental toughness. It is discussed constantly. Everyone mentions it. "Training camp this summer, we were getting a little sluggish in practice, so Reggie [Wayne] asked the coaches to leave the room, and Reggie spoke to the team," running back Donald Brown said.

"Reggie talked, and then Andrew stood up. You could hear a pin drop. He got the attention of the entire team. I saw it as almost his coming-of-age moment."

"His first year, we're playing Green Bay," Christensen said. "On a key third down, he shrugs off Clay Matthews, who came in on a blitz, and hit Reggie Wayne." It was a third-and-12 at the Packers 47, and the play went for 15 yards. That drive turned out to be the game-winner.

"I don't know how much [Luck] can bench press, but...it happened," Matthews said at the time, via ESPN Wisconsin. "It seems to be a theme amongst pass rushers with him. I guess I have to get back in the gym, work out a little harder. [He's a] big kid, elusive, slippery."

"We were playing Oakland" in 2013, Christensen said. "One of the linebackers came in on a twist and stuck Andrew right in the chest. He shook it off, kept going. The part a lot of people don't truly understand is that he's so physically strong." When Luck gets hit hard, he often tells the hitter, "nice job." Or he'll pat them on the helmet. This is also who Luck is. He is, in many ways, unflappable.

————

WHO IS ANDREW LUCK?

As it turns out, Andrew Luck is terrible talking about Andrew Luck. He is always respectful, but there is a force field that prevents the media from getting too close. There are moments, however, when Luck lowers his shields. One came during a Pro Bowl press conference in 2015. Luck was asked how tough it was to lose to the Patriots in the AFC Championship

Game. He said it was deflating; then, realizing the joke, he chuckled.

Another of those genuine Luck moments came when I interviewed him, and we were walking down a long, carpeted hallway at the team's practice facility. He was wearing a dark T-shirt, white hat, black sweatpants, and no shoes or socks. Luck was asked about his work ethic, which is documented and renowned. His explanation is typical Luck; it's brilliant:

"When I grew up, my father taught us the value of hard work. He wanted us to enjoy ourselves, but he also wanted to know what it took to be successful. He coached a lot of our sports teams growing up. We weren't very good, but we learned about hard work and enjoying life and your teammates.

"I took these lessons to high school, college and then here [the NFL]. I love this team and what we're doing, but I also realize we haven't done anything yet. You have to prove yourself every weekend.

"Biggest lesson I learned my first year in the NFL is no one gives a crap about what you did last week. This league is about 'what have you done for me now?' That's the NFL. It's also our culture. So you keep working hard because that's the biggest truth about football."

And with that, Luck said good-bye, then walked away, bare feet and all.

That, and many other things, many great things, finally answer the question. We know who Luck is. Like Wilson, he's the future.

7   THE MONSTER

ON A NOVEMBER NIGHT IN 2012 IN TEMPE, ARIZONA, AT APPROXI-
mately 2:00 in the morning, a woman awoke groggy and disoriented on a gray sectional couch in a modest apartment. Her night—the night she claimed she was drugged and sexually assaulted—actually began much earlier.

She lived in downtown Tempe, her apartment located near the red-bricked sidewalks, perfectly cut grass, and neatly aligned recycling bins. The Arizona State University football stadium and sloping hills could be seen in the distance. It seemed like the last place where something awful could happen. In full view of her building was the City of Tempe Police and Courts. Buses and trolleys maneuvered through the nearby transportation center. Dozens of people strolled on the street below, some going in the Mad Hatter Brew Pub to get two brats with fries for $0. In her apartment, she and friends mixed some Ketel One Vodka with flavored water. They chased it with pineapple juice. Just a little drink. Just something to get the night started.

Their first stop, the woman says, was a club in Scottsdale called the Mint. They arrived at 11:30 PM. A gaudy chandelier that looks like a jellyfish hung over the dance floor. The champagne room had couches and footstools. The coed bathroom resembled a Vegas hotel suite, an actual champagne bar not far from the stalls. A large LED cube dominated the club.

The group grew to about eight strong, she says, and after 15 minutes moved several blocks west to the far less pretentious American Junkie. Once at that bar, everyone initially sat outside on the patio, under the skinny tree draped with lights, before moving to a table inside. It was loud and crowded. The women servers were scantily clad, the menu reasonable. The drinks flowed. There was music and food, comfort and trust. No one felt they were in danger.

One of the woman's friends had ordered a Cîroc and water. She didn't finish it. Nonetheless, when the group arrived back at the apartment later, the friend began to throw up. She told police that she believed her drink had been spiked, and that the drugging caused her to black out, leading to her sexual assault.

Then came one last drink, at approximately 2:15 in the morning. The woman would later tell police the last thing she remembered was a man handing her that drink. That man was Darren Sharper.

———

THE SHARPER ALLEGATIONS CARRIED WITH THEM THE SAME REVERberations that the Rice and Peterson cases had. Obviously, comparing one horror to another—domestic violence and child abuse to rape—isn't a worthwhile discussion. All victims deserve justice and sympathy. But the Sharper allegations would cause the NFL to look at itself in a much harsher light. Around

the sport, former coaches, teammates, and front-office executives who were around Sharper began to wonder, *What did we
miss? Could we have stopped this? Are we even, in some ways,
at fault?*

Sharper would become the football analog to Bill Cosby.
Cosby had been accused of drugging and raping numerous
women going back decades. Sharper faced similar accusations.
Both men would cause two highly visible sectors of the entertainment industry to pose a series of uncomfortable questions.
Did Cosby's nice-guy persona blind people to the monster he
might be? Did the male penchant to question the authenticity
of rape victims—despite overwhelming proof that rape victims
rarely lie—allow Cosby to allegedly become such a rapacious
predator while being one of the most high-profile celebrities
ever?

And was the same thing true of Sharper? Many of us who
have covered the NFL extensively over the last two decades
came to know Sharper well. I met him dozens of times. I met
women who dated him. I met his close player friends. Sharper,
a multiple Pro Bowler, was a charmer, to be sure, yet there was
an element of phoniness to him. He'd compliment you on the
clothes you wore or your shoes, tell you a story you wrote was
terrific even though you'd suspect he hadn't actually read it.
Still, I liked him. He charmed me. He charmed a lot of journalists. I thought he was at times full of it, but I liked him. Yes,
I was fooled, but I wasn't alone. All the men who ever interviewed Sharper liked him.

No man around him, in any way, spoke of him in any manner
that would suggest he was a serial rapist. Were we in the media
ignoring obvious signals because of Sharper's charm? Or were

we violating one of the edicts of sports journalism: you never truly know the men you cover. Never believe that you do.

This would become horribly evident with Sharper when allegations surfaced. The Tempe woman's experience was just one part of a frightening odyssey that expanded over years and intersected the lives of at least eight women in five states. Each of them accused Sharper of sexual assault. A ninth woman accused him of sexual battery.

Not long after the story broke, I spent several months examining the Sharper case—interviewing law enforcement officials, examining court documents, speaking to former teammates and coworkers, as well as retracing the path of both Sharper and his alleged victims.

Sharper's story isn't solely about the dramatic downfall of a man who may have inflicted great pain using drugs and deceit. It's about one of professional football's favorite sons, considered a charitable man by almost all who knew him professionally and personally, being accused of secretly being a predator and chameleon. The totality of the accusations stunned the NFL, leading many to wonder if one of the league's most visible personalities—a member of the NFL's 2000s All-Decade team and analyst on the NFL's flagship NFL Network—was leading a double life during a career that spanned 13 years, three teams, and two Super Bowls.

The Sharper case is part crime mystery, but the case is also about hubris and arrogance and the possible belief that Sharper's looks and wealth could immunize him against anything, even the crime of date rape. After a charity softball game in 2013, Sharper took a picture with New Orleans Saints quarterback Drew Brees and receiver Lance Moore. Brees put his arm around Sharper and smiled. The picture was then posted to Brees' Facebook page. That was his life not so long ago. Today, Sharper is in jail, a pariah to former teammates and an entire league.

The morning after that November night in Tempe, the woman awoke around 8:35 AM. She remembered nothing after being handed a shot by Sharper, she told police. She was confused and scared and immediately departed, driving to her parents' nearby home. She went into the bathroom and felt pain and discomfort in her vaginal area. She was certain she had been raped and she told police she was equally certain that Sharper did it.

In one of the more stunning moments in a number of them, around noon that day, the woman drove back to the apartment to confront Sharper, she told police.

"What happened?" she asked him.

"You tell me," he responded.

Sharper, she says, was acting like he was the one drugged. What was I drinking?, he asked. Did I throw up? Sharper told the woman he couldn't remember anything from the night before. The woman didn't believe him. To her, Sharper was acting like he was the victim.

"I'm going to the doctor now," the woman told Sharper. "You know what's coming." She left the apartment, got into her car, and began the five-minute trip to Tempe St. Luke's Hospital. A light rain fell. The sky had darkened. She walked through the sliding front doors of the emergency room where a sign posted on them read: No Weapons. No Cell Phones. The two dozen chairs were mostly unoccupied. The television in the room was on and loud. She told hospital officials she believed she had been drugged and raped. Eventually, an emergency room nurse, Renee Little, phoned police.

In the end, three women told police they were drugged by Sharper that night in Tempe. One of them believed that Sharper had drugged her at one of the clubs. Two of them said he raped them while they were unconscious. In one instance, one woman said she saw her friend lying on the couch, appearing to be sleeping. Sharper was on top of her, with no pants on, moving in a thrusting motion. She feared Sharper would be violent, so she didn't say anything at that moment.

Another woman said she woke up naked from the waist down, with no recollection of how her clothes were removed. The third woman, also claiming to be drugged by Sharper, believes she escaped being assaulted because before she went to sleep, she locked her bedroom door.

———

POLICE ACCUSED SHARPER OF DRUGGING AND SEXUALLY ASSAULT-ing at least eight women in Los Angeles, New Orleans, Las Vegas, and Tempe. A ninth woman accused him of sexual battery in Florida.

Los Angeles prosecutors say Sharper had the same M.O. He'd meet the women, often in a bar or nightclub, then take them to his home or hotel room. He'd offer them a drink and they would black out, waking up with no memory of their night but feeling like they had been sexually assaulted. What we now know is that while Sharper purposely crafted an image as a humanitarian, philanthropist, teacher of children, actor, television analyst—even fighter for women's rights—he was also, according to police reports, secretly, methodically, and cruelly drugging and raping numerous women.

In March 2015, Sharper was convicted on nine counts of rape and sentenced to nine years in prison. It wasn't just that Sharper lived a double life, it was that he potentially created a public persona to hide devious criminal activity. Sharper was the smiling every-dude, the antipredator. Some women friends of Sharper's even set him up on blind dates with their female acquaintances. Sharper went on these dates as police were investigating him for sexual assault.

Few details about Sharper's accusers have been made available by law enforcement. Police have been extremely tight-lipped, but one law enforcement source told me the biggest strength of the cases against Sharper is the large number of women accusers and the similarity of their stories. (This is also why the Cosby case captured the attention of the country.) Many of the women complainants against Sharper, a review of court documents show, aren't just similar in their allegations, but also similar in appearance: many are white, with long hair, in their early twenties or younger, thin, and approximately 5'6". Law enforcement officials privately believe there could be more victims out there who have declined to come forward, possibly many more.

———

TWO YEARS EARLIER AND 2,300 MILES FROM TEMPE, TWO WOMEN embarked on an annual rite of passage: they went to Florida for spring break. They met Sharper, and eventually he invited them to his $4 million, 3,000-square-foot condo in Miami Beach. The condo had a close view of the Atlantic Ocean—so close you could see the beach chairs, umbrellas, and people sitting along the sand with great clarity. Inside, it was a typical bachelor pad.

A gray, four-piece sectional couch with dark blue pillows sat in the middle of the room. A large, circular kitchen stood to left. Nearby was a pool table. The bedroom had a queen-size bed with a fish tank just an arm's length away. That room also had a sofa and two ample chairs, all sitting atop a brown carpet.

The condo was stunning, a part of Sharper's allure. Also there that day was Sharper's brother Jamie—a former member of the Super Bowl–champion Baltimore Ravens—and several other men. The woman drank with them, sitting at a circular table near the kitchen, and later, the casual atmosphere would transform into something darker. One of the women awoke at 6:00 in the morning to a man standing before her, exposing his penis and moving it closer to her face. She told him to stop. After falling back asleep, the woman awoke again. This time, a man was attempting to lift her dress. She would tell police that, startled, she woke her friend. Both would discover that their underwear was missing.

A doctor stated that an examination of the accusers revealed no evidence of sexual assault. However, the woman said the man exposing himself could have been Sharper or his brother. Nonetheless, Sharper's trail was hot.

———

BACK IN NEW ORLEANS, SEVERAL YEARS AGO, TWO WOMEN MET Sharper, then a New Orleans Saints player, and a friend at a bar. Sharper invited them back to his Central Business District apartment on the 700 block of Tchoupitoulas Street. Sharper was a trusted face. He was well known. He was on television. He could be seen all around the city. The women looked at his smile and experienced his charm. He was disarming. They felt safe. The two men and two women talked and drank and talked some more. Then came sleep.

The women would later tell police it was not sleep by choice. One awoke with Sharper completely nude and on top of her. He was sexually assaulting her, the woman said. The second woman, later in the morning, said she too awoke to Sharper nude, on top of her, and sexually assaulting her. Both women told investigators they did not consent to sex with Sharper and both believe they were drugged.

———

THERE ARE SO MANY WOMEN ACCUSERS WHO CAME FORWARD there is a natural question: Are there more out there? How far back does this go? Looking far into Sharper's past, there are no other known accusations or past investigations. A spokesperson for William & Mary, where Sharper played college football, said there were no police investigations involving Sharper when he was a student there. A spokesperson for the Green Bay Police Department—the Packers were Sharper's first NFL job in 1997—said there were no investigations into Sharper there either. Yet the evidence thus far shows that Sharper recruited alleged victims in proximity to where he lived and worked.

Former FBI profiler Dr. Mary Ellen O'Toole, who still consults for the agency, has examined hundreds of rape cases, and also worked on the Unabomber and Zodiac Killer cases, says that if the Sharper allegations are true, his case would be highly unusual. O'Toole explained that she has rarely seen "a date-rape case involving a celebrity that has both this many accusers and crosses multiple jurisdictions." O'Toole said getting one woman to come forward in high-profile rape cases is extremely difficult. The fact so many women have in this situation could be significant in itself.

Sharper was able to parlay his good looks and football prowess on the field into a broadcast career that started in New Orleans and ended at the NFL Network. Now, in the NFL and elsewhere, he is a pariah. Close friends across the sport contacted about Sharper have distanced themselves; none wants anything to do with him. The people who scouted him, drafted him, coached him, played alongside him, bled with him...they have all run away from him. "Mentioning his name here now," said an NFL Network employee to me, "is like mentioning Hitler. He's been wiped from existence here."

———

HOW WAS SHARPER, A HIGH-PROFILE PERSON, ABLE TO STEALTHILY assault women without anyone in football knowing? Or anyone knowing period? And to do so for years on end?

The images of Sharper throughout his career have been of positivity. Sharper at a charity event. Sharper smiling. Sharper being interviewed. Sharper charming fans. After the Saints won Super Bowl XLIV, of Sharper repeatedly kissing the Lombardi Trophy. There was no hint of an ugly side. "I feel like New Orleans is a second home to me," Sharper told a half dozen reporters prior to a charity basketball game in May 2013. "I enjoyed my time here. I feel like I have a great connection with the city, and that's why I come back to do these events...I still try to keep my face in the community."

Sharper was a well-known face who could be seen across the city in various restaurants and bars, everywhere from the wealthiest quarters to the not-so-wealthy. He'd sit with a big group of teammates or simply a friend or two. When approached by fans, as often happened at a popular steakhouse in town, Sharper would always be friendly and sign any autograph requests. What people remember most about Sharper is that he seemed to be constantly flanked by attractive women.

He was always impeccably dressed when in public. At an event for Louisville Slugger, while others were dressed more casually, Sharper wore a tan suit, buttoned to the top, with a red tie and a perfect haircut. Standing on the red carpet for a charity event benefitting the James Graham Brown Cancer Center, he wore a perfectly tailored black suit with a white shirt and silver tie.

Sharper dated actress Gabrielle Union, who has appeared in dozens of film and television shows. After that, he dated several models. When the NFL-sanctioned Super Bowl Gospel Celebration was held in New Orleans several days before the big game, it was noted that a portion of the proceeds of the event would go to Sharper's charity.

In December 2010, not long before police say he committed his initial series of rapes, Sharper and one of his closest friends on the Saints, Roman Harper, in conjunction with the United Way, paid for two homes to be rebuilt that had been damaged by Hurricane Katrina. Harper declined repeated requests for comment. He's never spoken publicly about his once-close friendship with Sharper. In one of his more ironic moments, Sharper, along with then-Saints running back Reggie Bush, once gave a football seminar to women Saints fans. More than 300 attended.

Some of the area's top politicians and even high-profile law enforcement officers attended Sharper's charity events. At one, many of the proceeds of which went to the American Cancer Society, Jefferson Parish sheriff Newell Normand took a swim several times in a dunk tank. That event, held in 2011, was called Home Runs for Kids. Indeed, Sharper was close to many law enforcement officials in New Orleans. Interestingly, when Sharper was indicted in 2014, just three years after Home Runs for Kids, one of the others indicted along with Sharper was Brandon Licciardi, who was a sheriff's deputy from St. Bernard Parish. (As of press time, Licciardi had pled not guilty to the charges.)

Sharper and Harper would combine again to make their mark in the New Orleans community. They threw a series of football camps for kids ages 6 to 18, and Sharper was once photographed instructing an enthusiastic and smiling 10-year-old boy. The picture was the kind of thing that cemented Sharper as a good citizen in the minds of fans and others. While some teammates photographed with Sharper sometimes looked uncomfortable in the spotlight, Sharper never did. He basked in it.

At one of the camps, Sharper was speaking with a group of parents, who thanked him repeatedly for having the camp. One parent asked if he would ever go into politics. Sharper flashed his smile. "My main thing," Sharper said, "is to make things better for the kids."

After Sharper left football, he rose quickly through the ranks of the ex-player media. He was known around the NFL Network as gregarious and friendly, according to high-ranking personnel who work there. He'd chat with people in the hallways between shows or go out to dinner or a bar with coworkers. He was always smiling and charming, they said. "When a bunch of us heard about this," said one NFL Network official, "we all looked at each other and said, 'What the fuck is this?' We were stunned. We had no clue."

The Sharper case also showed the limits of even the NFL's pervasive security and psychological testing procedures, famous for catching almost every human vice, or predicting them. "They can find out if a player drinks too much or uses drugs," said a former team executive, "but if someone has a dark demon, you can't test for that."

———

IN 2010, SHARPER WAS ONE OF THE STARS WHO CONTRIBUTED to a book called *NFL Dads Dedicated to Daughters: Inspiring Personal Accounts of Fatherhood from the Men of the NFL.* It was a book that promoted women's safety.

Sharper wrote in part: "Money cannot buy the women we love everyday security, which men take for granted. So, it's going to take strong, accountable men to educate young boys and influence other men to deal with women respectfully, honorably and fairly at all times." About his daughter, Sharper added: "As my first born, she is definitely special, and I am thankful for the positive influence she has had on me. Sacrificing for her instilled selflessness in me that I know I wouldn't have gotten any other way. Playing football can be glamorous at times, but being a father keeps me humble…My daughter makes [me] mindful of how women are treated, undervalued and exploited, which is why I felt compelled to take advantage of this opportunity to speak up about domestic violence."

There was more. Sharper once sent out a tweet promoting a women's football camp in Slidell, Louisiana. The same day of that tweet, police documents show a woman met Sharper at a bar near the event. Sharper handed her a drink. The next thing she remembered, the woman told police, was Sharper on top of her, sexually assaulting her. It was approximately 10:00 the following morning. She went to the hospital and received a sexual assault examination. The Louisiana State Police crime lab said DNA taken from the woman matched the DNA of Sharper, court documents say.

Just four years after publication of the book, and a month after he was accused of raping yet another victim, Sharper was in West Hollywood on October 30, 2013, where he met two women at a nightclub called Bootsy Bellows. The club is located among a cluster of restaurants and boutiques and high-end car dealerships just outside Beverly Hills. The BOA steakhouse is across the bustling intersection. Nearby is Rivabella Ristorante, sometimes staked out by the paparazzi.

The entrance to the club is almost inconspicuous. Black doors blend into the side of the building. The velvet rope and line of people waiting to get in are the only exterior signs of its existence. Katy Perry hangs there. So has Kobe Bryant, and many other celebrities besides. It's a magnet for them.

Directly outside the club, one pair of long legs after another pile out of pricey sedans and other vehicles. The women are all young. Inside, there are women everywhere. There's dancing everywhere, there are glow sticks, more dancing, more women, lots of alcohol, booming music, a DJ booth that looks like the control panel on the Mars rover, more women, and more drinking. It is chaotic, appealing, and overdone all at the same time.

Sharper was apparently a regular at the club and would sometimes go after his duties at the NFL Network. (Its L.A. studio is about a 20-minute drive away.) In January 2013 the club was about to close when the two women were approached by Sharper to go to an afterparty. The women said yes. "I need to stop at my hotel to pick up something," Sharper told them.

Sharper did yet again what he had accomplished so many times before: he was able to charm the women back to his apartment or hotel room. Then, according to court documents, as he had done so many times before, Sharper offered the two women a drink. "It's coffee Patron," he told them, a mixture of coffee and Patron silver tequila. And, as had also happened so many times before, the women told police that after consuming the drink Sharper provided, they soon passed out.

One woman told police that upon waking at 8:30 AM, she found Sharper on top of her, sexually assaulting her, in one of the hotel bedrooms. The second woman, waking up on the couch, stumbled into the bedroom and interrupted the assault.

Several months earlier, on October 30, this entire scene had almost duplicated itself. The same club. Two women. Back to a hotel room. They were given drinks by Sharper, police say. They passed out. In this instance, also at 8:30 AM, both women awoke on a pullout couch, feeling as if they had been sexually assaulted. They also suffered intermittent memory loss in the hours previous, they told police.

The women from the October 30 assault left Sharper's hotel confused, scared, and angry. They proceeded to receive medical treatment and an examination for sexual assault. Sharper, meanwhile, went off to promote a breast cancer awareness event.

His tweet on October 31 is chilling: "Get your tix! You will be touched in many ways."

———

AFTER THE ALLEGED 2011 INCIDENT IN MIAMI BEACH, SHARPER went back to being the public Sharper—the non-suspect. In none of his television appearances on the NFL Network did he ever show a hint of stress or duplicity. No one ever looked at Sharper and thought, *rapist*.

Former FBI specialist O'Toole said serial rapists are often not easily discovered. They can be predators who hide their true natures until they are isolated with their victims. (Since O'Toole had not examined Sharper, she was speaking of rapists in general terms, not Sharper specifically.)

Stealth is part of the date rapist's toolkit, explained O'Toole. She said it's extremely common that the people around the rapist—even family, friends, and coworkers—have no clue about the rapist's acts.

O'Toole also addressed several critical aspects of the case. The first was the suspicion by some NFL players that the violence of the NFL may have caused Sharper to turn malevolent. Some scientists who study the brain believe CTE—or chronic traumatic encephalopathy—can cause a player to become violent off the field when he otherwise would not be. O'Toole discounted that theory, explaining that the type of violence "associated with traumatic brain injury is more impulsive violence. A date rape is more predatory violence."

In other words, a date rape is meticulously planned. She also explained the one question that is asked repeatedly by everyone interviewed for this story: Why would a man of Sharper's looks, wealth, and power need to allegedly rape? O'Toole said there have been numerous rape defendants who were handsome with good jobs. "Most people who commit violent crimes don't look like criminals," she said. "This isn't Hollywood. [There are] few scary-looking offenders." She added, "Rape is not about sex. Rape is about power, control, and dominance. It can be about being sadistic, being aroused by the victim's pain. Sex is just the conduit."

———

LAS VEGAS. IN 2013. ANOTHER NIGHTCLUB. ANOTHER GROUP OF women. Another invite from Sharper to hang out in his hotel room. More women who felt safe in Sharper's presence, who didn't see any danger.

In this instance, Sharper invited two young women and a young man to an afterparty at his room. Police say when the three arrived in Sharper's room, they were surprised to see that no one else was present. Sharper offered the three drinks. Afterward, each of them told police that they blacked out after consuming them.

One of the women told police she woke up in bed next to Sharper. She got up to go to the bathroom and upon seeing her face in the mirror noticed visible injuries. She couldn't remember how they got there. She went back to sleep. When she woke a second time, Sharper asked how she was feeling. "You got sick the night before," he told the woman. "This will help you feel better." It was another drink. The woman says after consuming it she again passed out, and upon waking up a second time, found Sharper sexually assaulting her.

The other woman woke up on a couch in the sitting room of the hotel suite, feeling physically as if she had been sexually assaulted.

The man accompanying the women had also blacked out. He told police after consuming the drink, his next memory was of him sitting at the hotel bar downstairs. He had no memory of how he got there.

———

WHEN I WAS WORKING ON THE SHARPER STORY, I HEARD FROM one law enforcement source familiar with the investigation that Sharper had allegedly introduced the concept of drugging women to rape them to other NFL players, and that those players were doing the same thing. I could never corroborate that. Then came a bombshell in December 2014.

At a pretrial hearing, FBI special agent Robert Blythe testified that one of Sharper's codefendants, Brandon Licciardi, told federal agents that at a Las Vegas convention attended by NFL players, that one player told Licciardi he had spiked drinks with drugs. The agent declined to state any names for fear of getting them wrong. But he testified there were several players. The agent also testified that Licciardi called the drinks "horny juice."

Names emerged in the media in 2015 of NFL players who were alleged to have participated with Sharper in drugging women's drinks. I won't name the popular player (for legal reasons), but I do not believe, and never have, that Sharper was the lone NFL player participating in this vile practice. At the very least, and this was buoyed by law enforcement sources, my belief was that Sharper bragged about the practice to friends and teammates.

The Sharper case goes beyond the fact he may be a lone

sociopath. There are actually things that pertain today's football environment and lessons that need to be learned. If other players not only knew what Sharper was doing but also engaged in similar conduct, something I believe to be true, then Sharper was not acting without the knowledge of others in the sport. *And no one said a word.*

In speaking to dozens of players, many of them feel there was a much simpler thing at work: hubris. As one player told me, the same mental and physical powers that enable players to excel at the highest level in the most violent sport in the country may have enabled Sharper to believe he could get away with such ugly criminal behavior. "I think players believe they're invulnerable," said another player.

There are many things we don't know about Darren Sharper, but there are many things we do. Sharper developed into one of the best defensive backs of his generation. He has the seventh-most interceptions of all time with 63, just a handful fewer than legends "Night Train" Lane and Rod Woodson and ahead of greats Ronnie Lott and Mel Blount. We do know that he was well-liked and respected by his peers in the football and broadcasting worlds, that he was a leader in the football locker room and a public spokesman for women's rights.

Sharper pleaded no contest to six criminal counts ranging from drugging and rape to sexual assault and attempted sexual assault. This is the dilemma the league faces. Any negative action by a player becomes more proof that NFL players—all of them—are troubled. This isn't true of course. Far from it. But this is where we are, and this is why the problem is such a threat to the league's dominance and will be for some time.

8 ENDING THE VIOLENCE

MEMORANDUM

To: Chief Executives Club Presidents

From: Commissioner Goodell

Date: September 10, 2014

Re: Investigation of Ray Rice Incident

As you know, there has been a good deal of specu-lation about the investigatory process that preceded the decision to suspend Ray Rice for his involvement in an incident of domestic violence last February. I want to use this opportunity to address this matter and provide a full understanding of the process that was followed.

First, we did not see video of what took place in-side the elevator until it was publicly released on Monday. When the new video evidence became available, we acted promptly and imposed an indefi-nite suspension on Mr. Rice.

Second, on multiple occasions, we asked the proper law enforcement authorities to share with us all relevant information, including any video of the incident. Those requests were made to different law enforcement entities, including the New Jersey State Police, the Atlantic City Police Department, the Atlantic County Police Department and the Atlantic County Solicitor's Office. The requests were first made in February following the incident, and were again made following Mr. Rice's entry into the pretrial diversion program. None of the law enforcement entities we approached was permitted to provide any video or other investigatory material to us. As is customary in disciplinary cases, the suspension imposed on Mr. Rice in July was based on the information available to us at that time.

Our understanding of New Jersey law is that casino security is regulated by the Division of Gaming Enforcement in the State Attorney General's office. Once a criminal investigation begins, law enforcement authorities do not share investigatory material (such as the videos here) with private parties such as the NFL. In addition, the state's Open Public Records Act excludes material that is generated in the context of an active law enforcement proceeding. The law enforcement agencies did nothing wrong here; they simply followed their customary procedures. As the New Jersey Attorney General's office said yesterday, "It would have been illegal for law enforcement to provide [the] Rice video to [the] NFL."

We did not ask the Atlantic City casino directly for the video. Again, our understanding of New Jersey law is that the casino is prohibited from turning over material to a third party during a law enforcement proceeding, and that doing so would have subjected individuals to prosecution for interference with a criminal investigation. Moreover, our longstanding policy in matters like this—where there is a criminal investigation being directed by law enforcement and prosecutors—is to cooperate with law enforcement and take no action to interfere with the criminal justice system. In addition, in the context of an ongoing criminal investigation, information obtained outside of law enforcement that has not been tested by prosecutors or by the court system is not necessarily a reliable basis for imposing league discipline.

Finally, it is our understanding that the criminal proceedings involving Mr. Rice are considered an open matter, and that so long as he is in the pretrial diversion program, no information will be made available to third parties or the public.

As always, we will continuously examine our procedures. I believe that we took a significant step forward with the enhanced policies on domestic violence and sexual assault that were announced last month. I also know that we will be judged on our actions going forward. I am confident that those actions will demonstrate our commitment to address this issue seriously and effectively, and will reflect well on the NFL, all member clubs, and everyone who is a part of our league.

The letter was Goodell's attempt to explain how the NFL mishandled the Rice case. But was Goodell misleading the owners? Did the NFL really make every effort to get the second Rice tape? I find it difficult to believe Goodell lied to his bosses. My contention in the Rice case all along has been that Goodell was swayed by the Ravens organization—especially the owner and general manager, who adored Rice—to be lenient on the player. Goodell obliged them. Then the second tape emerged and Goodell was caught in an impossible position. He had to reverse course and issue a more stringent punishment.

It wasn't the first time the NFL, with Goodell as its leader, made a mistake when it came to players and domestic violence. Far from it. There is a statistic that perhaps, as much as anything, shows why the image of the NFL has been atomized. It's one of the most damning things during his regime. The statistic was composed by the site Sidespin.com under the banner "Roger Goodell Is a Domestic Violence Enabler Who Must Be Stopped." While the headline was extreme, the reporting was grounded but staggering. From 2006, when Goodell first became commissioner, to the publication of the story in September 2014, there were 56 reported instances of NFL players committing domestic violence. However, in those instances, those 56 players were suspended a total of only 13 games by the NFL. Though no act of domestic violence should ever be minimized, the crimes these players were accused of and, in most instances, convicted of, were not minor acts. The fact that there was such little punishment—and only 10 players were kicked off their respective teams and of those 10, three were later signed by other teams—speaks to the attitude of the NFL toward the problem of domestic violence—until the Rice case.

"And the only reason the NFL cared about the Rice case," Gretchen Shaw, the director of strategic partnerships and projects for National Coalition Against Domestic Violence, said to me in 2014, "is due to the fact it was caught on videotape. I don't know how much the NFL would have cared had there not been so much public outrage due to that videotape."

The site assembled the arrests during Goodell's tenure. They are damning, to say the least.

2006

SAM BRANDON - S - DENVER BRONCOS
Violated the conditions of a restraining order (that came about as a result of previous domestic violence arrests).
Legal punishment: None.
NFL punishment: Suspended two games.

MARKUS CURRY - CB - SAN DIEGO CHARGERS
Allegedly attacked the mother of his child. He was previously arrested for domestic violence while in college.
Legal punishment: Charges dropped after witnesses failed to cooperate.
NFL punishment: Immediately released from the team.

ROBERT REYNOLDS - LB - TENNESSEE TITANS
Shoved his wife, smashed her cell phone, punched a hole in a wall.
Legal punishment: Pleaded guilty; $3,000 fine.
NFL punishment: Suspended one game by Titans head coach Jeff Fisher.

DONTE WHITNER - S - BUFFALO BILLS
Accused of harassment in a domestic dispute with his girlfriend.

Legal punishment: Charges dropped.
NFL punishment: None.

2007

BRANDON MARSHALL - WR - DENVER BRONCOS
Charged with false imprisonment in dispute with girlfriend, accused of hitting her car window and blocking her taxi. She later said that Marshall attacked her the day before as well, but that she did not report the attack to the police.
Legal punishment: Charges were dismissed after Marshall completed anger management counseling.
NFL punishment: None.

LIONEL GATES - RB - TAMPA BAY BUCCANEERS
Assaulted a pregnant woman. From ESPN.com at the time: "Gates kicked in the front door of Peggie Lavender's apartment Thursday night, destroyed two televisions and two doors, put a hole in the bedroom wall and assaulted her, a Hillsborough County Sheriff's Office report said. He was arrested later at his apartment in the same complex."
Legal punishment: Diversion program, anger management, $3,200 in restitution.
NFL punishment: None.

A.J. NICHOLSON - LB - CINCINNATI BENGALS
Accused of punching a woman in the face (she later recanted her statement, though police observed bruising around her eye).
Legal punishment: Diversion program; charges dropped after 40 hours of community service.
NFL punishment: Released by Bengals three days after arrest.

CLAUDE WROTEN - DT - ST. LOUIS RAMS
Accused of damaging property on LSU campus in argument with girlfriend, kicking down her door.
Legal punishment: None.
NFL punishment: None.

NAJEH DAVENPORT - RB - PITTSBURGH STEELERS
Accused of slapping and punching the mother of his child, endangering a child.
Legal punishment: Acquitted.
NFL punishment: None.

CLAUDE TERRELL - OG - ST. LOUIS RAMS
Charged with assaulting his wife.
Legal punishment: Pleaded guilty; sentenced to 30 days in jail, deferred adjudication, $1,000 fine.
NFL punishment: Cut by the Rams shortly after charges were filed. Terrell would later be charged with rape, aggravated kidnapping, and aggravated sexual assault.

2008

DANIEL GRAHAM - TE - DENVER BRONCOS
Accused of harassing his ex-girlfriend.
Legal punishment: Charges dropped.
NFL punishment: None.

JEROME MATHIS - WR - DENVER BRONCOS
Accused of choking his pregnant girlfriend.
Legal punishment: Charges dropped.
NFL punishment: None.

FABIAN WASHINGTON - CB - OAKLAND RAIDERS
Accused of domestic battery of girlfriend.
Legal punishment: Diversion program for first-time offenders.
NFL punishment: Suspended one game.

LARRY JOHNSON - RB - KANSAS CITY CHIEFS
Accused of shoving a woman in a nightclub. Later accused of spitting on a different woman in a nightclub.
Legal punishment: Pleaded guilty to disturbing the peace for this and the later spitting incident; given two years of probation, counseling.
NFL punishment: Suspended one game. Would go on to demonstrate a long pattern of violence against women.

BRANDON MARSHALL - WR - DENVER BRONCOS
Numerous allegations of domestic violence against his girlfriend from February and March 2008.
Legal punishment: Acquitted.
NFL punishment: Suspended one game.

JAMES HARRISON - LB - PITTSBURGH STEELERS
Accused of hitting his girlfriend during argument about whether to baptize his son, simple assault, mischief.
Legal punishment: Charges dropped; underwent anger counseling.
NFL punishment: None.

CEDRICK WILSON - WR - PITTSBURGH STEELERS
Charged with punching his estranged girlfriend in the face at a suburban restaurant.
Legal punishment: Charges dropped; underwent anger counseling.
NFL punishment: The Steelers released Wilson the day after the incident.

ROCKY BERNARD - DT - SEATTLE SEAHAWKS
Accused of punching a woman in the face at a nightclub.
Legal punishment: Diversion program, agreed to have no contact with woman for two years, domestic violence treatment.
NFL punishment: Suspended one game.

KALVIN PEARSON - S - DETROIT LIONS
Accused of aggravated battery of pregnant woman, domestic battery by strangulation, obstructing officer in southwest Florida.
Legal punishment: Domestic charges dropped.
NFL punishment: None.

DARRION SCOTT - DE - FREE AGENT
Accused of putting dry-cleaning bag over two-year-old son's head.
Legal punishment: Pleaded guilty to child endangerment.
NFL punishment: None; he later signed with Washington.

MICHAEL BOLEY - LB - ATLANTA FALCONS
Arrested after physical altercation with his wife.
Legal punishment: Charges dropped.
NFL punishment: Suspended one game.

WILLIE ANDREWS - CB - NEW ENGLAND PATRIOTS
Allegedly pointed a gun at his girlfriend's head during a physical altercation.
Legal punishment: Charges dropped.
NFL punishment: Released by the Patriots later that day.

2009

BRANDON MARSHALL - WR - DENVER BRONCOS
Accused of disorderly conduct in confrontation with fiancée. An off-duty officer saw Marshall and Michi Nogami-Campbell kicking

and punching one another on the sidewalk outside a building
Marshall owned.
Legal punishment: Charges dropped.
NFL punishment: None.

CORNELL GREEN - OT - OAKLAND RAIDERS
Police say Green slammed the mother of his children into a wall
and hit her arm with a mop handle.
Legal punishment: Undetermined.
NFL punishment: None.

QUINN OJINNAKA - OT - ATLANTA FALCONS
Accused of throwing his wife down a staircase and out of the
house after an argument over Facebook.
Legal punishment: Undetermined.
NFL punishment: Suspended one game.

SHAWNE MERRIMAN - LB - SAN DIEGO CHARGERS
Accused of choking and restraining girlfriend Tila Tequila.
Legal punishment: Charges dropped.
NFL punishment: None.

RICHARD QUINN - TE - DENVER BRONCOS
Accused of grabbing and shaking his girlfriend.
Legal punishment: Charges dropped.
NFL punishment: None.

WILL BILLINGSLEY - CB - MIAMI DOLPHINS
Charged with assaulting his girlfriend.
Legal punishment: Undetermined.
NFL punishment: None.

TERRELL SUGGS - LB - BALTIMORE RAVENS
Allegedly knocked down his fiancée, climbed on top of her, and
spilled bleach on her and their one-year-old son.
Legal punishment: None.
NFL punishment: None.

2010

JERMAINE PHILLIPS - S - TAMPA BAY BUCCANEERS
Charged with trying to choke his wife during an argument.
Legal punishment: Diversion program.
NFL punishment: None.

TONY MCDANIEL – DT – MIAMI DOLPHINS
Accused of shoving his girlfriend, whose head then hit the pavement.
Legal punishment. Pleaded no contest to amended charge of
disorderly conduct; six months probation, counseling.
NFL punishment: Suspended one game.

LEROY HILL - LB - SEATTLE SEAHAWKS
Charged with assaulting his girlfriend.
Legal punishment: Diversion program, 18 months probation,
treatment program.
NFL punishment: Suspended one game.

PHILLIP MERLING - DE - MIAMI DOLPHINS
Accused of attacking his pregnant girlfriend.
Legal Punishment: Charges dropped.
NFL Punishment: None.

WILL SMITH - DE - NEW ORLEANS SAINTS
Accused of grabbing his wife by the hair during a verbal dispute
outside a nightclub.

Legal punishment: Diversion program; charges were dropped when Smith completed community service and counseling.
NFL punishment: None.

PERRISH COX - CB - DENVER BRONCOS
Accused of raping and impregnating an unconscious woman in his home.
Legal punishment: Acquitted (despite DNA evidence).
NFL punishment: None.

KEVIN ALEXANDER - LB - DENVER BRONCOS
Accused of hitting his girlfriend in the face and shoving her.
Legal punishment: Charges dropped.
NFL punishment: Released by the Broncos the day after he was arrested.

2011

BRANDON UNDERWOOD - CB - GREEN BAY PACKERS
Accused of pushing wife to the ground and ripping a necklace from her neck.
Legal punishment: Pleaded no contest to disorderly conduct; paid an undetermined fine.
NFL punishment: None.

RYAN MCBEAN - DT - DENVER BRONCOS
Accused of stalking an ex-girlfriend.
Legal punishment: Charges dropped.
NFL punishment: None.

CHRIS COOK - CB - MINNESOTA VIKINGS
Accused of domestic assault (felony strangulation) after a neighbor called 911 to report argument.

Legal punishment: Acquitted.
NFL punishment: Suspended for remainder of season by the Vikings.

ERIK WALDEN - LB - GREEN BAY PACKERS
Accused of assaulting his live-in girlfriend.
Legal punishment: Pleaded no contest; deferred sentence of 12 months.
NFL punishment: None.

2012
JARRIEL KING - OT - SEATTLE SEAHAWKS
Charged with having forcible sex with an incapacitated woman.
Legal punishment: Found not guilty.
NFL punishment: Released by the Seahawks immediately following the arrest.

DEZ BRYANT - WR - DALLAS COWBOYS
Arrested for assaulting his mother.
Legal punishment: Undetermined.
NFL punishment: None.

CHAD JOHNSON - WR - MIAMI DOLPHINS
Crime: Accused of head-butting his wife.
Legal punishment: Pleaded no contest to misdemeanor domestic violence; received probation.
NFL punishment: Immediately released by the Dolphins.

BRYAN THOMAS - LB - NEW YORK JETS
Accused of assaulting his wife.
Legal punishment: Probation, pretrial intervention program.
NFL punishment: None

JOVAN BELCHER - LB - KANSAS CITY CHIEFS
Fatally shot his girlfriend (and mother of his child) 10 times before killing himself.

TERRELL SUGGS - LB - BALTIMORE RAVENS
Accused of punching his girlfriend in the neck and dragging her alongside a moving car.
Legal punishment: Temporary restraining order granted; Suggs was also forced to surrender his guns. No criminal charges were filed.
NFL punishment: None.

2013
ROBERT SANDS - S - CINCINNATI BENGALS
Accused of assaulting his wife, who was treated at a local hospital for minor injuries.
Legal punishment: Undetermined.
NFL punishment: None.

CHRIS RAINEY - RB - PITTSBURGH STEELERS
Accused of slapping a woman in an argument over a cell phone.
Legal punishment: Charges will be dropped. From ESPN.com, "He was ordered to pay $50 for the cost of prosecution, undergo evaluation and counseling for anger management / domestic violence issues, and either donate $100 to a domestic violence shelter or perform 10 hours of community service."
NFL punishment: Rainey was released by the Steelers the next day. Rainey was previously arrested for domestic violence while in college.

LEROY HILL - LB - SEATTLE SEAHAWKS
Accused of hitting and restraining his girlfriend.

Legal punishment: Felony charges were dropped.
NFL punishment: Technically none. He was on a one-year contract at the time of the arrest and has not played in the NFL since.

AMARI SPIEVEY - S - DETROIT LIONS
Arrested for third-degree assault and risk of injury to a child after a domestic dispute with his girlfriend over child support.
Legal punishment: Undetermined.
NFL punishment: None.

WILLIAM MOORE - S - ATLANTA FALCONS
Accused of grabbing a woman during a dispute.
Legal punishment: Undetermined.
NFL punishment: None.

DARYL WASHINGTON - LB - ARIZONA CARDINALS
Allegedly grabbed his ex-girlfriend by the throat and shoved her to the ground.
Legal punishment. Undetermined.
NFL punishment: None (however, he was suspended four games in 2013 for violating the NFL's substance abuse policy).

A.J. JEFFERSON - CB - MINNESOTA VIKINGS
Arrested on probable cause of domestic assault after allegedly choking his girlfriend.
Legal punishment: Undetermined.
NFL punishment: Released by the Vikings immediately following arrest.

2014
RAY RICE - RB - BALTIMORE RAVENS
Accused of punching his wife and rendering her unconscious.

Legal punishment: Diversion program; charges will be dismissed.
NFL punishment: Suspended two games. After a subsequent video of the full incident was made available, Rice was released by the Baltimore Ravens seven months after the incident, and the NFL suspended Rice indefinitely. He was reinstated by an arbitrator.

GREG HARDY - DE - CAROLINA PANTHERS
Assaulted and threatened his girlfriend.
Legal punishment: 18 months probation.
NFL punishment: Placed on commissioner exempt list.

RAY MCDONALD - DE - SAN FRANCISCO 49ERS
Arrested and charged with felony domestic violence for allegedly attacking a pregnant woman.
Legal punishment: Undetermined.
NFL punishment: Currently playing.

———

TO BLAME GOODELL EXCLUSIVELY IS OF COURSE SILLY. IT'S ALSO fair to say that the domestic violence problem in professional football was an issue long before Goodell came along. One of the most frightening and notorious (but little known) cases of an NFL player committing domestic abuse was that of former New York Giants player Tito Wooten. While comparing abuse and tragedies is self-defeating, it must be said that Wooten's actions were among the worst cases of domestic violence in recent NFL history. The 200-pound Wooten was arrested and accused of punching his girlfriend, Akina Wilson, in the face and choking her. It was the third time Wooten had been accused of physically attacking a woman. Wilson would later be found dead, of carbon monoxide poisoning, on the floor of Wooten's garage in his New Jersey home. Her death was ruled a suicide.

While it's impossible to say why she took her own life, her friends and family believed it was due, at least partially, to her violent relationship with Wooten. The Giants knew of Wooten's troubles and domestic violence history but still signed Wooten to a multiyear contract worth $8 million. When the case went to court, just four days before the Giants were to play Dallas, a judge, incredibly, told Wooten, "Have a good game."

That case happened in 1998, nearly a decade before Goodell became commissioner. In the five years before that, there were 37 total players arrested or accused of family violence crimes. Many of those crimes were serious ones, including assault and kidnapping. The NFL, at that time, had just initiated a violent crime policy, but it had no teeth. For example, it was left to individual teams to decide whether or not a player would receive counseling. Counseling. That was it.

Some of the domestic violence cases under Commissioner Paul Tagliabue's tenure were equally ugly, and the subsequent NFL punishment almost nonexistent. In 2005, Tagliabue's last year as commissioner, nine players were arrested on domestic violence accusations. Only one was punished by the NFL, and it was a ridiculously light one-game suspension.

The NFL never understood domestic violence. It didn't have to—because for so much of its existence, a significant portion of its fan base didn't care. A significant portion of the legal system didn't care. A significant portion of America didn't care. If the legal system and country didn't care, then why should the NFL? The problem of domestic violence in the NFL has always been presented as a nearly impossible problem to solve. But now, in this post–Ray Rice era, the league appears to at least partially give a damn. It's not difficult to solve at all. Caring was 50 percent of the problem.

I saw some of this care in my interview with Troy Vincent, the NFL's executive vice president of football operations, in late 2013. "We are caught up in this 'us versus them,'" he said. "Can we for five minutes think about the kid [Adrian Peterson's son]? Can we think about all kids who have to go through that? Can we think for five minutes about the woman [Janay Rice] and all women who have to suffer through that? For five minutes?

"Forget what's negotiated, what Article 46 is. For two minutes even, can we think about the victims instead of egos? All I hear is about Adrian Peterson. Well, what about his son? Can we think about that? Imagine for a second if that was your child or your wife or your daughter. Drop the egos at the door. Think about the community for once before thinking about yourselves. For two minutes? Just two minutes. Think about who was attacked. Think about the survivors. Just two minutes. That's it. That's all I ask.

"Think about the families for once. I don't see them (the union) doing that. I don't want to hear about redemption (for Ray Rice or Peterson). Not someone's career. I don't want to hear about how someone feels they need to be back on the field playing. I want to talk about the families affected by domestic violence. Can we do that? Just two minutes. Two minutes is all I'm asking."

Vincent has been one of the bright spots in a league that's been extraordinarily troubled. He's led on a number of issues, including the league's fight to address its domestic violence problem as well as changing the NFL's rules to make the game less barbaric. During the 2013 preseason, Vincent videotaped a message to all players about the rules changes. "In some instances, the rules may cause you to alter your play. But they are in place to protect you from unnecessary risk," Vincent stated. "As a former player, there are few things as frustrating as being fined for something you didn't realize was a fineable offense, or worse, having to sit and watch somebody else play your position. If you have a clear understanding of the rules, your chances of staying on the field are higher. That's best for you, your team, and the league."

The changes led to predictable objections from some players. Then-Washington safety Ryan Clark criticized Vincent as "soft." But Vincent was right. Players notorious for angering the league office with their play adjusted their game and didn't find themselves running afoul of the rules in 2014. More than that, the changes led to safer play. Through the first 13 weeks of the 2014 season, unnecessary roughness penalties decreased 26 percent from the same period in 2013, according to the NFL. Illegal hits on defenseless players fell 68 percent. Illegal hits on quarterbacks had been cut nearly in half.

Just as rule changes led to predictable complaints, the domestic violence plan changes did as well. Nonetheless, they were fairly substantial changes for the better. Among the key changes were that the NFL would no longer defer to the criminal justice system. Instead, it will conduct its own investigation into the allegations by embracing the use of independent investigators. The NFL would also continue paid leave for employees accused of violent crimes, but would remove Goodell from initial disciplinary proceedings. However, Goodell retains a substantial amount of power in the process because he has the final say in the discipline process.

On the CBS pregame show late in 2014, three of the NFL's top media stars discussed the new policy, and their conversation showed the complexity of the issue. Amy Trask, the former Raiders executive who should get into the Hall of Fame, argued the more nuanced position. Bill Cowher, who might get into the Hall of Fame, backed the NFL. Tony Gonzalez, the former tight end who will get into the Hall of Fame, backed the union position.

"A great step in the right direction," said Trask. "There needs to be and presumably we're on the road to a clearly articulated, comprehensive policy which is consistently interpreted and consistently applied. My hope now is that the league and the union set aside their legal differences as to who yielded what rights under the CBA and who has what obligations to collective bargaining. Put that aside, work together collectively, cooperatively, embrace this new program. And as we know, most players in the NFL are terrific, terrific human beings. It's a very, very small percentage to whom this applies. Let's make it work."

"A rocky road to get there," said Cowher. "No question. And mistakes were made along the way. But as you stated, we're there. It's very specific. It's very comprehensive, and to me, we're headed in the right direction."

"When you look at it, it hasn't really changed," said Gonzalez. "Because right now [Goodell is] still the guy. Even after it's all said and done, whether you like what he has to say about whatever judgment he passes down, he's still going to have that final say. They're going to hire somebody to handle these cases and it's going to be hired by the league. Your allegiance lies where you're getting the paycheck from. So from a player's perspective, I don't see that much of a difference."

"I think the biggest challenge is to make sure that a policy is consistently interpreted and consistently applied," said Trask. "If we look at this as a baseline, there is a new policy in place, and I respect those concerns. I understand those concerns. Coach [Cowher] makes the point that they were yielded in the negotiations and the players arguably should talk to the union about that. But now you have a new baseline policy. Let's consistently apply it, consistently interpret it, and let's hope that the NFL can be at the center point of fostering some social change. Look, domestic violence and issues of that nature aren't only an issue in the National Football League. These are societal issues. Now, if the league can use this new policy and its application to demonstrate to other businesses how to do this, that's terrific…Communicate, collaborate, coordinate, cooperate: the four Cs that make businesses work."

Senator Jay Rockefeller, the West Virginia Democrat who in late 2014 chaired a Senate Commerce Committee hearing about domestic violence in professional sports, issued a lengthy statement after the NFL's policy announcement:

> I know domestic violence is not unique to sports, but when a celebrity athlete is charged with committing an act of domestic violence it uniquely reverberates through our society. Sadly, it seems that it took a series of very public embarrassments and backlash for professional sports leagues to begin responding appropriately when their athletes or employees commit violent acts. I'm encouraged to see the NFL moving

to address its past mistakes with this effort toward establishing uniform rules and standards around domestic violence and other problematic acts. The other leagues should take comparable steps without delay. No more excuses. Until recently, the leagues have long looked the other way and, in doing so, have been arguably complicit. While the problem of domestic violence goes far beyond sports, the era of league complacency on this issue must come to an end and those who are involved in misconduct must face the consequences.

Rockefeller also addressed a key problem with the issue, and that's due process. Said Rockefeller: "Within the context of professional sports and the leagues' disciplinary penalties on players as employees, league and union officials frequently invoke 'due process' but this term should not be conflated with the legal guarantees afforded by the U.S. Constitution." Interestingly, what Rockefeller said contradicted a position publicly taken by the 49ers after the McDonald arrest just four months earlier. Rockefeller added, "Nonetheless, the leagues and their players' unions have grappled with conceiving standards and procedures that avoid being arbitrary and treat players fairly. In so doing, the leagues and the unions must determine how the criminal justice system interacts with league-wide policies and procedures, determinations of fact, and the meting out of punishment.

"The biggest question is how league policies should treat players who have been accused of committing acts of domestic violence but have yet to be convicted or have their charges resolved by the criminal justice system. A uniform league-wide policy must establish what punishment, if any, to impose on a player who has not had his day in a court of law."

There is also the issue of second chances. They are a part of our country's genome, but the sports universe has always had a difficult time with the concept. It has always been counterbalanced with the concept in sports that it's a privilege to play. The former belief was expressed by Nick Saban in late 2014 about one of his players, D.J. Pettway, who was kicked off the Alabama team for second degree robbery a year earlier. Pettway returned and was a key contributor on the field. And Saban claimed that Pettway had changed his life off the field. Saban's speech on second chances, albeit extremely self-serving, was nonetheless compelling: "It's really, really good for me and I think for some of our administrators around here who, our president, who shakes hands with all of our players when they walk across the stage and graduate, when we give somebody a second chance and they do well and graduate from school," Saban explained. "There's always a lot of criticism out there when somebody does something wrong. Everybody wants to know how you're going to punish the guy. There's not enough—for 19- and 20-year-old kids—people out there saying, 'Why don't you give them another chance?'

"So I'm going to give a speech right now about this. Where do you want them to be? Guy makes a mistake. Where do you want them to be? You want him to be in the street or do you want them to be here graduating?"

Saban also spoke about one of his former players, Muhsin Muhammad, whom Saban had coached at Michigan State, and also got into trouble off the field. Saban suspended Muhammad, who then returned to the Spartans. He would go on to a 15-year NFL career, found a charity foundation for young children, and become a father of seven. His oldest daughter is at Princeton. "Everybody in the school, every newspaper guy, everybody was killing a guy because he got in trouble and they said there's no way he should be on our team," Saban said. "I didn't kick him off the team. I suspended him. I made him do some stuff.

"So who was right? I feel strong about this now, really strong, about all the criticism out there of every guy that's 19 years old that makes a mistake, and you all kill them. Some people won't stand up for him. My question to you is, 'Where do you want him to be?' You want to condemn him to a life sentence? Or do you want the guy to have his children going to Princeton?"

The concept of second chances, and innocent until proven guilty, are the stuff of a great rift between the union and NFL. The union wants players to stay on the field while his case goes through the court system. The NFL wants players off the field immediately while that case proceeds. This gap may never be bridged.

The conduct policy changes were substantial, yes, but they're not enough. More needs to be done. How do you truly start to fix the problem? This is one way:

1. Each NFL player must volunteer one hour at a domestic violence center every year.
2. Each player, every year, must take a one-hour domestic violence prevention seminar.
3. Any player accused of domestic violence is immediately placed on paid leave.
4. A domestic violence council is established. It's composed of one lawyer appointed by the union, one appointed by the NFL, and a judge agreed upon by both sides.

The attorneys will each have an equal investigative staff, funded by money from the television contracts (which the players and owners split). The purpose of the council is to determine if there is probable cause to remove the player from the exempt list. The judge, not Goodell, would make the final determination—within two weeks of initial allegations. The council is created to ease player concern that the commissioner, who now has the final say on many discipline issues, has too much power. This way, the power is shared equally between player and management, and an independent person has the final say.

5. If the council determines there is no probable cause, the player is reinstated immediately.

6. If the council determined there is probable cause that the player committed the crime, he would remain on the exempt list pending outcome of the case in criminal court.

7. If the player is found guilty or pleads guilty to any domestic violence crime, he would be suspended eight games, or half of the regular season.

8. A second accusation would lead to the process starting all over again, but with more severe consequences, as stated below.

9. A second plea or conviction would lead to a lifetime ban without possibility of reinstatement.

10. Another unit composed of two attorneys appointed by the union—again with investigative staffs and again paid for with television money—would be used to determine if any NFL player was wrongly convicted.

11. If the group finds credible evidence that a player was wrongly convicted, or a jury or judge verdict is overturned,

the wrongly convicted player would receive the salary he missed while out of football plus treble damages. He would also be free to sign with any NFL team.

———

THERE IS ONE LARGER POINT ON TEAMS SIGNING PROBLEMATIC players overall. If a team signs a player with a violent criminal record, I believe the team should be held more accountable. This is one of the biggest problems the NFL faces. The league office can enact changes to make players face stiffer punishments, but none of those initiatives stops a franchise from signing a turd. This is where a team's desire to win conflicts with the NFL's desire to improve the league's overall image. So the NFL needs to punish teams that take chances on troubled players. If a player with an arrest record for violence, or who is found liable in civil court for violent crime, signs with a team, and that player gets in trouble again, the team is docked a first-round pick and fined one million dollars. This would be called the Stupidity Tax.

There is a version of this "tax" being proposed in England. The Prudential Regulation Authority, the Bank of England's regulatory branch, wants to make senior bank managers more accountable if they take reckless actions that cause the bank to collapse. Football needs a version of this.

———

SUCH A PLAN, ANY PLAN REALLY, WOULD REQUIRE EXTENSIVE CO-OPeration between the players' union and NFL. Right now, that cooperation does not exist, in any way; in fact, the relationship between the two is at its worst since the strike years in the 1980s. So any plan to stop domestic violence in the NFL must begin with a healing of that relationship.

In July 2014 the website FiveThirtyEight.com, run by the seemingly prescient Nate Silver, the metrics genius who started in politics but branched into sports, examined arrest records compiled in *USA TODAY*'s NFL Arrest Database. The site found that the NFL's arrest rate for crimes such as burglary or drug use was far lower than the general population. In fact, the NFL arrest rate for all crimes was lower than the general population—except one, for which it was dramatically higher: domestic violence.

"Perhaps the question of how the NFL should 'police' its players is the wrong analogy entirely," the site suggested. "This situation may be more akin to tort law than criminal law: If the NFL is capable of reducing any harm its players are causing—whether through harsher suspensions or other policies targeting behavior—it may have a legal (or at least moral) duty to do so."

One last thing. The NFL, after the Rice case, partnered with No More, an organization that raises awareness and funds for victims of domestic violence and sexual assault. In June 2014, which was prior to the Rice video release, No More's website had 35,000 page views, reported the *New York Times*. In December 2014, that number had ballooned to 275,000 views. That's the power of the NFL—and the NFL should keep using that power to make change for the better.

9   THE HERO

BEFORE THE BRAVE MICHAEL SAM, THERE WAS SOMEONE ELSE. OR rather, there was *almost* someone else. It happened about a year before Sam would become the first openly gay player in NFL history.

The team had decided yes. The player had decided the same. It was set. It was going to happen. An NFL player was going to publicly say he was gay and then play in the NFL. What happened before that moment showed how parts of the NFL are progressive and ready for change. But what happened next showed how the sport is still in some ways fearful of it. (Likewise, what would happen to Sam after his brave act was also indicative of how even in modern times there is a backwardness across the sports world and the NFL isn't immune from this backwardness.)

The following account is based on interviews with approximately a dozen people, including team and league officials, current and former players, and gay rights advocates. Some were directly involved with the discussions that nearly led to the first openly gay NFL player. Further illustrating the intense secrecy, delicacy, and fear surrounding the subject, none of the principals wanted to be identified. They also refused to identify the team or the player.

The story begins with a closeted gay player, a free agent, reaching out to a small group of friends and telling them about his sexual orientation. The friends, both current and former players, and others with NFL connections, then contacted a handful of teams to gauge their interest in the player and their comfort with that player talking openly about being gay if they signed him.

A number of teams contacted passed. The player was told the teams didn't have a need at his position. However, the player reportedly told a recently retired player that he believed the teams declined because they feared the attention a gay NFL player would receive from the public and media.

Yet some teams were interested, and one team actually said yes. It wasn't a lukewarm yes or a conditional one. It was a definite yes. The team, in the NFC South, expressed that it didn't care if the player was gay and had no issue with him announcing he was gay after signing. The player expected the signing, and subsequent announcement, to happen in the early summer. This would give the team, fans, and media a month to adjust to the news before training camp began.

It was during these talks that reports surfaced about the possibility of an openly gay player emerging. In effect, word of the impending signing had leaked. I reported, based on speaking to several NFL sources, that a player was strongly considering coming out. Word of an openly gay player signing was spreading among the player base.

Gay rights advocate and former Baltimore Raven Brendon Ayanbadejo at the time stated he believed several gay players might come out. He later backed away from that number but stood by his statement that a gay player would soon emerge onto the NFL stage. It's possible Ayanbadejo may have been right. The feeling among team officials, as well as current and former players, is that there wasn't just one gay player ready to shed his secret but many.

The sources painted a remarkable picture. At least two or three gay players, each unaware of the other, living in different parts of the country, with different sets of friends and agents, were each contemplating the same thing: coming out. That period was, as one gay rights advocate described it, "the spring of optimism for the NFL and gay rights." There was a feeling that the NFL was on the verge of crossing a significant barrier. There was great excitement. It was going to happen.

Until it didn't.

THE QUESTION LINGERS: WHAT HAPPENED?

In some ways, that extraordinary moment became moot with the emergence of Sam. Yet in some ways, they are interconnected.

Sam's bravery cannot be overstated. While he has always publicly maintained he was unconcerned about potential bigotry, those concerns have kept (and keep) other gay athletes from coming out, especially in the big four American professional sports of football, basketball, baseball, and hockey. A number of NFL sources including players, coaches, and team executives give varying estimates of the number of gay players in football but those estimates range from several dozen to several hundred of the NFL's thousands of players.

To date, there is only one known NBA player, Jason Collins, who publicly said he was gay while still an active player. There have been none in baseball or hockey. So of all the many thousands of professional athletes in those sports, across decades, there have been only two *openly* gay players.

So what is stopping gay players from being open about their sexuality? Said veteran kicker Jay Feely, who has also been a longtime union representative, "Players, in general, don't care what other players do in the bedroom, whether that is being celibate, having an affair, being happily married for 20 years or being gay. No one cares. The only thing they care about is winning games [and getting paid]. That's the honest truth."

Along with the initial player discussed earlier, there was a fairly well-known defensive back. He drew interest from an AFC North team that knew he was gay. Coaches on the team were asked if they were okay with a gay player. They were. Some defensive players were casually queried, according to an official on the team. All of the players asked said it wouldn't be an issue. (They were not told the name of the player.) According to the team, the potential deal collapsed when the player wanted too much money. If that was the case—and there is doubt about that among gay rights advocates—then it stands apart from everything else league insiders are saying about an NFL that they know includes many gay players (rather than not a single one until Sam would publicly acknowledge he's gay).

The first player who drew interest was told he would not be signed out of fear he would be a distraction. This is the biggest reason why Sam, despite showing immense promise with the Rams in the preseason, has not found employment since he was first released by the Rams and then the Dallas Cowboys.

There is no question that as the spring of 2015, when Sam was drawing almost no interest from NFL teams, that his sexuality was factor. If Sam was not gay, he'd have been on a team much sooner. There's little doubt about this. I've been criticized for making that point, as well as my assertion that Sam is not on an NFL roster because he's gay. The response of homophobes (and those who think they aren't but really are) is that the media only writes about Sam because he's gay, not because he's a good player. But he was the co–defensive player of the year in the SEC, perhaps the toughest conference in college football.

What became clear with Sam is that being gay hurt him in the football world. The data clearly shows that something highly unusual happened to Sam in the NFL. This was documented by journalist Cyd Zeigler on the website Outsports.com:

> Since 2000 (not including this past 2014 season) 73 different men have won the defensive player of the year award in the big five football conferences: ACC, Big Ten, Big XII, Pac-12 and SEC. Of those 73 men, only four have fared worse in the NFL Draft than Sam, all of whom went undrafted. Sam was taken in the seventh round.

Zeigler goes on to list the other four as: Jackson Jeffcoat (Big XII Defensive Player of the Year, 2014), who was signed by the Seahawks, cut, then signed by Washington; Mark Herzlich (ACC Defensive Player of the Year, 2008), who was signed by the Giants in 2011, and as of this writing is still with the team; Nick Reid (2005 Big XII Defensive Player of the Year), who went back and forth between NFL Europe and the Kansas City

Chiefs; and Dale Robinson (2005 Pac-10 Defensive Player of the Year), who had the shortest run, getting cut by the Colts before the start of his first season.

Let's stop there for a moment. Reid, Robinson and Sam are the only players in recent NFL history—going back 14 years—to fail to make an active NFL roster after being named Defensive Player of the Year in a major conference. Even that fact is interesting. Reid was signed to a two-year deal by the Chiefs and then allocated to NFL Europe in 2007. Remember, back then, teams used NFL Europe almost as an extension of their roster, almost like a farm system. Players who teams thought had potential but couldn't make active or practice squads—which were smaller back then—were sent there. So ostensibly, Reid made a roster as well.

More from Zeigler: "The three former Defensive Players of the Year to go in the sixth round: Michigan State linebacker Greg Jones in 2011, Oklahoma linebacker Rufus Alexander in 2006, and Oregon State DE Bill Swancutt in 2005. All three men were on active rosters in the NFL for at least three seasons. None of these players—except Sam—were drafted in the seventh round. It's interesting, though, to compare Sam to Nick Reed [not the same (Nick) Reid as above], the 2008 Pac-10 Defensive Lineman of the Year. He was selected 247th in the 2009 NFL Draft (two spots ahead of where Sam was drafted five years later). Like Sam, Reed was a defensive end (for Oregon) who had an 'undersized' label. In fact, Reed was an inch shorter and 10 pounds lighter than Sam. Unlike Sam, Reed made the Seahawks' active roster that season after a strong preseason. Sam was cut by the Rams after his strong preseason in which he was fourth in the NFL in sacks."

So in many ways, what happened to Sam is one of the most unusual things to ever happen to a player of his caliber. Ever. Over the past 15 years, we've never seen anything like this. This from Zeigler is damning for the NFL: "To put it another way, of the 73 DPOYs in the big conferences since 2000, 95 percent were selected earlier than Michael Sam; all but two since 2000 (97 percent)—and 100 percent in the last eight years—made an active roster his rookie season...all except for Sam." (This does not include this past 2014 season.)

What does that mean? What people say is, if Sam was good enough, he'd be on a team. Maybe that's true, but teams still fear Sam. Fear is a dynamic in play. Despite Sam handling himself like a professional, keeping a low profile, fear of an openly gay man in the locker room is still a factor. Otherwise, he'd be on a team. I don't believe in coincidence or anomalies. There is something wrong here. There was also the alleged circus aspect that Sam might bring to a team, but Sam, again, has done everything the right way. There's been no circus. Nothing.

When I think of Sam's story, I think of past players like Warren Moon. When Moon came out of college, every NFL team passed on him. They all justified why they did it. He can't play. He's not good enough. But it was simple bigotry—the NFL wasn't ready for a black quarterback—and Moon had to start his pro career in Canada. It's possible Sam might have to do the same. Sam's experience teaches future closeted gay athletes an important and unfortunate message about the NFL: it's still not ready for you to be open about who you are.

———

IN JANUARY 2015, SAM PROPOSED TO HIS BOYFRIEND, VITO Cammisano, in Vatican City. It was a nice moment both in the proposal (which Sam posted on social media) and the symbolism of asking Vito to marry him at a place that is the heart of the Catholic Church, which is against gay marriage.

In an interview with Oprah Winfrey not long before he proposed, Sam said he heard from closeted gay NFL players who thanked him and wished him well. Sam stated explicitly what was already well known: there are gay men in professional football, hiding who they truly are out of fear of discrimination. Probably *many* more. But they are afraid to come out, and after Sam's experience, it's understandable why.

"There's a lot of us out there," Sam told Winfrey. "I'm not the only one. I'm just the only one who's open."

———

THROUGHOUT THE 2014 SEASON, I ASKED 50 PLAYERS, 20 COACHES (head coaches and assistants), and 15 front-office executives and scouts two questions. One: Are you okay with an openly gay player in the NFL? Two: What percentage of the NFL is gay? All respondents were guaranteed anonymity.

I've been writing on this issue for decades and the responses still surprised me. Thirty-seven players said they did not want a gay player in the locker room, nine said they didn't care. The last four said they needed more time to think about the question. Twelve players said the NFL was 30 percent gay. Ten said 20 percent was gay. Another 10 said 10 to 15 percent. Eight said less than 10 percent. Five said the number was 1 percent. The remaining five said there are no gay players in the NFL.

Of the 20 coaches, 15 said they did not want a gay player in the locker room; five said they didn't care. Four coaches said the NFL was 10 percent gay, six said 5 percent, and 10 coaches said there were no gay players in the NFL.

Of the front office executives and scouts, 11 said there were no gay players in the NFL. Three said that number was 1 percent.

Other polls have shown overwhelming support from NFL players for openly gay athletes. I believe some of those polls are slightly misleading because the players aren't always comfortable telling pollsters how they truly feel. I went to players I know who told me their honest thoughts.

Here are five notable comments from five different NFL sources:

PLAYER 1: "I have nothing against gays. I think the problem is I don't want any man looking at me while I'm in the shower." [Author's note: This was by far the most prevalent comment made by players. It's ridiculous on many obvious levels but it apparently remains a common fear among straight men that non-straight men might look at their ding-dong.]

PLAYER 2: "Last month of the [2014] season, a group of us were in the locker room, and Michael Sam's name came up. It was some of the most vile antigay shit I ever heard. If I [were] a gay NFL player, I would never come out. The prejudice against gays in the NFL is real and far more prevalent than the NFL wants to admit."

PLAYER 3 (who is a star in the NFL): "If we ever drafted an openly gay player, the first time he came into the locker room I'd give him a big hug in front of every player on the team, welcome him, and dare anyone to have a problem with it."

HEAD COACH: "The truth is no team wants to draft an openly gay player because of the distraction that would come with it." [Author's note: the distraction excuse was most common among coaches and personnel men. There was also never a satisfactory response when I would raise the point of why a gay man is a distraction but a domestic abuser isn't. Or a child abuser. Or a dog murderer. Or…)

GENERAL MANAGER: "The unfair thing for an openly gay player is that after Michael Sam, teams won't draft an openly gay player unless that player is above and beyond really talented. Their situation reminds me of what it was like to be a black quarterback maybe 30 years ago. Some teams refused to draft them, thinking they were a distraction, and they only got drafted if they were exceptional."

———

AND WHAT DO FANS THINK?

A *Huffington Post* poll in May 2014 showed that 60 percent of Americans said they would approve of their favorite sports team signing an openly gay player, the site reported, while 20 percent said they would disapprove. Among NFL fans, 65 percent said they would approve and 21 percent said they would disapprove. Interestingly, those same fans who backed openly gay players in football said they disapproved of Sam kissing his then-boyfriend when Sam was drafted by the Rams, and 47 percent in the poll said it was "inappropriate" for networks to show the kiss. This is interesting because non-gay players kiss their girlfriends on camera after being drafted all the time.

What you see with the issue of gay players is there are still some fans who hate the notion. They don't want them damn gays in their damn sport 'cause their damn sport is for real damn men and them damn gays aren't real damn men. This is what some homophobes say while sitting on their fat asses watching games. But what you also see—and you saw this with Sam—that there is a growing number of fans who don't care if a player is gay.

So what happens if the league, in the aftermath of Sam, is perceived as antigay? Such a perception would not be a great threat to football, but it would be a problem in a country that increasingly doesn't care who loves whom. A Pew Research poll taken in 2014 showed just how far the country has come on the issue of gay marriage. In 1996, just 33 percent of the nation favored same-sex marriage; in 2014, 54 percent. Those who opposed same-sex marriage in 1996 totaled 55 percent and those in favor made up 39 percent. And now it's legal.

There are openly gay men and women in every aspect of society—politics, sports, and the media—except in the biggest sport in America. What does it say about the NFL when we know there are gays in the sport, yet among its thousands of players, there isn't a single openly gay player?

Sam in 2015 did a commercial for Coca-Cola. In it, he talked about both the bigotry he faced and the hopes he has that people will overcome their prejudice. It was wonderfully done. It was, in many ways, typical Sam and underscored what is a missed opportunity for football. To me, NFL teams allowed their prejudices to blind them to a good player and a good person.

"I actually didn't get into social media until this past year," Sam says in the commercial. "Not on Twitter, not on Instagram, Facebook—never had any of that. My friends used to say I was always old school. [But] social media kind of had to be a big role in my life because I'm in the spotlight…I see negativity daily. I've gotten nasty Tweets, Instagram messages. People have sent me YouTube videos saying how they hate me, how they wish I was dead. One nasty e-mail [the writer] pretty much told me that we don't belong. We're evil. She's really the only hate message I ever replied to.

"And what I said was, 'I am sorry you feel that way. But even though you hate me so much, I still love you, and I wish you had a great day.'" Then Sam smiles. "She never replied back," he said.

"All the negativity that comes to me, I turn it into positivity," he continued. "I have to prove the haters wrong. If I can use social media to make somebody understand and accept people I [will] do so…I will be that person to stand against bullying. To stand against hate."

———

IN THE SPRING OF 2015, SAM WOULD SIGN WITH THE CANADIAN Football League's Montreal Alouettes. Sam would later abruptly depart the team with little explanation, and later return. But his troubles in Canada and his inability to stay in the NFL do not change an important fact: Michale Sam will always be a hero.

10   SCOOPAGE

IT WAS DECEMBER 2014 AND JAY GLAZER DID WHAT JAY GLAZER
always does: break a huge story. This is what he has done for
more than two decades probably better than anyone covering
the NFL ever has.

The Browns were deciding between Brian Hoyer and Johnny
Manziel, and much of the football media were attempting to get
the story first. Glazer did. Again, Glazer getting the story first
is a regular phenomenon. Glazer tweeted the Manziel scoop,
clearly the first to get it. Just minutes after Glazer broke the
news, ESPN reported that Manziel was going to start, except
they initially failed to attribute the information to Glazer, who
clearly broke the story. What ESPN did was the media insider
equivalent of grand theft.

ESPN has outstanding journalists. Few are better than Adam
Schefter, who covers the NFL for the network. If you started
an NFL insider team and you had the first pick in the insider
draft, Glazer and Schefter would be your first picks. There's
also Buster Olney, who covers baseball. Jim Trotter is the best
combination of writer and reporter in the business. Perhaps the

most well-rounded talent in all of sports journalism is ESPN's Jemele Hill, who does print, radio, and television as well as anyone.

Yet ESPN, for whatever reason, has a blind spot when it comes to crediting other media organizations. It's a bully move, and if there is one thing I've learned about Glazer it's that he can't be bullied, not even by one of the biggest media companies in the world.

A FOX public relations person approached ESPN and asked why they stole Glazer's story. A person at ESPN said they didn't. That person was then asked who broke the story for ESPN and the ESPN representative declined to say who it was. It's fairly unprecedented for a news organization not to identify which of their staff reported a story.

Glazer went to Twitter and, rightfully so, vented. He wrote it was an "all-time low from @ESPN on their constant thievery of [others'] work. FOX PR guy calls them to call BS on their claim they had Manziel scoop. News desk guy @sportscenter tells him their reporter didn't want to be identified. Huh? What reporter doesn't want credit for hard work paying off? Lying bastards."

To Glazer, a scoop is about hard work, the product of hours— thousands of hours, a career, a lifetime of work. Ripping off information isn't just stealing in the moment, it's stealing from someone's future. "I get judged by one thing and one thing only: scoops," Glazer later told *The Rich Eisen Show*. So when ESPN steals people's work, I'm not going to sit by. I'm going to rip the hell out of them for it until they stop doing it. Whether it's me or they did it to C.J. Nitkowski today for baseball, they did it to *[The] Dan Patrick Show* yesterday. It makes you wonder, everything that they claim, did anything they do they break [themselves]? It hurts great reporters like Adam Schefter and Chris Mortensen and guys like that. Guys, there's enough to go around. They have such a lying, cheating, stealing policy over there. I don't agree with lying, cheating, and stealing in anything in life."

Readers and viewers may not care who gets the scoop, but all of the main insiders—names like Glazer, Schefter, Ian Rapoport at the NFL Network, Mike Florio at NBC and ProFootballTalk.com, Peter King at *Sports Illustrated*, Jason La Canfora at CBS, Jason Cole from *Bleacher Report,* and Chris Mortensen at ESPN, among others—definitely do care. It's a huge deal.

There are no true insiders at newspapers any longer. Newspapers can no longer afford to have someone on staff just to break news and barely write. All of the true insiders work for television and websites. And none of the insiders do true comprehensive writing; their sole jobs are getting scoops.

(A brief aside: one insider who has quickly grown into a dominant force is Rapoport. He had something happen with one of his stories that I've never seen before. Rapoport reported the Bears were having buyer's remorse when it came to their quarterback, Jay Cutler, perhaps the greatest coach killer of all time. This led to initial denials from the apparent source of that information, the team's offensive coordinator. The coach would later admit he was the source and, as the *Chicago Tribune* reported in December 2014, tearfully apologized to the entire team during a meeting at the Bears complex. It was excellent reporting by Rapoport.)

There are excellent NFL journalists, including Josina

Anderson from ESPN, Jarrett Bell from *USA TODAY*, Mike Silver and Judy Battista from the NFL Network, and Sam Farmer from the *Los Angeles Times*, among others. But they aren't true insiders. One other thing on the insiders: they are male and they are white. The insider business is one of the least diverse subgroups of sports journalism.

NFL journalism is among the most transformative of all journalism. NFL writers are also, by turns, the most manipulated and the most manipulating. I've been used by the NFL and union to get their messages across (rarely, but it's happened). Some NFL writers are used almost daily. NFL teams in particular are skilled at preying upon the insecurity and vulnerabilities of journalists, particularly journalists who are fans. (There are an abundance of local radio and writer types who nothing but glorified team PR people.) Teams excel at making a writer or television reporter feel as if they are part of something important by leaking a story that makes the journalist seem like an insider. Most aren't. They just think they are.

One key place where many of us in the football media have erred (myself included) is in glorifying the violence of the sport while not detailing the toll that violence took on the body. "Unlike other forms of popular entertainment, NFL football is real—the players actually do what they appear to be doing—yet at the same time it is a creation of the media, and it generates some of the most powerful fantasies in our culture," wrote Michael Oriard, a former Notre Dame and Kansas City Chiefs offensive lineman, now a distinguished professor of American literature at Oregon State University. He wrote this in the book *League of Denial*. "The actuality of football is the source of its cultural power, but media-made images of that reality are all that most fans know."

This was the great fail of many NFL writers in the pre-concussion crisis. Our mistake was not being *too close* to the NFL (though some journalists were and are), but in glorifying the violence of the sport. We didn't know about CTE in the '70s or '90s or even into the 2000s, but we did know that the bodies of players were being wrecked, and we still wrote glowingly about the violence of the sport, and condemned players we perceived as soft.

CTE grew in this environment, like the Andromeda strain, and we were its incubating agents. The challenge now for NFL writers is to provide balance when reporting on the violence of the sport and how the NFL handles the results of that violence. Where the NFL's future goes, in some small part, will be determined by how the media handles this battle, and how the NFL manages the media's handling of it. This means that if the sport gets another free pass on how the body is affected by football it will help ease the threat to its long-term future. But if the media continues critical looks at CTE, and there remains constant negative news about how the violence of the sport makes it not just risky to play but also erodes the mind, then this can shift how fans view the sport.

Many insiders don't deal with the underbelly of football. They report on the latest trade news or coaching rumors or who will start at quarterback for the Browns. Glazer has always been slightly different. Some of his stories, back when he covered the Giants, showed how brutal the game was on the bodies of players. This earned him the respect of almost everyone in that locker room. "He didn't see players as just something to rip or criticize," his longtime friend, Hall of Famer Michael Strahan, told me. "Jay treated players like human beings. That's why he inspired such loyalty from so many players."

Glazer has been breaking significant stories regularly for two decades. When we first met, both covering the Giants football beat, Glazer was working for a weekly publication. While working for a weekly—a *weekly*!—Jay would break stories about the team. And not just a few, a lot. I had never seen that in sports journalism before. One of the more remarkable things I've witnessed in my career was Glazer not just breaking those stories in the weekly, but also in a weekly picks column he had in the *New York Post* as a freelancer. In the *Post*, he'd break down each game, and in those vignettes, many of them would contain some type of scoopage.

Full disclosure: Jay is my friend, and I purposely chose not to speak to him for this. I know. Weird. But I didn't want to be influenced. I just wanted to write on him from the heart. But I would write this about Jay if he was my friend or not.

Jay remains one of a handful of journalists whom I've met in my career who wasn't mean-spirited or petty or bigoted or misogynistic. Or overly egotistical. Sure, if he's wronged, Jay will let you know, but that's it. He isn't like that significant number of people in my business who enjoy bullying the weak. (Case in point: at a playoff game last year there was a writer who verbally abused a 21-year-old woman intern because the writer didn't like his seat location in the press box.)

What Glazer does, and why he's the most important sports journalist working today, is he accomplishes something exceedingly rare in 21st-century journalism: he offers uniqueness. His information is almost always something no one else has. In this era of extreme pack journalism, uber-laziness from many in the media, and athletes who often provide little true insight into themselves, Glazer has breached this barrier. How has he done it? By outworking everyone else.

11   THE PLAN

IN DECEMBER 2014, AMY TRASK, THE SKILLED FORMER RAIDERS executive, appeared on the CBS Sports Network and outlined one of the key steps needed to keep the NFL from imploding.

"There needs to be a clearly articulated codified [player conduct] policy that's consistently interpreted and consistently applied," said Trask. "And while the league has every right from a legal standpoint to say to the players that they are not entitled to participate in a collective bargaining process, with respect to a new policy, the smartest thing the league could do is to extend a hand to the players and say we're putting legal issues aside [and say] 'Come formulate this new policy with us. Let's be partners.'"

That is the most crucial concept that will keep the NFL on top: it needs to work closely with the players. That is the core of this 25-point plan to save professional football. The plan begins with stark honesty.

1. Football should offer a cigarette-style warning for the game. There must be an understanding, more than anything, that concussions in football cannot be prevented. No type of

helmet technology can stop them, only reduce them. So anyone who plays the sport will always be at risk for serious brain trauma and CTE.

The warning would be simple and short. It would go something like this: "Playing football can cause potentially serious long-term damage to the brain. It can cause a condition known as chronic traumatic encephalopathy, or CTE. CTE can lead to impaired decision-making, even to suicide or violent behavior."

Harsh? Blunt? Well, yes. But there needs to be a harsh, blunt understanding of what football truly is. So everyone playing it— from Pop Warner to the pros—knows the risks. *All* of the risks.

2. Mandatory mental health evaluations every six months. Results will be kept confidential unless the result of an examination shows a player may be trending towards off-field violence.

3. One of the greatest threats to the NFL is the lack of trust between players and management. Make it part of the CBA that the union head and commissioner meet once a month at a neutral location for a minimum of two hours. Just the two of them. No recording devices.

4. Give all assistant coaches more money. They are not poor, sure, but the amount of compensation they receive compared to head coaches is remarkable. Some assistants get a fraction of the pay they deserve while putting in insane hours.

5. Any player who plays in the NFL at least five years, upon leaving the NFL—because of retirement or medical reasons— gets a $1 million, one-time payment. NFL revenues are approximately $9 billion per year and rising; the league can afford it. The payment would help to guarantee that players don't go broke once they leave the game.

6. Along those lines, as part of the CBA, every player in the league must show proof to the union that he meets with a union-approved financial advisor once every six months.

7. A panel of four former players—all high achievers on the field who have excelled off of it in retirement—would form part of a think tank that would advise the NFL on a number of issues. Those players would be Scott Fujita, Roman Oben, Jay Feely, and Michael Strahan. A fifth person would be part of the panel in Amy Trask.

8. Eliminate all chop blocks.

9. Start a minor league. This would go a long way to ending what is basically a form of indentured servitude within college football. I know, I know…they get scholarships! But those scholarships aren't even close to commensurate to the dizzying amount of money players generate for football. A minor league would allow players who truly only want to play professional football to do so and bypass the sham of the college system. These players would take courses in money management and public speaking, among other subjects. Any courses they take would go toward a college degree that the NFL would pay for once their playing days are over.

At the Super Bowl, Seahawks players Richard Sherman and Michael Bennett absolutely savaged the NCAA scam and demonstrated why a true minor league system is needed. Said Sherman, "I don't think college athletes are given enough time to really take advantage of the free education that they're given, and it's frustrating because a lot of people get upset with student athletes and say they're not focused on school and they're not taking advantage of the opportunity they're given.

"I would love for a regular student to have a student athlete's schedule during the season for just one quarter or one semester and show me how you balance that. Show me how you would schedule your classes when you can't schedule classes from 2:00 to 6:00 on any given day. Show me how you're going to get all your work done when after you get out at 7:30 or so, you've got a test the next day, you're dead tired from practice and you still have to study just as hard as everybody else every day and get all the same work done...

"[Those] aren't the things that people focus on when talking about student athletes. They are upset when a student athlete says they need a little cash. Well, I can tell you from experience, I had negative-40 bucks in my account. Usually my account was in the negative more time than it was in the positive. You've got to make decisions on whether you get gas for your car or whether you get a meal for the day. You've got one of the two choices. People think, 'Oh, you're on scholarship.' They pay for your room and board, they pay for your education, but to their knowledge, you're there to play football. You're not on scholarship for school and it sounds crazy when a student athlete says that, but those are the things coaches tell them every day: 'You're not on scholarship for school.'"

Said Bennett, "I think the NCAA is one of the biggest scams in America, because these kids put so much on the line, and they study hard, they play football as hard as they can, but if they don't crack the NFL, then [the NCAA] says, 'We gave you a free degree.' That's like me owning a restaurant and saying, 'I'll give you a free burger.'...I'm just giving you something I already have. Athletes don't get enough credit, and a lot of the schools don't really do anything for the guys after they graduate. I think there are very few schools that actually care about the players...

"Guys break their legs and they get the worst surgeries you could possibly get, they see the worst doctors, they get the worst treatment, then they're stuck with injuries for the rest of their life, and to say that you get a degree doesn't mean anything to me.

"I think the NCAA should come up with a plan for college athletes to receive some of the money they bring in for the schools. I think my school, Texas A&M, averaged $50 million just on jersey sales. They sell numbers of guys that don't have names on the back of the jerseys, but we all know who No. 2 is for College Station: Johnny Manziel. He makes so much for the university but he doesn't see any of the money.

"They need to come up with some kind of program. I would say, maybe $60,000 for every year you stay in college, and then at the end of the year they keep it in some kind of 401k. You stay in college, you graduate, you keep that money until you're a certain age, and then after that you get that money and you get to determine what you want to do with it. And that gives you the chance to do something special in life, because you give so much to the schools, and they just move on.

"Of course they can pay Jim Harbaugh $48 million, because they don't have to pay any of the athletes. The athletes are the ones that make the school. It's not really the coach. If Nick Saban doesn't have those athletes that he has, can he still be Alabama?...

"When I was in college, I'd be going to class, some student comes to me and says 'I pay your tuition.' I'm like, 'You don't pay my damn tuition. My mom paid my tuition when she worked two jobs, and I woke up every morning at 6:00 AM and I worked hard.' To think about it, it makes me so mad and irate that people are so simple-minded when it comes to something like that."

The championship games in my fictional minor league world would be televised and likely generate huge ratings. It would also introduce America to its future stars. They'd be paid just below the minimum salary for NFL veterans and be afforded union protection.

10. No more commercials after kickoffs. It slows the game down—and the NFL already makes plenty of cash.

11. Change the pass interference penalty from a spot foul to a 15-yard penalty. It's stupid to punish a defense so severely for one play. I know the NFL wants points, but the rule is overly punitive.

12. Study the possibility of returning to leather helmets or the modern equivalent. Or even no helmets. Seriously. What we know is that no helmet can stop concussions. Leather helmets would force players to tackle properly and it would slow the game to sub–light speed instead of warp speed. There'd still be enough violence to make the average American happy but fewer brain-concussing collisions.

13. Pay players more by increasing the salary cap by 25 percent. We now know that it's highly likely anyone who plays this sport risks long-term brain damage. Increasing pay does two things: It treats the players more humanely and helps to alleviate guilt that we're cheering gladiators who might be unable to function as normal members of society decades from now.

14. The NFL should no longer accept public tax dollars to build new stadiums. The league doesn't need welfare.

15. In 2013, Goodell earned $44 million; the league's executive vice president for media, Steve Bornstein, earned $26 million; and Jeff Pash, the head lawyer for the NFL, earned almost $8 million.

The NFL refusing to accept tax dollars for stadiums would go a long way to help change its image as the Company. (The Company was a fictional corporation from the movie *Alien* that was a ruthless monolith concerned only with making money. The league's image as a greedy corporation is one of the biggest threats to its future.)

16. Get rid of the taunting rule. It's the dumbest rule ever created.

17. Let players celebrate in groups again, like Washington's Fun Bunch from the good old days.

18. Keep pushing the player safety rules no matter how much the players complain. The data shows the rules changes are making football safer. There's no question about that.

19. Put a damn team in Los Angeles, for Christ's sake. From the site FiveThirtyEight.com: "There are 3.66 million total NFL fans in Los Angeles with 590,000 of them being Raiders fans, another 590,000 being Chargers fans and 490,000 being Cowboys fans. That leaves an astounding 1.99 million unaffiliated fans." These could potentially be 1.99 million future fans of the Los Angeles Stars. That's my name for the future team—the Stars. Don't laugh. It's perfect.

20. Teams need to have more patience with younger stars. In fact, everyone, including the media and fans, should have more patience with young stars. But I'm only dealing with the NFL's side of this. One thing that's happened is that owners—yes, owners—have been the root of the cause for impatience with younger players. Leigh Steinberg, once the most powerful agent in all of sports, wrote on this phenomenon recently for RantSports.com. While Steinberg correctly stated that there's always been pressure on young players and draft picks, things

are far different now. He stated five reasons.

   A. New owners have entered football. They have made their fortune in other businesses, where they were often under pressure from investors for instant returns and were therefore used to quick judgment. They often carry heavy debt service from the astronomical cost of buying a franchise and want to see a return.

   B. The exponential explosion of hundreds of television, radio, and Internet platforms for analysis and commentary on the NFL means that those shows thrive using drama and conflict. The public is treated to nonstop questioning of coach and player performance and speculation as to these figures' futures. Controversy sells.

   C. The huge salaries paid to coaches and players [encourage] expectation that there will be instant success. Higher compensation leads to expectation of perfection.

   D. Higher ticket and suite prices create less patience in fans for poor performance.

   E. A salary cap system was designed to create parity. It forces teams with the good judgment to assemble and coach a group of players to discard valuable veterans because of an inability to have too many highly compensated players grouped on one roster. This system is specifically designed to thwart dynasties. More rapid turnover is a side effect, and this undermines stability.

21. Have openly gay athletes speak to NFL locker rooms once a year. This would help to end some of the homophobia still rampant within NFL teams.

22. Make players sit for at least one game after a concussion,

no matter if they pass concussion protocol tests or not. These tests are not infallible, and while sitting one game isn't a perfect solution, it helps prevent players from circumventing the system post-concussion.

23. Eliminate kickoffs. I used to hate this idea because I love kickoffs. But this is the violent American in me. The truth is, kickoffs are concussion generators. Giants co-owner John Mara told reporters in 2012 the issue with kickoffs was "that the concussions come from everywhere—from the wedge, from the crossing blocks where a guy goes from one side of the field to another, from a full-speed collision between a return guy and a tackler." One general manager estimated to me that if kickoffs were eliminated, concussions would be reduced by one-third.

24. This suggestion from ESPN's Jeff Chadiha is brilliant: "It feels ironic to hold up boxing as a positive example, but bear with me. Boxers have to face a medical advisory board before they're allowed to step into a ring, and maybe the NFL should think about doing the same. In many ways, it would be a logical extension of the NFL sideline concussion exam, which already establishes a cognitive baseline for each player. The league might as well make that test an annual event for each player. It shouldn't just be administered when a player is wobbling to the sideline like a drunken sailor on leave. An approved medical board could re-administer that test every 12 months to check for noticeable changes. If a player's results were drastically declining, he could be required to sit a certain amount of games the following season—with full pay—until he's deemed ready to go. That would eliminate concerns about players hiding symptoms from coaches or losing their jobs because they're

injury risks. If the league is serious about helping players, it has to put its money where its mouth is."

25. Bring back male cheerleaders. This would make the whole cheerleading thing on the NFL level far less sexist. Or maybe just eliminate cheerleaders on the NFL level altogether.

12   FOOTBALL 2039

TIMOTHY RICHARDS ALWAYS WANTED TO PLAY FOOTBALL, EVEN when so many people in his life told him not to. He started playing tackle football at 18 years old, as early as the law would allow. He played in all of the NFL-sponsored flag football and touch leagues. He liked those leagues, but he had the same thought many other kids his age did: *football isn't football unless there's a collision.*

Timothy's mother hated the sport. She was a Yankees and Knicks fan and constantly reminded her son that basketball and baseball were the premier American sports. "All your friends play basketball," she'd say. "Why don't you?"

For years, while he grew up playing football, he heard so many people talk about the NFL's decline. How congressional intervention weakened it. About the deaths of dozens of players in their forties in the 2020s, which one sportswriter called "the NFL's great plague." He heard about the science that says football can destroy your mind before you turn 50. He saw insurance companies distance themselves from the sport. And since no one would insure them, high schools dropped football.

Lawsuits ended college football. There was also the NFL's forced admission (one similar to the one cigarette makers had to make) that the NFL had lied for decades about its knowledge that concussions caused serious and long-term brain damage.

To Timothy, football was his future. Yet to many in American society, football was toxic—a relic from the past, like fossil fuels. Its low television ratings seemed to prove that. But to players who loved the sport, nothing else mattered but their passion for the game.

Timothy remembers reading about how the NFL was once 32 teams. And it was the biggest thing in America. He was a quarterback, so posters on his walls were of the great Hall of Famers of old who were his favorite players: Aaron Rodgers, Russell Wilson, and Andrew Luck. That was then. These days, there were 12 teams in the NFL—and all he wanted was to be on one of them.

Which is what brought him to this moment. It was his 24th birthday, so legally—and finally—he could play in the NFL. The law required he take the football gene test, the F-test, as it was commonly called. He remembers reading the words on the box after he got the test in the mail. They seemed so…strange. So final. "This test will determine if you carry the gene that predisposes you to significant brain impairment if you receive blows to the head from playing a sport such as boxing or football. The test is highly accurate, and if you carry the F-gene, participating in contact sports could lead to dementia, Alzheimer's, or even suicidal thoughts." Timothy peed into the bottle, sealed it, put the container in the preaddressed package, and waited.

Five days later, he called a phone number from the instruction packet. He had the F-gene, but he didn't care. The money was too good. *And who knows*, he thought, *maybe the test was wrong*. As far as Timothy was concerned, he was going to be fine. Just fine.

At his kitchen table was his mother, father, and a recruiter for the Dallas Cowboys. He was the 10th recruiter to visit in the past three days, but was offering the sweetest deal, one of the highest they'd offered to a rookie in decades: three years at $100,000 a year with a $20,000 signing bonus. That money could change everything for Timothy's mom and dad. He could get them out of the apartment and into a house. What's more, the Cowboys had the best health care plan of any team. And he would see plenty of action at QB; the offense last season averaged 62 passes a game.

Playing in the NFL's minor league system, the league would pay for classes in finances and public relations. He would leave with the equivalent of an associate's degree and the Cowboys would pay partial tuition for him to finish a four-year degree if he wanted. But for the moment, that wasn't on his mind. He just wanted to play football.

Timothy felt a sense of urgency. No, it wasn't the robots. Timothy had heard about the damn robots and how they were no longer just cooking and cleaning or working in the sex trade. They were now playing sports, and some asshole in Massachusetts had started a robot league. No, it wasn't the robots. Timothy felt he needed to hurry because the NFL's clock was ticking. He wasn't sure how long the NFL was going to be around, and that ate at him. It scared him.

The recruiter stepped out of the house for a moment. Timothy and his parents stayed at the table. "I don't want you to do this," his mom said. She made sure, yet again, to regale Timothy with stories of football's dangers. How 10 years ago 75 of the world's top brain specialists at a press conference in New York declared that football reduces life spans. This was no longer a question; this was a scientific fact. In one of the documents, she highlighted the now infamous quote from Dr. Nesbitt Pike, the Harvard-educated neurologist, the same quote that led every newscast and piece of social media the day it was released: "Playing football will significantly shorten your life."

Timothy's father was less adamant, but also worried. He had played football 20 years ago as starting at linebacker for the Las Vegas Warriors. His memory was failing, and he sometimes screamed at Mom or retreated to his den for hours. He was just 42.

Despite it all, Timothy didn't care about the dangers. If he hit the incentives in the proposed deal, he could make millions. What would happen in 30 years—*if* it happened—wasn't of consequence to Timothy. The moment, today, was everything.

He invited the Cowboys recruiter back inside. "Where do I sign?" he asked him.

13 WHEN FOOTBALL RIGHTED A WRONG

ONE FALL NIGHT SOME 25 YEARS AGO, ART SHELL CLIMBED INTO bed. He was watching *Nightline* when the phone rang. It was Al Davis, owner of the Los Angeles Raiders. It was a call that would begin to change everything.

"I'm thinking about making a switch," Davis told Shell. "I'm thinking about making you head coach of the Raiders." Shell sat up in bed. His heart began beating rapidly. Mike Shanahan was the current head coach, and Shell the offensive line coach under him. Davis had caught Shell totally by surprise. So much went through Shell's mind, including the fact that, if he accepted, he would be the first black head coach in the modern era of the sport. Shell climbed out of bed.

"You understand the Raider way," Davis said. "You're a leader. You're smart. You work hard. Everyone respects you, so you're the perfect choice. Think about it and get some sleep." Then Davis hung up.

Shell had dreamed of being a head coach. Arguably the best

offensive tackle in history, he prepared like a coach anyway. During his playing days, he had impressive physical skills, but it was his studious nature and workaholism that led Davis to call him "coach" in passing. Then–head coach John Madden agreed, telling him he would make a great coach if that's what he wanted to be.

"How do I become a head coach in this league?" Shell had once asked Raiders head coach Tom Flores. On the surface, it was a crazy question. Not only were there no black head coaches in the NFL, but also there were almost no black assistant coaches. In 1980, nine years before Shell got that phone call, there were only 14 black assistants among 262 assistants. But Flores didn't blink. He told Shell to study and work hard. Shell already knew how to do both of those things. From that point on, Flores was among Shell's supporters in becoming a head coach.

Suddenly there he was, on the verge. An all-time Raider great who would become not just the head coach of the team he loved, but also the first black coach since Fritz Pollard headed the Akron Pros in the 1920s. That phone call from Davis would begin Shell's historic, brilliant odyssey, which in turn would open the door for many more African American head coaches to come. A legion of men owe so much to Shell, from Denny Green to Tony Dungy to Marvin Lewis to Herm Edwards to Mike Tomlin. In many ways, all of their careers trace back to Shell.

But the hire meant something else, too. Davis was a thorn in the league's side, but his hiring of Shell represented a time in the NFL when men of principle corrected wrongs with simple measures. Davis, for all of his faults, was one of those men.

The game today isn't as diverse as it should be, but it has grown considerably, and in many ways that growth can be traced directly to Shell. While the growth in African American coaches was excruciatingly slow, it has reached a point, where the color of a coach's skin, while not irrelevant, is almost so.

Not so long ago, black men who wanted to coach were often thought of the same way as the black men who wanted to quarterback. To some, they were regarded as intellectually inferior and incapable of producing the work ethic required to do the job. (To some degree this is the same bigotry black men breaking into the general manager ranks also faced.) I remember a story a black assistant coach once told me. He was interviewing for a head-coaching job when the owner asked him, "Is a black man ready to be a head coach in this league?" The candidate was stunned—especially since the question was asked several years after the Raiders had hired Shell as a head coach. Not that one needed to prove such a thing, but Shell had already answered that question.

A second assistant coach said a general manager asked him during an interview "if he believed in the teachings and principles of Malcolm X." The coach, admitting he was momentarily flummoxed, explained the civil rights leader had contributed positive and negative aspects to his life. "I disagree," the general manager said. The coach never received a second interview.

Davis wouldn't have cared if Shell wore Malcolm X T-shirts to practice. The owner only cared if Shell could do the job or not. And because of persistence from Shell and others, along with the efforts of the NFL, including former commissioner Paul Tagliabue, the number of black assistant coaches rose from a paltry 14 in 1980 to 199 in 2012, 32.6 percent of the total coaching staff. Two and a half decades ago, Shell was the only black head coach; now, after years of denied opportunities, there are five current African American head coaches in the league: Lovie Smith at Tampa Bay, Mike Tomlin at Pittsburgh, Jim Caldwell at Detroit, Todd Bowles with the Jets, and Marvin Lewis at Cincinnati. That isn't exponential progress, but it's progress all the same. Slow, deliberate progress. And much of the credit, again, goes to Shell.

Shell learned how to coach by listening and preparing. "I'd listen to Gene [Upshaw] answer the questions," Shell said in an interview with the *New York Times'* Thomas George in 1989. "He always said the right things and he was so good, so quotable...I paid close attention. I learned a lot that way about football, about life, by just listening."

He told *Sports Illustrated*'s Jill Lieber in 1989 what he learned from the various coaches he worked under. "John Madden taught me about the game of people," Shell said. "I learned that you have to understand each individual, when to push his buttons and when not to. From Tom Flores, I learned patience. He was a quiet, stoic leader. Mike Shanahan was one of the most organized people I ever met."

Shell was ready. Yes, so much went through Shell's mind after that phone call, but one thing that didn't was going back to bed. "I don't know how in the hell Al thought I was going back to sleep after that call," Shell said.

Shell went to the Raiders facility the morning after the call, and Davis made it official. "You understand the Raiders," Davis said. Shell's next stop was a press conference. It was packed. The story had become national news, but Shell remained calm and measured. He didn't, however, downplay the importance

of the moment. "It is an historic event. I understand the significance of it," he said at the time. "I'm proud of it, but I'm also a
Raider. I don't believe the color of my skin entered into this decision. I was chosen because Al Davis felt I was the right person
at the right time. The significance in this is I am now the head
coach of the Los Angeles Raiders. We're going to try and regain
the power, toughness, and explosiveness we had in the past."

"If this is an historic occasion," Davis said at the press conference, "it will really only be meaningful and historic if he is a
great success."

Davis told the *New York Times'* Dave Anderson in 1989, "I
wanted a Raider. When we went back to Oakland for an exhibi-
tion game two months ago, the one thing lacking was a link to
the past in our coaching leadership."

For his second order of business, Shell had to do something
uncomfortable. Shanahan's relationship with Davis had become toxic. By the end, Shanahan and Davis came to truly despise one another. After Shanahan's ouster, Shell called a staff
meeting, and in that meeting were assistants who were loyal to
Shanahan. "There may be some of you that don't want to be
here," Shell told the room. "My office will be open all the time.
If you want to talk, we can talk." Shell wasn't certain if any staff
members would quit out of loyalty to Shanahan. None did. It
was a testament to the respect Shell had earned in his decades as
a player and assistant coach.

Monday night came, and hours before the game Shell sat in
his hotel room. He thought about everything, but mostly his
thoughts focused on the football game. Then he smiled. "Al
wanted this history to be made on *Monday Night Football*,"
Shell said in 2014, as part of an extensive interview on the

anniversary of his hiring, the only such interview Shell has done. "He wanted the extravaganza. He wanted that big stage."

The Raiders were in last place in the AFC West, and their opponent, the New York Jets, were last in their division. The game was scoreless in the first half, and Shell knew what was wrong. The players were tight because they wanted to win the game for him. His halftime speech to the players addressed the problem directly. "I want to win this game, too," Shell told the team, "but not for me. I want to win for the Raiders. So relax and play smart."

They did. A 73-yard touchdown pass put the Raiders on the board, and with the score tied in the fourth quarter, the Raiders intercepted Jets quarterback Ken O'Brien for an 87-yard pick six. Shell had implored the Raiders to play the game for themselves, but what they ended up doing was winning it for him after all. They beat the Jets 14–7, and that game went down in history. It was a desperately needed win, but everyone knew it was more than that.

The locker room afterward was electric. Every player hugged Shell. He remembers one of the biggest congratulations coming from Raiders defensive lineman Howie Long, now an NFL analyst on FOX, who would later join Shell in the Pro Football Hall of Fame. And throughout the rest of the season, Shell would be congratulated by opposing players and staff on his achievement. The Raiders that year went 7–5 under Shell, finishing 8–8 overall and narrowly missing the playoffs by a single game. The next year, they went 12–4 and reached the AFC title game.

Shell wasn't the only one making history. One year earlier, at the beginning of the 1988 season, Johnny Grier had become the NFL's first black referee. Shell remembers speaking to Grier a couple weeks after he was hired as head coach. Shell had recently received some hate mail, and he relayed the contents of one letter in particular to the ref: "You and your n——r referee," the letter read, "cheated the Jets out of a win."

Shell told Grier, "You know you're my n——r referee, don't you?"

Grier and Shell both chuckled. It was their way of mocking the hatred.

To understand how Shell became a part of history, you have to understand the man who made the decision. For all of his quirks and faults, Davis was a pioneer, far ahead of his time. The things Davis did to diversify the Raiders may never be equaled. When Davis coached the Raiders, then a part of the AFL, he made a statement against segregation when his team was scheduled to play a game in Mobile, Alabama. Davis pulled his team from the contest to protest Alabama's segregation laws. He also got the American Football League's All-Star Game moved from New Orleans to Houston because of the former city's segregation laws. He was also one of the first to sign players from historically black colleges to pro contracts. One of those men was Shell, whom Davis signed out of Maryland State College (now called University of Maryland Eastern Shore).

Decades later, as Raiders owner, his hiring of Shell and others demonstrated Davis' beliefs in balancing winning with equal opportunity. He'd also hire Tom Flores, the first Latino coach to win a Super Bowl, and Amy Trask, the first female chief executive to run Raiders business operations. Shell was an excellent coach, Flores won two Super Bowls, and Trask is a Hall of Fame candidate.

"Al hired Art for all the right reasons—he hired Art as he

always hired: without regard to race, ethnicity, religion, or gender," Trask wrote in an e-mail to me. "Al did this well before anyone else—and to a greater extent than any others do to date."

This is one of the most salient points of the Shell story. The NFL could learn a lot by looking back at Al Davis. Today, so much of the communication between all sides—players, coaches, and ownership—is so strained that the league is taking steps backward on the issue of equal opportunity. Like almost every other aspect of NFL life, that lack of communication and trust is its Achilles' heel.

I've known Shell for decades, and there are few men, in any walk of life, who are smarter and more decent. But Shell's most defining quality, calmness, is what made him the perfect pioneer. Some criticized Shell for it, saying he was too distant, but they didn't understand. As a player, Shell always believed that you played smarter when you were under control. As a coach, he felt the same way. It was more than that, though. Shell knew full well that everyone was watching. He wasn't just coaching for himself or the Raiders; he was coaching for black men who would follow.

A white coach could be boisterous or scream or leave tickets for Elvis the way Jerry Glanville did. Or he could get cocky with the press like Bill Parcells. However, the double standards of race meant Shell had to constantly be uber-professional. Still, this wasn't a problem for him, because that's who he was.

Shell had two coaching stints with the Raiders. His second lasted a single season, but it's that first one, the historic one, when Shell made his mark. Shell coached the team in that first stint for six years, going 54–38. To this day, that stretch is one of the most successful in Raiders history. Davis fired Shell after the 1994 season, something Davis would later say he regretted. After the Raiders came NFL assistant coaching jobs, but then Shell went to New York City to work for the league office, first in the office of college relations and then in the appeals office, handling player discipline. He then served as the NFL's senior vice president of football operations and development beginning in 2004.

And now? "I'm totally retired," Shell said.

Yet his legacy endures. Twenty-five years ago, a forward-thinking owner gave Shell a unique opportunity, and his performance proved Davis right—while simultaneously making history. "Fairly early in my career, and after Art was named head coach, we were at a league owners meeting," Trask remembered. "One night while there, the Raiders contingent went to dinner, and as I listened to Art share stories, reflections, and anecdotes from his career, I understood that not only was Art a giant of a man on the field, but off the field as well. Art exemplifies the best of not only the Raiders, but the National Football League."

The NFL wasn't as wealthy or powerful or watched then. It had its flaws, but it was better despite those flaws because men like Shell were a part of it. Today's NFL needs more people like him to guarantee its survival.

14   THE LAST WORD

WHERE I COULD BE WRONG

One of my favorite people in the world is Greg Aiello, the NFL's top PR man. He's funny, creative, and smart. He is also one of the key people who will handle one of the most important parts of the NFL's future: its image.

This is where I could be wrong—if the NFL, using people like Aiello, learns from its mistakes. One of the issues with the sport in recent years is it has not done that. Instead, it has made mistakes of arrogance repeatedly. Where the NFL could prove me totally wrong is if it tones down that arrogance. If it takes better care of fans by not bleeding them for every penny. If it restricts how much football is on television, preventing saturation. If it doesn't bully people. If it continues to genuinely care about domestic violence. If it does everything in its power to handle the concussion and CTE crisis. Of course, those are all big *ifs*.

The last point, about CTE, remains an important one—and we are seeing progress where it comes to lowering the incidence of concussions. According to the NFL, concussions were down 25 percent in the 2014 regular season from 2013 and 36 percent compared to 2012. Further, concussions due to helmet-to-helmet hits were down 28 percent in 2014 from the previous year. What this tells us is that the NFL's rules that now punish players harshly for tackling helmet-to-helmet are working. This makes the game safer, no question, but still doesn't account for the growing science that playing football and enduing even minor hits that don't cause concussions can lead to permanent brain damage. This fact remains one of football's greatest foes.

One day after the NFL released those statistics, Arizona defensive lineman Darnell Dockett wrote an opinion piece for *Sports Illustrated*. The key passage of the article, which attacked the media for focusing on Marshawn Lynch's reticence with the press instead of real issues, read:

> I met Moose Johnston once. His knuckles and fingers are twisted and jagged. Tony Siragusa hurts all over his body. Junior Seau killed himself. But the NFL says concussions are down 25 percent and you don't even blink. You want to know when the next Lynch press conference is going down. You're not asking the question many of us players are: Why aren't our contracts guaranteed? And I'm not talking about every contract. I'm talking about established veterans on their second and third deal getting fully compensated on those big contracts that make headlines but never actually get fulfilled...
>
> We go out there...with bad knees and shoulders and headaches. Because we know if we don't play hurt and injured, we'll be released just the same. I look at guys like Richard Sherman and Earl Thomas,

laying it on the line in this Super Bowl with their elbow and shoulder injuries. In three months everybody will forget what they did and assume those injuries are 100 percent fine, but there is no such thing as 100 percent [health] in the NFL. You play with a bad shoulder, you retire with a bad shoulder and you die with a bad shoulder. Same goes for brains.

Overall, if the NFL tried for a more human touch in all of its dealings, it could transform its current image, which is nestled somewhere between a Wall Street crook and ISIS member.

Indeed, a problem the league continues to face is perception. Originally, Ray Rice was suspended for two games for knocking out his then-fiancée. Prior to the Packers and Seahawks NFC title game in 2015, Glazer reported that the NFL initially threatened to eject Marshawn Lynch if Lynch wore his spiffy new gold cleats. (The cleats were a uniform violation.) The NFL later softened its stance, saying he would be removed from play until he removed the cleats, if he wore them. Lynch backed down and never sported them. Perhaps Lynch wore a gold jock strap instead.

Lynch faced a one-game suspension for wearing gold cleats. And the NFL originally gave a domestic abuser a *two*-game suspension. This is where things get interesting for the NFL. Now, I get why the NFL has a uniform code. If the league didn't have one, some player would go beyond gold cleats, maybe wear something more offensive. Still the optics of a two-game suspension for violence against women and a one-game suspension for unauthorized cleats presents a huge problem for the NFL. Something has to change.

In January 2015, something happened that demonstrated a massive change in the NFL's approach to domestic violence. Indianapolis backup player Josh McNary was accused of rape. He was placed on the NFL's version of paid leave—a new initiative under Goodell. The fairness of removing a player from his employment based on an accusation is an interesting test of one of the core principles of our democracy, which is that a person is innocent until proven guilty. The move was historic, the first such one under the new policy, and one the NFL had never done before. It demonstrated for the first time, at least in the decades I've been covering the sport, that the NFL takes domestic violence accusations seriously. Would the NFL place a star on paid leave after similar accusations? I believe the league now would, and that's one of the extremely new changes in attitude. These are the kinds of changes in the right direction that could prevent an NFL recession.

The NFL also adapted in one important way. It took its time during the Deflatriots scandal, investigated thoroughly, and didn't rush to judgment. That is also a new thing for the NFL.

My main point is that all of the ugliness the NFL has faced, should it continue, will eventually act as a counteragent to its popularity. The league will continue to face some of these issues, but if it changes how it handles them in the future? Well, I'll be dead wrong.

There is also another simple reason why I might be wrong, and it lies in fans, not the league. The NFL satisfies a primal need among many humans. It provides a conduit for tribalism; allows us to watch gladiators destroy one another, giving us an opportunity to exorcise our violence vicariously; and provides us a superficial guiltlessness because those gladiators are paid so handsomely. It also allows people to get publicly and legally smashed on alcohol. For some, football allows people to be their alternate-universe, debauched selves.

Other sports do not satisfy these urges in the same way. Baseball does not. Basketball does not. Mixed martial arts does, to some degree, but it has so far demonstrated no momentum to overtake the NFL. This is all good news for football. No other sport has come close to challenging it in decades.

Football could also be helped by the next generation of televisions. Their resolution is supposed to be unbelievable—far superior to HD. We'd get to see our violent sport even more clearly. (This would be good for the NFL in terms of television viewership, which would obviously be fantastic for football, but I know league executives who worry that next-gen TVs will lead to decreased stadium attendance.)

One last point. The players are key, obviously. There are many good ones, like J.J. Watt or Larry Fitzgerald, to name just two. These men do incredible deeds outside of the NFL. But in fact there are legions of good men in football. They could turn the image of football around if somehow they can control some of the bad guys in the league.

There was a moment during NFL Honors in 2015 that really hit home. Carolina Panthers linebacker Thomas Davis was named the league's Walter Payton Man of the Year in recognition of his outstanding humanitarian efforts. His speech brought many to tears. "To the guys in this league, I just want to say to you, let's take charge," he said. "Dare to be different. We are a village. Let's step up and be a village of guys that make a difference. Let's change this world. We're well compensated for what we do. Let's show these kids how much we care about them. Let's give the media something positive to talk about instead of bashing our league."

WHERE I COULD BE RIGHT

If the NFL and its players don't change a damn thing, then football doesn't stand a chance.

Just days after Davis' excellent speech, an NFL player was arrested for allegedly punching a pizza deliveryman in an argument over a parking space. Another was arrested with $200,000 in cash, some weed, and a firearm in his possession. Another was arrested for marijuana possession after police were called to a hotel room following a domestic violence complaint (the player's second arrest in four months). Three arrests, just two days into the off-season.

But the ugliness didn't end there. The Browns were facing penalties over allegations that members of Cleveland management had been texting coaches on the sideline during game play, which is not just a violation of decorum—management should never, ever tell coaches what plays to call—but also expressly against league rules. Cleveland wide receiver Josh Gordon was also banned for at least one year after numerous violations of the NFL's substance abuse policy. Then there were the Atlanta Falcons, who were being investigated for pumping fake crowd noise into their stadium. And Deflategate dragged on.

Assault. Firearm possession. Systemized cheating. Domestic violations accusations (again). Animal cruelty. Failed drug tests. And in one of the most bizarre black eyes to the league, it was announced several days after the Super Bowl that Seattle receiver Doug Baldwin was fined $11,025 for his obscene gesture during the game. He simulated taking a poop.

It seems few in football learned any lessons from what was indeed the worst year in NFL history—and this in itself is one of the biggest problems the league faces.

Nothing exemplified this lack of perspective more than when the Buffalo Bills signed renowned awesome American Richie Incognito in 2015. Icognito, of course, was at the center of one of the great scandals in league history, the Bullygate scandal of the Miami Dolphins. Need more proof that Incognito is one of the NFL's truly bad bad guys? According to a police report and numerous media reports, Incognito allegedly sexually harassed a 34-year-old African American woman who was volunteering at a golf tournament in 2012. The woman told police Incognito touched her genitals with a golf club and emptied bottles of water in her face. He settled the case out of court, paying her $30,000.

It wasn't just crimes or rules infractions that were a problem. Take this case of NFL hypocrisy. Toward the end of the 2014 season the NFL fined Seattle running back Marshawn Lynch $20,000 for grabbing his crotch during the NFC Championship Game. Then, prior to the Super Bowl, the NFL threatened to fine Lynch if he grabbed his junk during the upcoming game. It seemed like a principled stance of a corporation looking to improve its image. But then the NFL, just days after threatening Lynch with an illegal junk-grabbing fine, sold a collection of Seahawks photographs from the NFC title game. One of the pictures was, yes, Lynch grabbing his crotch. So the same league that fined Lynch for his obscene gesture profited from the act not once but twice—an act they forbade! The price of the Seahawks collage with Lynch's clutched crotch?: $149.95. The NFL would later state publicly that it was a mistake to sell the item.

There was one other significant piece of news during the NFL off-season. While not directly NFL-related, it was big. A Wisconsin mother sued Pop Warner youth football—and the organization's insurer—claiming her 25-year-old son hanged himself because of mental health issues sustained from playing youth football. "Tackle football with helmets is a war game. It is not only a 'contact' sport, it is a 'combat' sport," the complaint read. "Joseph Chernach's suicide was the natural and probable consequence of the injuries he suffered playing Pop Warner football." The lawsuit claimed Chernach suffered from CTE and post-concussion syndrome. Whether or not the lawsuit will be successful is one thing, but the fact Pop Warner was being sued over CTE is one of the NFL's worst nightmares, particularly from an image standpoint. The idea that mothers might see football as a CTE generator is potentially devastating.

Journalist Gene Collier in a story called "Football's Concussion Issue Won't Just Go Away" in the *Pittsburgh Post-Gazette* hit on one of the pivotal issues: "the potential implications of the Chernach case probably can't be overstated. If the broad structure of youth football, which has already seen a 7 to 10 percent decline in participation over the past five years, is going to be held liable for the unpredictable results of brain injuries, the sport could begin to atrophy from the bottom up."

The other damage the NFL needs to fix is the level of distrust between the players and the league office. The union and Goodell despise one another. From the players' side, I've been told this many dozens of times, actually, from their wives. By my own policy, I never write what the wives say; I stay away from covering families. Yet the wives constantly complain about how the NFL treats their husbands, particularly when it comes to injuries.

This leads to the story about Miko Grimes, wife of Miami Dolphins Pro Bowl player Brent Grimes. Miko went on an epic Twitter rant in January 2015 about her husband's treatment during the Pro Bowl. The rant is run here in its entirety because it shows how some wives, in particular, feel about the NFL but rarely say publicly.

Miko Grimes @iHeartMiko
Twitter rant directed at @nfl in 5.. 4.. 3.. 2.. 1
2:29 PM - 26 Jan 2015

Miko Grimes @iHeartMiko
For those of u that dont know, i had emergency oral surgery on Thursday. My husband was concerned for me, so he asked coach Garrett if he
2:34 PM - 26 Jan 2015

Miko Grimes @iHeartMiko
could miss practice to be there for me bcuz i was stressed and in a lot of pain. Coach Garrett and an NFL exec excused him from practice
2:35 PM - 26 Jan 2015

Miko Grimes @iHeartMiko
to be there for me. Well... Apparently, the right hand of the @nfl didnt tell the left hand he wouldnt be there that day, so they yanked
2:36 PM - 26 Jan 2015

Miko Grimes @iHeartMiko
his paid appearances & are not happy with him.

What kind of message does that send to the players?
Do they think they are above family?
2:37 PM - 26 Jan 2015

Miko Grimes @iHeartMiko
WTF was he supposed to do? Stay at a PRO BOWL
practice while his wife is in pain that equates child
birth? Was him missing a fan autograph
2:39 PM - 26 Jan 2015

Miko Grimes @iHeartMiko
session worthy of shitting on him @nfl? Havent u
guys shit on him enough? Him missing practice
made u guys take the MVP from him?
2:40 PM - 26 Jan 2015

Miko Grimes @iHeartMiko
There is NO REASON ALL ALL why Brent
Grimes shouldnt have been MVP of the defense!!!
NONE!!!! Do u hear me??????
2:43 PM - 26 Jan 2015

Miko Grimes @iHeartMiko
I have friends that were beaten, thrown down stairs
WHILE PREGNANT, guys arrested, & @nfl sus-
pended them 1 FUCKING GAME! Now yall care?
FOH
2:47 PM - 26 Jan 2015

Miko Grimes @iHeartMiko
Im contemplating naming SEVERAL players that
the @nfl violated the concussion rules with players

but that would take down ppl i care about.
2:52 PM - 26 Jan 2015

Miko Grimes @iHeartMiko
My food was just served but fuck that im preaching
right now! It can wait!!
2:57 PM - 26 Jan 2015

Miko Grimes @iHeartMiko
Do u know most injuries early in the season are bcuz
training camp is TOO FUCKING MUCII ON
THE BODY, U IDIOTS? @nfl But yall care huh?
GTFOH!
3:02 PM - 26 Jan 2015

Miko Grimes @iHeartMiko
Brent signed a 4yr 32M contract with 16M guaranteed. U better beleve he wont see that other 16M!
They can opt out after the guaranteed.
3:06 PM - 26 Jan 2015

Miko Grimes @iHeartMiko
See how @nfl set that shit up? But if u wanna leave
after ur deal is up, they can tag u, TWICE!!! To make
u stay! That shit is comedy!
3:07 PM - 26 Jan 2015

Miko Grimes @iHeartMiko
Keep fuking my husband over and im gonna put a
map out to the world and expose this league for what
it truly is! @nfl #TryItBitch
3:10 PM - 26 Jan 2015

Miko Grimes @iHeartMiko
#DropsMic
3:11 PM - 26 Jan 2015

Grimes hit on a key issue during her rant: the perception of the NFL among women. A poll from Public Policy Polling in January 2015 found that 55 percent of women surveyed do not approve of how the NFL handles domestic abuse issues and 67 percent believe the NFL should do more to prevent players and others in the sport from assaulting women. This is important because while the NFL has a significant number of women fans, some analysts believe the NFL could lose them should their domestic violence issues continue. Or, at the very least, the league won't be able to make further gains among that segment of the population. "Conventional wisdom suggests that every man who could be a football fan already is," *Business Insider* reported in September. "The NFL has squeezed everything it can from that segment of the population. There's still potential to convert more women into full-time fans, and that's where the league's revenue growth must come from."

I keep emphasizing this but it's important: the league has to humanize the NFL. So far that isn't happening. "Unless there is a radical shift in management and tone," wrote Sally Jenkins for the *Washington Post*, "20 years from now NFL owners are going to find themselves presiding over a league that is not only less popular but that actively repulses people."

"We have grown to love the NFL up to this point because—amid natural complications and foibles—it can show humanity at its strongest, highest and fastest and with its highest pain threshold," Jenkins added. "But when the game and the people who run it start showing humanity at its very worst—reckless disregard for others, prioritizing profit over people—then the audience begins to ask, 'Is watching this game making us feel better or worse?' And the answer is getting murkier all the time. The NFL is beginning to make its audience feel guilty and uneasy."

Maybe the most vicious of the many obstacles the league faces are the optics of the men living their lives after a career in football. The hobbled men, the men who can't remember, the men who cannot use their minds. Men like Hall of Famer Tony Dorsett. Dorsett is struggling with severe brain trauma. In 2015 he told radio station 1310 The Ticket: "I'm in a battle, obviously. I got diagnosed with CTE, and it's very frustrating at times for me. I've got a good team of people around me: my wife and kids, who work with me. When you've been in this town for so long and I have to go to some place I've been going to for many, many, many years, and then all of a sudden I forget how to get there. Those things are frustrating when it comes to those things. I understand that I'm combating it, trying to get better. But, you know, some days are good. Some days are bad.

"I signed up for this when, I guess, I started playing football so many years ago, but, obviously, not knowing that the end was going to be like this. But I love the game. The game was good to me. It's just unfortunate that I'm going through what I'm going through. I'm in the fight, man. I'm not just laying around letting this overtake me. I'm fighting. I'm in the battle. I'm hoping we can reverse this thing somehow."

There are others, too. Men like the ones who played on one of the greatest teams of all: the 1985 Chicago Bears. That team was one of the hardest hitting—and violent—the NFL has ever seen. But since then, as a January 2015 HBO Sports story detailed, many of those Bears players have become debilitated. Jim McMahon, the quarterback from that team, has early onset dementia and struggles to complete even simple tasks around his home. Richard Dent, a defensive lineman, says readily available painkillers turned him into "damaged goods." Dave Duerson, a safety on that team, took his own life. Twenty-three players from the team, about half of the roster, have sued the NFL saying football destroyed them.

"When I first heard about these guys killing themselves, I couldn't figure out how they could do that," McMahon told HBO. "But I was having those thoughts myself, feelings of inadequacy, and just like 'you're a dumbass.' Once the pain starts getting that bad, you figure you'll take the only way out. If I would've had a gun, I probably wouldn't be here."

These stories are brutal, and they are the NFL's worst nightmare. One of the more head-shaking quotes came actually from the head coach of that team, Mike Ditka. Ditka is in the Hall of Fame, and in many ways he is one of the symbols of the brutality of the sport. His nickname, after all, is Iron Mike. So when Ditka said if he had a young son he would not allow him to play football, it was nothing less than a staggering moment in the sport's history. Maybe in some ways Ditka saying it is more of a problem for the NFL than President Obama saying it.

"If you had an eight-year-old kid now, would you tell him you want him to play football?" Ditka asked interviewer Bryant Gumbel. Gumbel answered he would not. Then, he asked the same question of Ditka. Ditka shook his head no. "Nope, and that's sad," Ditka said. "I wouldn't. My whole life was football. I think the risk is worse than the reward. I really do."

In yet another example of how football's troubles have leapt with great rapidity and ferocity outside of the sports universe and into everyday American culture, comedians Bill Maher and Mel Brooks discussed the Bears story on the show *Real Time With Bill Maher*. Brooks offered this humorous (and interesting) bit about football: "I think from [ages] five to ten… no football. From 10 to 15…touch. Touch. No tackling and no helmets. Just touch football. After 15…no football."

Then Maher said something that is not uncommon among fans, something that remains problematic for the sport that boasts massive Super Bowl ratings and seemingly unending popularity. "I love football," Maher said, "but it's kind of like, I feel like I'm watching a Bill Cosby show at this point. I don't know if I really want to patronize this anymore. There's something really icky about it."

15 THE LAST, LAST WORD

THERE WAS A FASCINATING DOCUMENT RELEASED TO A SMALL number of media members in the winter of 2015 by a former NFL player named Sean Gilbert. Gilbert had been a talented player in the NFL for more than a decade. In 2015 he challenged incumbent union leader DeMaurice Smith. The document was effectively Gilbert's résumé, but it was much more. It was a look at the struggles of a highly prosperous sport from a player's perspective. Gilbert represented a certain faction of players who, despite the massive wealth the league was earning, felt a degree of nervousness about its future. And his letter tapped into that. It was certainly self-serving and semipropaganda, but I can tell you more than a few NFL players agreed with everything he wrote:

> My passion is for every current NFL Player to be successful both on the field and in transitioning to his life after football. Any CEO or similar business executive will tell you that experience is just as valuable as a degree. Industry knowledge and work ethic usually trump

anything that can be learned in a classroom. While the classroom can provide a foundation for success, an individual can only get there with determination, life experience and discipline. I understand what happens on and off the field. I understand how the game challenges every Player both physically and mentally. I understand the business of the game. I know what players go through and the objectives of the owners.

I have more than 25 years of education and experience in football. The NFLPA already acknowledges in its agent bylaws that every credited season of playing in the NFL is equivalent to one year of negotiating experience toward becoming an agent. I played 11 years in the NFL and have counseled players ever since. I have spent more than two years preparing to be the Executive Director of the NFL Players Association. I started this process by writing a book about our business. It's a concise look at how we were beaten in the last negotiation with the owners in 2011. We have already seen a shift of $2.5 Billion from the Players to the Owners in the first four years of that deal and it will grow to $10 Billion by the time this 10-year deal expires.

We have a $10 Billion problem from the 2011 CBA. I believe it can be attributed to DeMaurice Smith's lack of institutional football knowledge. Smith is a lawyer. He is a litigator, not a businessman. He has no background in football. Gene Upshaw was not a lawyer. He was a former Player. During Upshaw's time leading the union, the salary cap increased every year. When the NFLPA hired a litigator with no institutional football knowledge, the cap went down for three straight years. Since Smith took over, Owners didn't just roll back the cap. They slashed it.

How? In addition to Smith's inexperience, NFL Commissioner Roger Goodell is an expert in the business of football. He's not a lawyer. He doesn't have a post-graduate degree. Instead, he has 30 years of education and experience in the NFL. The ONLY place he has ever worked is in the NFL. He possesses institutional football knowledge. His expertise in the industry showed in the 2011 CBA negotiations. In 2006, the NFL hired Goodell over some of the top business executives and lawyers in the country. The league hired one of its own. The results are evident. The NFLPA needs to do the same.

Let me give you a little story about another person in the NFL who has found success without a formal education: He was a student at Washington State University in 1974. He dropped out as a sophomore to get a job and follow his passion. He later convinced a good friend of his to also drop out so that they could start a company.

More than 40 years later, I don't think anybody will question the resume of Paul Allen, co-founder of Microsoft, owner of the Seahawks and the richest owner in the NFL worth $17 Billion. And his friend Bill Gates hasn't done too badly, either. Neither of them have a college degree. Like them, I left school to chase my passion.

Football has taught me that in order to win you need a strong team. I take pride in cultivating good relationships with strong people. I have learned the value of surrounding myself with a team of exceptional football experts. My team already has more than 150 years of experience in the NFL. We are prepared and equipped to effect positive change for our players. In the same [vein], President Ronald Reagan put a great team around him and was considered one of the greatest leaders in the history of our country.

Before Reagan entered politics, he was an actor who once played a famous football player.

I was a football player.

As I wrote in my book: "The bottom line is that after you strip away all the legalese and strategy, I feel our union needs a new leader. Yes, we need great lawyers, accountants and other business people to guide us. But we also need to develop leadership from within our ranks, finding someone who completely understands the game, both on and off the field...I have been in the game and the business of football my entire life.

———

ONE DAY, BECAUSE OF THE TOLL FOOTBALL TAKES ON THE HUMAN body, perhaps not so far in the future, robots will play football.

That is the premise of a science fiction book called *Ultra Bowl*. In the book, published in 2014, the concern over football violence combined with technological innovation leads to a future

100 years from now in which the violence of football is out-sourced to robots. Go ahead and laugh. They laughed at Galileo, too. (Actually, they imprisoned him, but you get the point.)

"Robot football became the perfect vehicle for Corporate America's relentless drive to sell and profit," the author, I.J. Weinstock, explained in one interview. "Where once the Super Bowl was the most prized, viewed and expensive ad space, an actual game of robots, showcasing the latest technology while competing in a world championship, would become one big ad. The game's point-spread would determine tech supremacy, stock price and ultimately market share. It would be called the Ultra Bowl because if a nation stumbled, stocks tumbled and economies crumbled.

"The financial interests of Wall Street will combine with the political support of a growing segment of Main Street for whom football is too violent, to make robot football not only plausible, but probable," Weinstock said. "Science fiction writ-ers try to imagine what tomorrow might look like, and they've often been right. Credit cards, radar, solar power, voice mail, flat-screen TVs, virtual reality, even atomic bombs were all first imagined by science fiction authors."

I'm not laughing.

ADDENDUM

MAY 2015

The same owner at the beginning of this book, talking about how the league could be Rome, was now talking about a civil war.

"My fear is that Deflategate will tear ownership apart," the owner explained. "I'm greatly concerned about that."

The reality is the NFL was never going to totally fracture. There is too much money to be made. Yet Deflategate was one of several forces (just from 2015 alone) that demonstrated despite the great wealth and power of football, it's also quite vulnerable. More vulnerable than perhaps people think or the league wants to believe. Scandal fatigue isn't as draining as fans not going to games or television money drying up, but it's close. It took a series of scandals—boxers applying plaster to their hand wraps, bribes, PEDs, Mike Tyson biting an ear, Mike Tyson serving time in prison for rape—to wreck boxing's popularity. Drug scandals in the 1970s led to NBA weekday championship games being shown on tape delay at 11:30 at night. The steroid era in baseball severely injured the popularity of the sport. It's not a leap to say that Tiger Woods stepping out on his wife was as problematic for him as his bad golf.

Scandal fatigue isn't a palpable metric, yet it's an important one. Lawyer Ted Wells' report on Deflategate wasn't perfect, but it was thorough and believable. The NFL used it as a vehicle to suspended Tom Brady four games, dock the Patriots draft picks (including a first rounder), and fine the organization $1 million (pocket change). Fans and some media decried the ruling as draconian. The *Boston Herald* responded with the tried and true homer-trolling column: you hate us because you can't be us and eviscerated other cities, all in order to defend Brady.

In a column called "National State of Envy," columnist Tom Shattuck wrote in part:

> Sorry, losers. The fact is that everything about Brady is awesome.
>
> Even his adopted hometown is cooler than yours. And that bothers you.
>
> Boston has never looked better—never been better, and that only serves to fuel the irrational, national hate for Brady even further.
>
> New York City is badly in need of Febreze, and its clown mayor has solidified himself as national donkey.
>
> Philadelphia is home to the worst fans in sports and has nothing to offer the many visitors who don't have the heart to tell them that their cheesesteaks are synthetic rubbish.
>
> Baltimore…well…Baltimore is Baltimore. Enough said.

Ditto Detroit.

Indianapolis has relegated itself to the home of The Tattletale. It has an airport and a convention center. Maybe they can have the tattletale convention there. "Trust no one."

These are just a few of the hater hot spots.

What the NFL was truly trying to beat back with its Deflategate ruling was the erosion of believability. PEDs destroyed baseball's believability. Drugs the NBAs. On it goes. Believability is the currency a sports empire must have. It's the lifeblood of a league. Any league without it is doomed.

The punishment of Brady was an attempt to fortify the NFL's believability after a brutal year in which the NFL's credibility took massive hits. No, there will be no civil war in football. But there is vulnerability. It is there.

ACKNOWLEDGMENTS

IN THE SPRING OF 2015, THE FORMER GREEN BAY PACKERS EXECU-
tive, and current analyst, Andrew Brandt, wrote about NFL
arrogance. Again, as I've stated, it remains the league's biggest
future opponent. Brandt touched on this in his writing on the
MMQB.com site.

He wrote of how *New York Times* writer David Brooks
told the owners at their meetings in Arizona that despite their
power, and the success of the NFL, they were still failing because of arrogance.

Wrote Brandt: "Brooks' message was for these titans of the
football industry to be more contrite, more respectful and to
stay humble. That may be their most difficult—and most important—task ahead.

"The NFL can be an intoxicating workplace. Just as constant
praising can affect players' egos and attitudes, it does the same
with owners and executives. I have seen it firsthand, with some
NFL owners and executives needing to get over themselves. I
was, at times, one of them: I had to check myself a few times
with the Packers and wondered about the type of person I was
becoming. I know I am a better person out of that environment.

"I have suggested that Roger Goodell sometimes let down his guarded and unrevealing posture to show a more human and vulnerable side. I would say the same about others at high levels of the NFL hierarchy. That will go a long way with a public they claim to care so much about."

One thing I had hoped to do was not be arrogant and make totally declarative statements. I've made an impassioned case here, but I also know I could be wrong.

I first want to thank Triumph for believing in this book, specifically Michelle Bruton, who is brilliant. Thank you also to my terrific editor, Jesse Jordan. I also want to thank my researcher Jennifer O'Neill. And everyone at Bleacher Report simply for being cool-ass people.

SOURCES

Adler, Lindsey. "Here's How Sony Plans To Fight The NFL On Its Upcoming Concussion Film." BuzzFeed. 11 Dec. 2014. Web. <http://www.buzzfeed.com/lindseyadler/sony-leak-nfl-concussion-movie-1418334/396#.bszyMQlP3Z>.

"An Indian Hunt." Atchison Daily Champion 9 Oct. 1885. Web. <http://indiancountrytodaymedianetwork.com/2015/01/26/seeking-250-reward-settlers-hunted-redskin-scalps-during-extermination-effort-158865>.

Anderson, Dave. "The Silver And Black Head Coach." The New York Times. The New York Times, 5 Oct. 1989. Web. <http://www.nytimes.com/1989/10/05/sports/sports-of-the-times-the-silver-and-black-head-coach.html>.

"Another Death Knell for the Middle Class." Rochester Homepage. CBS, 22 Oct. 2014. Web. <http://www.rochesterhomepage.net/story/d/story/another-death-knell-for-the-middle-class/24724/r53BD595rkCGOuWy2_UvGQ>.

Badenhausen, Kurt, Michael Ozanian, and Christina Settimi. "The Business Of Football." Forbes. Forbes Magazine, 20 Aug. 2014. Web. <http://www.forbes.com/nfl-valuations/>.

"Ban on Football by Trinity School; Boys, Grieving at Death in Their Match on Friday..." The New York Times 21 Nov. 1909. Print.

Banks, Paul. "Troy Aikman Says Tom Brady Was Complicit in 'Ballghazi' The Sports Bank. 21 Jan. 2015. Web. <http://www.thesportsbank.net/new-england-patriots-2/troy-aikman-tom-brady-ballghazi/>.

Bell, Jarrett. "Sen. John McCain Joins Critics of Roger Goodell." *USA Today*. 25 Jan. 2015. Web. <http://www.usatoday.com/story/sports/nfl/columnist/bell/2015/01/25/john-mccain-rips-roger-goodell-handling-of-controversies/22327257/>.

Belson, Ken. "Brain Trauma to Affect One in Three Players, N.F.L. Agrees." The *New York Times*. The *New York Times*, 12 Sept. 2014. Web. <http://www.nytimes.com/2014/09/13/sports/football/actuarial-reports-in-nfl-concussion-deal-are-released.html>.

Belson, Ken. "Goodell's Pay of $44.2 Million in 2012 Puts Him in the Big Leagues." The *New York Times*. The *New York Times*, 14 Feb. 2014. Web. <http://www.nytimes.com/2014/02/15/sports/football/goodell-nfl-commissioner-earned-44-2-million-in-2012.html>.

Bensinger, Graham. "Brett Favre after Final Concussion: I Never Looked Back." Yahoo Sports. 16 Jan. 2015. Web. <http://sports.yahoo.com/video/brett-favre-final-concussion-never-110000170.html>.

Bensinger, Graham. "Brett Favre: It Was Not My Job to Mentor Aaron Rodgers." Yahoo Sports. 27 Jan. 2015. Web. <http://sports.yahoo.com/video/brett-favre-not-job-mentor-110000456.html>.

"Best of NFL Commissioner Roger Goodell." NFL. 30 Jan. 2015. Web. <http://www.nfl.com/videos/super-bowl-live/0ap3000000465897/Best-of-NFL->.

Brady, Erik. "Daniel Snyder Says Redskins Will Never Change Name." *USA Today*. 10 May 2013. Web. <http://www.usatoday.com/story/sports/nfl/redskins/2013/05/09/washington-redskins-daniel-snyder/2148127/>.

Brandt, Andrew. "The NFL's Reality TV Mess | The MMQB with Peter King." *Sports Illustrated*. 28 Jan. 2015. Web. <http://mmqb.si.com/2015/01/28/deflategate-benson-family-scandal-nfl-super-bowl-49/>.

Breslow, Jason. "76 of 79 Deceased NFL Players Found to Have Brain Disease." PBS. PBS, 30 Sept. 2014. Web. <http://www.pbs.org/wgbh/pages/frontline/sports/concussion-watch/76-of-79-deceased-nfl-players-found-to-have-brain-disease/>.

Brody, Anita. "In RE: National Football League Player's Concussion: Injury Litigation." US Courts. 7 July 2014. Web. <https://www.paed.uscourts.gov/documents/opinions/14D0537P.pdf>.

Broussard, Chris. "LeBron: No Football in My House." ESPN. ESPN Internet Ventures, 13 Nov. 2014. Web. <http://espn.go.com/nba/story/_/id/11866239/lebron-james-says-kids-allowed-play-football>.

Brown, James. CBS. 11 Sept. 2014. Television.

Burke, Monte. "Think The NFL Is In Decline Because Of Head Trauma Issues? Think Again." Forbes. Forbes Magazine, 14 Aug. 2013. Web. <http://www.forbes.com/sites/monte-burke/2013/08/14/think-the-nfl-is-in-decline-because-of-head-trauma-issues-think-again/>.

Casualties of the Gridiron. Perf. Ray Lucas, Brent Boyd, Terry Tautolo, and Jennifer Smith. GQ, 2013. Film.

"Change the Mascot Calls..." Oneida Indian Nation. 11 Dec. 2014. Web. <http://www.oneidaindiannation.com/pressroom/Change-the-Mascot-Calls-on-Commissioner-Roger-Goodell-to-Adopt-Proactive-Stance-on-Racism-By-Implementing-an-NFL-Owners-Code-of-Conduct-285530371.html>.

Chemi, Eric. "The NFL Is Growing Only Because of Women." Bloomberg. Bloomberg, 26 Sept. 2014. Web. <http://www.bloomberg.com/bw/articles/2014-09-26/the-nfl-is-growing-only-because-of-female-fans>.

Cohen, Rich. "How the NFL Reflects American Culture." WSJ. Wall Street Journal, 19 Sept. 2014. Web. <http://www.wsj.com/articles/how-the-nfl-reflects-american-culture-1411149452>.

Cook, Kevin. The Last Headbangers: NFL Football in the Rowdy, Reckless '70s, the Era That Created Modern Sports. 1st ed. New York: W. W. Norton, 2012. 288. Print.

Cox, John, and Mark Maske. "Civil Rights Group Closely Allied With..." *Washington Post*. The *Washington Post*, 19 Jan. 2015. Web. <http://www.washingtonpost.com/local/civil-rights-group-closely-allied-with-the-nfl-calls-for-the-redskins-to-change-its-name/2015/01/18/d8c692ce-9cfe-11e4-bcfb-059ec7a93ddc_story.html>.

"Curran: Goodell Deflategate Stance Shows He's a Fraud." Comcast SportsNet. 30 Jan. 2015. Web. <http://www.csnne.com/new-england-patriots/curran-goodell-deflategate-stance-shows-hes-fraud>.

Dowd, Maureen. "Throw the Bums Out: Roger Goodell, Ray Rice and the N.F.L.'s Culture." The *New York Times* 13 Sept. 2014, SundayReview Op-Ed Columnist sec. Print.

Dubin, Jared. "Chris Conte Would Rather Die Early than Not Play in the NFL at All." CBS Sports. 17 Dec. 2014. Web. <http://www.cbssports.com/nfl/eye-on-football/24897586/chris-conte-would-rather-die-early-than-not-play-in-the-nfl-at-all>.

Earnest, Josh. "White House Daily Briefing." C-SPAN. 23 Jan. 2015. Web. <http://www.c-span.org/video/?323967-1/white-house-briefing>.

Eisen, Michael. "Giants President John Mara on Rule Changes." Giants. 13 Apr. 2012. Web. <http://www.giants.com/news-and-blogs/article-1/Giants-President-John-Mara-on-rule-changes/4251e760-3ad7-431b-bbc8-b37cd5226de9>.

Eisen, Rich. "Jay Glazer Calls The RES to Talk Johnny Manziel." *The Rich Eisen Show*. 11 Dec. 2014. Web. <http://www.richeisenshow.com/2014/12/11/jay-glazer-calls-res-121114/>.

Exley, Frederick. *A Fan's Notes: A Fictional Memoir*. New York: Vintage, 1988. 385. Print.

Fainaru, Steve, and Mark Fainaru-Wada. "Questions about Heads Up Tackling." ESPN. ESPN Internet Ventures, 10 Jan. 2015. Web. <http://espn.go.com/espn/otl/story/_/id/10276129/popular-nfl-backed-heads-tackling-method-questioned-former-players>.

Fainaru-Wada, Mark, and Steve Fainaru. *League of Denial: The NFL, Concussions, and the Battle for Truth*. Crown Archetype, 2013. 432. Print.

Feldman, Bruce. *The QB: The Making of Modern Quarterbacks.* Crown Archetype, 2014. Print.

Florio, Mike. "40 Days and No NFL arrests." ProFootballTalk. 26 Dec. 2014. Web. <http://profootballtalk.nbcsports.com/2014/12/26/40-days-and-no-nfl-arrests/>.

Florio, Mike. "ESPN Confirms Existence of Seattle Locker-room Divide, in Unusual way." ProFootballTalk. 24 Oct. 2014. Web. <http://profootballtalk.nbcsports.com/2014/10/24/espn-confirms-existence-of-seattle-locker-room-divide-in-unusual-way/>.

Florio, Mike. "Memo from Jeff Pash to Owners regarding Ray Rice ruling." ProFootballTalk. 29 Nov. 2014. Web. <http://profootballtalk.nbcsports.com/2014/11/29/memo-from-jeff-pash-to-owners-regarding-ray-rice-ruling/>.

Florio, Mike. "NFLPA Reverses Course, Sends Witness to Senate hearing." ProFootballTalk. 2 Dec. 2014. Web. <http://profootballtalk.nbcsports.com/2014/12/02/nflpa-reverses-course-sends-witness-to-senate-hearing/>.

Foer, Franklin, and Chris Hughes. "Barack Obama Is Not Pleased." *New Republic.* 27 Jan. 2013. Web. <http://www.newrepublic.com/article/112190/obama-interview-2013-sit-down-president>.

"Football in 1909 Caused 26 Deaths." The *New York Times* 21 Nov. 1909: 9. Print.

Fowler, Jeremy. "Johnny Manziel Gets Starting Nod." ESPN. ESPN Internet Ventures, 9 Dec. 2014. Web.

Freeman, Mike, and Steve Strunsky. "A Pattern of Misconduct: A Special Report; The Violent Life of Tito Wooten." The *New York Times.* The *New York Times*, 27 Feb. 1998. Web. <http://www.nytimes.com/1998/02/27/sports/a-pattern-of-misconduct-a-special-report-the-violent-life-of-tito-wooten.html>.

Freeman, Mike. "Art Shell Reflects on Becoming NFL's 1st Black Head Coach in Modern Era." Bleacher Report. 9 Oct. 2014. Web. <http://bleacherreport.com/articles/2216541-25-years-later-art-shell-reflects-on-becoming-the-nfls-first-black-head-coach>.

Freeman, Mike. "Former NFLPA Head Troy Vincent Blasts Union for Ignoring Domestic Abuse Victims." Bleacher

Report. 12 Dec. 2014. Web. <http://bleacherreport.com/articles/2296816-former-nflpa-head-troy-vincent-blasts-union-for-ignoring-domestic-abuse-victims>.

Freeman, Mike. "In a Year of Big Offense and Big Controversy, J.J. Watt Stands as Brightest Star." Bleacher Report. 4 Dec. 2014. Web. <http://bleacherreport.com/articles/2264979-in-a-year-of-big-offense-and-big-controversy-jj-watt-stands-as-brightest-star>.

Freeman, Mike. "Is the NFL Going to Let Brady and Belichick Play It for a Fool?" Bleacher Report. 20 Jan. 2015. Web. <http://bleacherreport.com/articles/2339195-is-the-nfl-going-to-let-brady-and-belichick-play-it-for-a-fool>.

Freeman, Mike. "J.J. Watt Is a Young Michael Strahan, and That Is the Ultimate Compliment." Bleacher Report. 29 Sept. 2014. Web. <http://bleacherreport.com/articles/2214119-jj-watt-is-a-young-michael-strahan-and-that-is-the-ultimate-compliment>.

Freeman, Mike. "Mike Freeman's 10-Point Stance: Another WR Learns Not to Disrespect the QB." Bleacher Report. 22 Oct. 2014. Web. <http://bleacherreport.com/articles/2238790-mike-freemans-10-point-stance-another-wr-learns-not-to-disrespect-the-qb>.

Freeman, Mike. "Mike Freeman's 10-Point Stance: Will Knighton's Weight Keep Him from Greatness?" Bleacher Report. 14 Jan. 2015. Web. <http://bleacherreport.com/articles/2325698-mike-freemans-10-point-stance-will-knightons-weight-keep-him-from-greatness>.

Freeman, Mike. "Roger Goodell Exclusive: Looking Back on a Year of Regrets and Accomplishments." Bleacher Report. 30 Dec. 2014. Web. <http://bleacherreport.com/articles/2311297-roger-goodell-exclusive-looking-back-on-a-year-of-regrets-and-accomplishments>.

Freeman, Mike. "The Inside Story of How the NFL's Plan for Its 1st Openly Gay Player Fell Apart." Bleacher Report. 20 Nov. 2013. Web. <http://bleacherreport.com/articles/1831178-the-inside-story-of-how-the-nfls-plan-for-a-1st-openly-gay-player-fell-apart>.

Freeman, Mike. "Who Is Andrew Luck? Behind the Scenes with a Unique Personality and Tlanet." Bleacher Report. 25 Oct. 2013. Web. <http://bleacherreport.com/articles/1819612-who-is-andrew-luck-behind-the-scenes-with-a-unique-personality-and-talent>.

Freeman, Mike. "Who Is Darren Sharper? Date-Rape Allegations Raise Serious Questions." Bleacher Report. 16 Apr. 2014. Web. <http://bleacherreport.com/articles/2013700-who-is-darren-sharper-date-rape-allegations-raise-serious-questions>.

Freeman, Mike. "Why Snyder Won't Relent on 'Redskins,' and Why I Did." Bleacher Report. 10 June 2014. Web. <http://bleacherreport.com/articles/2088756-why-dan-snyder-wont-relent-on-redskins-and-why-i-did>.

"Full Transcript from Patriots Quarterback Tom Brady's Media Session." AZCentral. 26 Jan. 2015. Web. <http://www.az-central.com/story/sports/nfl/super-bowl/2015/01/27/full-transcript-patriots-quarterback-tom-brady-media-session/22387607/>.

Garriott, Khalil. "NFL Says Concussions, ACL Injuries Decreased This Season." NFL. 30 Jan. 2014. Web. <http://www.nfl.com/news/story/0ap2000000320373/article/nfl-says-concussions-acl-injuries-decreased-this-season>.

Gasper, Christopher. "Joe Montana Thinks Tom Brady Responsible for Deflategate." BostonGlobe. 30 Jan. 2015. Web. <http://www.bostonglobe.com/sports/2015/01/30/gasper/4fjyn5NWemEYnhkwjlLEYL/story.html>.

"Gay Marriage." Pew Research Center. 23 Feb. 2014. Web. <http://www.pewresearch.org/data-trend/domestic-issues/attitudes-on-gay-marriage/>.

George, Thomas. "Raiders Piece Their 'Family' Back Together." The New York Times. The New York Times, 8 Oct. 1989. Web. <http://www.nytimes.com/1989/10/08/sports/pro-football-raiders-piece-their-family-back-together.html>.

Glazer, Jay. "Breaking: Johnny Manziel and Brian Hoyer Have Been..." Twitter. Twitter, 9 Dec. 2014. Web. <https://twitter.com/jayglazer/status/542373280242356226>.

Glazer, Jay. "Haha an All-time Low From..." Twitter. Twitter, 9 Dec. 2014. Web. <http://m.tmi.me/1eTA0i>.

Glazer, Jay. "Marshawn Lynch Barred from Wearing Gold Cleats." FOX Sports. 18 Jan. 2015. Web. <http://www.foxsports.com/video?vid=385995843649>.

Gordon, Michael, Joseph Person, and Johnathan Jones. "Panthers Greg Hardy Guilty of Assaulting Female, Communicating Threats." CharlotteObserver. 15 July 2014. Web. <http://www.charlotteobserver.com/news/local/crime/article9140591.html#.U8WRnI1dUiK>.

Graham, Tim. "Kevin Turner's Rugged Road." ESPN. ESPN Internet Ventures, 18 Mar. 2011. Web. <http://espn.go.com/blog/afceast/post/_/id/26976/kevin-turners-road>.

Gregory, Sean. "The Tragic Risks of American Football." Time. Time, 18 Sept. 2014. Web. <http://time.com/3397085/the-tragic-risks-of-american-football/>.

Grimes, Miko. Twitter. Twitter, 26 Jan. 2015. Web. <https://twitter.com/iHeartMiko>.

Grimm, Andy. "Disturbing Details in Darren Sharper Rape Case Come out during Hearing." Nola. The Times-Picayune, 19 Dec. 2014. Web. <http://www.nola.com/crime/index.ssf/2014/12/disturbing_details_in_darren_s.html>.

Hannon, Elliot. "Listen to the Goodell-Bashing Comments That Got Bill Simmons Suspended by ESPN." Slate. 24 Sept. 2014. Web. <http://www.slate.com/blogs/the_slatest/2014/09/24/bill_simmons_suspended_listen_to_the_goodell_bashing_comments_that_got_the.html>.

Heller, Dean. "Heller Stands Up to NFL to Protect Survivors of Domestic Abuse." United States Senator Dean Heller. 10 Sept. 2014. Web. <http://www.heller.senate.gov/public/index.cfm/2014/9/heller-stands-up-to-nfl-to-protect-survivors-of-domestic-abuse>.

Holder, Larry. "Former Teammates Shocked, Disgusted with Charges Surrounding Former New Orleans Saints Safety Darren Sharper." Nola. The Times-Picayune, 21 Feb. 2014. Web. <http://www.nola.com/saints/index.ssf/2014/02/former_teammates.html>.

Hruby, Patrick. "The NFL Concussion Settlement Is Pocket
    Change for the League." VICE Sports. 12 Nov. 2014. Web.
    <https://sports.vice.com/article/the-nfl-concussion-settle-
    ment-is-pocket-change-for-the-league>.
"In The Ray Rice Situation, Everyone Must Go." Olbermann,
    Keith. Olbermann. ESPN. 8 Sept. 2014. Television.
"Interview: Pete Rozelle Pro Football Hall of Fame." Academy
    of Achievement. 15 May 1991. Web. <http://www.achieve-
    ment.org/autodoc/printmember/roz0int-1>.
Jaffe, Harry. "The Dan Snyder You Don't Know." The
    Washingtonian. 1 Sept. 2006. Web. <http://www.washingtonian
    com/articles/people/sports/the-dan-snyder-you-dont-know/>.
Jenkins, Sally. "How NFL Has Become the Coal Industry,
    and Why Congress Must Intervene." *Washington Post*. The
    Washington Post, 1 Oct. 2014. Web. <http://www.washington-
    post.com/sports/redskins/nfl-must-pay-for-its-handling-of-
    concussion-issues--or-congress-should-intervene/2014/10/01/
    8e0cc6ae-4984-11e4-b72e-d60a9229cc10_story.html>.
Jenkins, Sally. "Washington Redskins Are the Victims of Top-
    down Organizational Dysfunction." *Washington Post*. The
    Washington Post, 1 Jan. 2015. Web. <http://www.washington-
    post.com/sports/redskins/washington-redskins-are-the-vic-
    tims-of-top-down-organizational-dysfunction/2014/12/31/27
    05348a-913e-11e4-a900-9960214d4cd7_story.html>.
Jones, Barbara. "In the Matter of Ray Rice Decision." ESPN. 28
    Nov. 2014. Web. <http://espn.go.com/pdf/2014/1128/141128_
    rice-summary.pdf>.
Jones, Roxanne. "Roger Goodell, Start Respecting Women."
    CNN. Cable News Network, 31 Jan. 2015. Web. <http://
    www.cnn.com/2015/01/31/opinion/jones-roger-goodell/>.
"Junior Seau's Tragic Death & His Family's NFL Lawsuit."
    Keteyian, Armen. *60 Minutes Sports*. Showtime. 6 Jan. 2015.
    Television.
Kaplan, Daniel. "Rockefeller On Domestic Violence In Sports:
    'No More Excuses' *Sports Business Daily*. 11 Dec. 2014.
    Web. <http://www.sportsbusinessdaily.com/Daily/Closing-
    Bell/2014/12/11/Rockefeller.aspx>.

Kawakami, Tim. "Am I Suggesting That SJPD..." Twitter. Twitter, 2 Sept. 2014. Web. <https://twitter.com/timkawakami/status/506883111427121152>.

Kersevan, Chris. "A Boy Wrote A Letter To Every NFL Owner... Only One Wrote Back." Chat Sports. 13 Jan. 2015. Web. <http://www.chatsports.com/nfl/a/A-Boy-Wrote-A-Letter-To-Every-NFL-OwnerOnly-One-Wrote-Back-10-206-3237>.

Kilgore, Adam. "Ben Roethlisberger, Heath Miller Returned 'too Quick' to Properly Check for a Concussion." *Washington Post*. The *Washington Post*, 4 Jan. 2015. Web. <http://www.washingtonpost.com/news/sports/wp/2015/01/04/ben-roethlisberger-heath-miller-returned-too-quick-to-properly-check-for-a-concussion/>.

King, Peter. "Should We Still Like Football? | The MMQB with Peter King." *Sports Illustrated*. 15 Sept. 2014. Web. <http://mmqb.si.com/2014/09/15/monday-morning-qb-nfl-week-2/7/>.

King, Peter. "The 2014 MMQB Awards | The MMQB with Peter King." *Sports Illustrated*. 30 Dec. 2014. Web. <http://mmqb.si.com/2014/12/30/nfl-awards-mvp-rookie-coach/>.

King, Peter. "The Making of Modern QBs | The MMQB with Peter King." *Sports Illustrated*. 11 Dec. 2014. Web. <http://mmqb.si.com/2014/12/11/nfl-aaron-rodgers-bruce-feldman-the-making-of-modern-quarterbacks-the-qb/>.

King, Peter. "The Week 2 Mailbag | The MMQB with Peter King." *Sports Illustrated*. 16 Sept. 2014. Web. <http://mmqb.si.com/2014/09/16/nfl-week-2-mailbag/>.

Klein, Christopher. "How Teddy Roosevelt Saved Football." History. A&E Television Networks, 6 Sept. 2012. Web. <http://www.history.com/news/how-teddy-roosevelt-saved-football>.

Klemko, Robert. "Where Does It Come From? | The MMQB with Peter King." *Sports Illustrated*. 29 Jan. 2015. Web. <http://mmqb.si.com/2015/01/29/russell-wilson-seattle-seahawks-wisconsin-badgers-richmond-family/>.

Koblin, John. "The Team Behind the N.F.L.'s 'No More' Campaign." The *New York Times*. The *New York Times*, 2

Jan. 2015, Web. <http://www.nytimes.com/2015/01/04/style/
the-team-behind-the-nfls-no-more-campaign.html>.

League of Denial: The NFL's Concussion Crisis. PBS, 2013. Film.

Leive, Cindi. "How to Win at Work: Advice From the Youngest
Female Boss in the NFL." *Glamour.* Jan. 2014. Web. <http://
www.glamour.com/inspired/2015/01/indianapolis-colts-
owner-carlie-irsay-gordon-glamour-interview>.

Lieber, Jill. "Dreams Do Come True Art Shell of the Raiders..."
Sports Illustrated. 23 Oct. 1989. Web. <http://www.si.com/
vault/1989/10/23/120853/dreams-do come-true-art-shell-of-
the-raiders is-not-just-the-nfls-first-black-head--coach-in-
64-years-hes-silver-and-black-through-and-through>.

Lingebach, Chris. "Redskins, After 4-12 Season, Are 'Winning Off
The Field,' Bruce Allen Says." CBS DC. 31 Dec. 2014. Web.
<http://washington.cbslocal.com/2014/12/31/redskins-after-
4-12-season-are-winning-off-the-field-bruce-allen-says/>.

Lund, Jeb. "The 15 Worst Owners in Sports." *Rolling Stone.*
25 Nov. 2014. Web. <http://www.rollingstone.com/cul-
ture/lists/the-15-worst-owners-in-sports-20141125/
daniel-snyder-washington-redskins-20141121>.

"Malcolm Gladwell: 'Football Is a Moral Abomination'"
Bloomberg. Bloomberg, 13 Nov. 2014. Web. <http://www.
bloomberg.com/news/2014-11-13/malcolm-gladwell-football-
is-a-moral-abomination-.html>.

McCarthy, Michael. "Blood in the Water: NFL's Rivals Smell
Opportunity to Capitalise on League's Scandals, Failures."
Sportal. Web. <http://www.sportal.com.au/article/news/
blood-in-the-water-nfls-rivals-smell-opportunity-to-capi-
talise-on-leagues-scandals-failures/1djld1ju3ggxu105aiczrpt
8ax>.

McManus, Jane. "Enough with NFL's Refusal to Evolve." ESPN.
ESPN Internet Ventures, 11 Nov. 2013. Web. <http://espn.
go.com/espnw/news-commentary/article/9962548/espnw-
jane-mcmanus-says-enough-enough-nfl-refusal-evolve>.

"Michael Sam on Gay Players in the NFL | Oprah Prime."
YouTube. Oprah Winfrey Network, 28 Dec. 2014. Web.
<https://youtu.be/D9kFz8-4Az0>.

Mike and Mike. Golic, Mike, and Mike Greenberg. ESPN Radio. Radio.

Miller, Claire, and Chi Birmingham. "A Vision of the Future From Those Likely to Invent It." The *New York Times*. The *New York Times*, 1 May 2014. Web. <http://www. nytimes.com/interactive/2014/05/02/upshot/FUTURE. html?_r=0&abt=0002&abg=0>.

Moore, Chris, and Brian Jones. *MoJo Show*. CBS Sports Radio. 25 Mar. 2013. Radio.

Moore, Matt. "Adam Silver Wants the NBA to 'Rival' the NFL." CBS Sports. 8 Feb. 2014. Web. <http:// www.cbssports.com/nba/eye-on-basketball/24435509/ adam-silver-wants-the-nba-to-rival-the-nfl>.

Morris, Benjamin. "The Rate of Domestic Violence Arrests Among NFL Players." 31 Jul. 2014. FiveThirtyEight. Web. <http://fivethirtyeight.com/datalab/ the-rate-of-domestic-violence-arrests-among-nfl-players/>.

Moya-Smith, Simon. "Seeking $250 Reward, Settlers Hunted For 'Redskin Scalps' During Extermination Effort." Indian Country Today Media Network. 26 Jan. 2015. Web. <http:// indiancountrytodaymedianetwork.com/2015/01/26/seeking-250-reward-settlers-hunted-redskin-scalps-during-extermination-effort-158865>.

Mueller III, Robert. "Executive Summary." NFL. 8 Jan. 2015. Web. <http://static.nfl.com/static/content/public/photo/2015/ 01/08/0ap3000000455475.pdf>.

Newton, David. "Ex-GM on Pats: Culture of Cheating." ESPN. ESPN Internet Ventures, 26 Jan. 2015. Web. <http://espn. go.com/nfl/story/_/id/12216634/former-carolina-panthers-gm-marty-hurney-angry-spygate-amid-new-england-patriots-controversy>.

"NFL Owners Express Full Confidence in Roger Goodell in Wake of Mueller Report." *USA Today*. 8 Jan. 2015. Web. <http://www.usatoday.com/story/sports/nfl/2015/01/08/ john-mara-art-rooney-owners-statement-robert-mueller-report/21453495/>.

"Nineteen Killed on the Gridiron from the San Francisco Call."
Chronicling America. 27 Nov. 1905. Web. <http://chronicling-
america.loc.gov/lccn/sn85066387/1905-11-27/ed-1/seq-1/>.

Obama, Barack. *The Colin Cowherd Show*. 12 Dec. 2014.
<http://espn.go.com/espnradio/play?id=12019745>.

O'Neill, Terry. "NOW Calls for Roger Goodell's Resignation,
Appointment of Independent Investigator." National
Organization for Women. 9 Sept. 2014. Web. <http://now.org/
media-center/press-release/now-calls-for-roger-goodells-res-
ignation-appointment-of-independent-investigator/>.

Oriard, Michael. *Brand NFL: Making and Selling America's
Favorite Sport*. Chapel Hill: U of North Carolina, 2007. 344.
Print.

Orr, Conor. "Marvin Lewis: Concussions Seem to 'Linger
Longer' Now." NFL.com. 16 Oct. 2014. Web. <http://
www.nfl.com/news/story/0ap3000000411709/article/
marvin-lewis-concussions-seem-to-linger-longer now>.

Parcells, Bill, and Nunyo Demasio. *Parcells: A Football Life*.
Crown Archetype, 2014. 544. Print.

Payne, Marissa. "NFL Players Association President Eric
Winston Apologizes..." *Washington Post*. The *Washington
Post*, 31 Jan. 2014. Web. <http://www.washingtonpost.com/
blogs/early-lead/wp/2015/01/31/nfl-players-association-pres-
ident-eric-winston-apologizes-for-comparing-roger-goodell-
to-bad-spring-break-bartender/>.

Pelissero, Tom. "Goodell Tells NFL Employees League Is
Now 'Stronger and Better'" *USA Today*. 8 Jan. 2015. Web.
<http://www.usatoday.com/story/sports/nfl/2015/01/08/
roger-goodell-robert-mueller-report-memo-nfl/21463785/>.

Person, Joseph. "Panthers' Greg Olsen: NFL Should Suspend
Ankle-twisting Vontaze Burfict." The *Charlotte Observer*. 13
Oct. 2014. Web. <http://www.charlotteobserver.com/sports/
nfl/carolina-panthers/article9201446.html>.

Petchesky, Barry. "Richard Sherman And Michael Bennett
Savage The NCAA 'Scam' Deadspin. 30 Jan. 2015. Web.
<http://deadspin.com/richard-sherman-and-michael-bennett-
savage-the-ncaa-sc-1682752726>.

"Police Blotter." ProFootballTalk. Web. <http://profootballtalk. nbcsports.com/police-blotter/>.

"Public Policy Polling." Amazon Web Services. Amazon, 23 Jan. 2015. Web. <https://s3.amazonaws.com/s3.weareultraviolet. org/images/NationalSurveyofWomenResults.pdf>.

"Quotes From Divisional Round Editions of NFL Network's..." NFL Communications. 18 Jan. 2015. Web. <http://nflcommunications.com/2015/01/12/quotes-from-divisional-round-editions-of-nfl-networks-nfl-gameday-high-lights-nfl-gameday-final/>.

"Raiders Hire Jack Del Rio, Dismiss Tony Sparano as Only the Raiders Can." FOX Sports. 15 Jan. 2015. Web. <http://www. foxsports.com/video?vid=384985155586>.

Rapoport, Ian. "As for Jay Cutler, There Is Serious..." Twitter. Twitter, 7 Dec. 2014. Web. <https://twitter.com/RapSheet/status/541601574225977345>.

Rapp, Timothy. "NFL Settles Concussion Lawsuit with Players for $765 Million." Bleacher Report. 29 Aug. 2013. Web. <http://bleacherreport.com/articles/1754622-nfl-settles-con-cussion-lawsuit-with-players-for-765-million>.

Raushenbush, Paul. "Is Watching Football A Sin? ALL TOGETHER Podcast On Conscience And Concussions." The Huffington Post. TheHuffingtonPost.com, 27 Dec. 2014. Web. <http://www.huffingtonpost.com/2014/12/27/football-concussions-sin-_n_6383676.html>.

"Ray Rice—Dragging Unconscious Fiancee After Alleged Mutual Attack [Video]." TMZ. 19 Feb. 2014. Web. <http://www.tmz.com/2014/02/19/ray-rice-unconscious-fiancee-at-lantic-city-video-arrest//?adid=TMZ_Search_Results>.

Real Sports with Bryant Gumbel. Kronick, Jordan. "Monsters No More." HBO. 20 Jan. 2015. Television.

"Remarks by the President on Economic Mobility." The White House. The White House, 4 Dec. 2013. Web. <https://www.whitehouse.gov/the-press-office/2013/12/04/remarks-president-economic-mobility>.

"Robert Muller Is The World's Worst Person In Sports." Olbermann, Keith. Olbermann. ESPN. 8 Jan. 2015. Television.

"Roger Goodell Is a Domestic Violence Enabler Who Must Be Stopped." Sidespin. 9 Sept. 2014. Web. <http://sidespin.kinja.com/roger-goodell-is-a-domestic-violence-enabler-who-must-b-1632385955>.

"Roger Goodell's Letter to NFL Chief Executives and Club Presidents." *USA Today*. 10 Sept. 2014. Web. <http://www.usatoday.com/story/sports/nfl/2014/09/10/roger-goodells-letter-to-nfl-chief-executives-and-club-presidents/15400391/>.

Rovell, Darren. "USC Professor: NFL Lacks Trust." ESPN. ESPN Internet Ventures, 15 Sept. 2014. Web. <http://espn.go.com/nfl/story/_/id/11532940/poll-shows-image-nfl-already-deteriorating>.

"Saban on Second Chances." YouTube. AL.com, 20 Dec. 2014. Web. <https://youtu.be/xHYGeQGJRTY>.

Sanchez, Josh. "Former Player Terry Crews: NFL Is a Cult." *Sports Illustrated*. 21 May 2014. Web. <http://www.si.com/nfl/audibles/2014/05/21/terry-crews-nfl-cult>.

Schilken, Chuck. "NFL Great Lem Barney Calls the Sport 'Deadly,' Predicts Its Demise." *Los Angeles Times. Los Angeles Times*, 18 June 2013. Web. <http://articles.latimes.com/2013/jun/18/sports/la-sp-sn-lem-barney-20130618>.

"Sesame Street: Word on the Street -- Inflate." YouTube. Sesame Workshop, 5 Apr. 2013. Web. <https://youtu.be/Y9SYE21X0pQ>.

Shaughnessy, Dan. "World Series Isn't What It Used to Be." *BostonGlobe*. 25 Oct. 2014. Web. <http://www.bostonglobe.com/sports/2014/10/25/world-series-isn-what-used/zQc-6Q2OkZUuWgnvyToxzSN/story.html>.

Shepardson, David. "Obama: If I Were Lions Fan I'd Be 'Aggravated'" *Detroit News*. 6 Jan. 2015. Web. <http://www.detroitnews.com/story/news/politics/2015/01/06/obama-lions-fan-aggravated/21363661/>.

Sherman, Gabriel. "Roger Goodell's Season from Hell." *GQ*. 1 Feb. 2015. Web. <http://www.gq.com/sports/201502/roger-goodell-season-from-hell>.

Shook, Nick. "Menelik Watson Donates Game Check to 4-year-old Girl." NFL.com. 21 Dec. 2014. Web. <http://

www.nfl.com/news/story/0ap3000000447958/article/
menelik-watson-donates-game-check-to-4yearold-girl>.

Silver, Nate. "The NFL Should Expand To London. But First:
Canada, Mexico And LA." FiveThirtyEight. 11 Nov. 2014.
Web. <http://fivethirtyeight.com/features/the-nfl-should-ex-
pand-to-london-but-first-canada-mexico-and-la/>.

Smith, Michael. "Bill Parcells Still Thinks Bill Walsh Cheated
during 1980s playoffs." ProFootballTalk. NBC Sports,
25 Sept. 2011. Web. <http://profootballtalk.nbcsports.
com/2011/09/25/bill-parcells-still-thinks-bill-walsh-cheated-
during-1980s-playoffs/#comments>.

Sokolove, Michael. "How One Lawyer's Crusade Could
Change Football Forever." The *New York Times*. The *New
York Times*, 6 Nov. 2014. Web. <http://www.nytimes.
com/2014/11/09/magazine/how-one-lawyers-crusade-could-
change-football-forever.html>.

Steinberg, Leigh. "Leigh Steinberg Blog: Premature Judgment
on Coaches & Players Threatens NFL." RantSports.
19 Dec. 2014. Web. <http://www.rantsports.com/club-
house/2014/12/19/leigh-steinberg-blog-premature-judgment-
on-coaches-players-threatens-nfl/>.

Stern, Robert. "In RE: National Football League Player's
Concussion: Injury Litigation." NFL Concussion Litigation. 6
Oct. 2014. Web. <http://nflconcussionlitigation.com/wp-con-
tent/uploads/2014/10/6201-16-Dr.-Stern-Declaration.pdf>.

Strachan, Maxwell. "NFL Pulls $150 Poster Featuring Marshawn
Lynch's Fine-Inducing Crotch Grab After Getting Called
Hypocrites." The Huffington Post. The Huffington Post, 26
Jan. 2015. Web. <http://www.huffingtonpost.com/2015/01/26/
nfl-poster-_n_6546870.html>.

Taylor, John. "Spurrier: 'If You Hit a Girl, You're Not Going
to Play on Our team.'" CollegeFootballTalk. NBC Sports,
9 Sept. 2014. Web. <http://collegefootballtalk.nbcsports.
com/2014/09/09/spurrier-if-you-hit-a-girl-youre-not-going-
to-play-on-our-team/>.

"Team Marketing Report." Team Marketing. Team
Marketing Report, Chicago, 2014. Web. <https://www.

teammarketing.com/public/uploadedPDFs/FOOTBALL_
FCI_TWENTYFOURTEEN.pdf>.

That Other Pregame Show. CBS Sports Network. 30 Nov. 2014.
Television.

Triplett, Mike. "Payton Critical of Extra-short Week." ESPN.
ESPN Internet Ventures, 31 Oct. 2014. Web. <http://espn.
go.com/nfl/story/_/id/11795016/sean-payton-new-orleans-
saints-critical-sunday-night-thursday-night-turnaround>.

Turley, Kyle. "Kyle Turley: 'Roger Goodell Needs to Step
Down'" *Time*. *Time*, 9 Sept. 2014. Web. <http://time.
com/3313227/kyle-turley-ray-rice-roger-goodell/>.

"Two Dead From Football. Boy 13 Years Old at Harrisburg and
College Player in Sioux City." The *New York Times* 25 Nov.
1909: 5. Print.

Underwood, John. "An Unfolding Tragedy." *Sports Illustrated*
14 Aug. 1978. Print.

Visger, George. "The Devastating Repercussions of Football
Head Injuries that Began in Youth." *Slate*. Esquire Network.
Web. <http://www.slate.com/articles/sports/esquire_
fnt/2015/01/the_devastating_repercussions_of_football_head_
injuries_that_began_in_youth.html>.

Weinstock, I. J. *Ultra Bowl*. DreaMaster, 2014. 294. Print.

"When Deflategate Is Over, Robert Kraft Is
Coming for Roger Goodell." USA Today. 26 Jan.
2015. Web. <http://ftw.usatoday.com/2015/01/
new-england-patriots-robert-kraft-nfl-deflategate>.

"White House: NFL Needs to 'Get a Handle' on Domestic
Violence." CBSNews. CBS Interactive, 19 Sept. 2014. Web.
<http://www.cbsnews.com/news/white-house-nfl-needs-to-
get-a-handle-on-domestic-violence/>.

"Women Stop Football Game; Players Mothers in Montclair
Said They Wanted No Broken-Necked Sons." The *New York
Times* 22 Nov. 1909. Print.

Yahr, Emily. "CBS Scraps Plans for Triumphant '*Thursday Night
Football*' Opener as Ravens-Steelers Game Turns Serious."
Washington Post. The *Washington Post*, 11 Sept. 2014.
Web. <http://www.washingtonpost.com/blogs/style-blog/

wp/2014/09/11/cbs-scraps-plans-for-triumphant-thursday-night-football-opener-as-ravens-steelers-game-turns-serious/>.

Zeigler, Cyd. "Michael Sam's NFL Snub Already at Historic Level." Outsports. 4 Nov. 2014. Web. <http://www.outsports.com/2014/11/4/7152717/michael-sam-nfl-draft-snub-gay>.

"Zephyr Teachout." Stewart, Jon. *The Daily Show*. Comedy Central. 11 Sept. 2014. Television.

ABOUT THE AUTHOR

MIKE FREEMAN IS A FOOTBALL COLUMNIST FOR BLEACHERREPORT. com. He has previously been a writer for CBSSports.com, the *New York Times, Washington Post, Boston Globe, Dallas Morning News*, and *Florida Times-Union*. He is the author of eight books—five on football—and has been a contributor to CNN, MSNBC, and the CBS Sports Network. Freeman has been writing on the NFL for over 25 years. His last book, *Clemente: The True Legacy of an Undying Hero*, was written with the Clemente family and published in 2013.